THEODORE METOCHITES

New Directions in Byzantine Studies

This series showcases the work of writers who are setting new agendas and working at the frontiers of the field, exploring Byzantium's peripheries (geographically, socially), promoting innovative research methods and demonstrating the empire as dynamic, complex and fluid – the crossroads between East and West.

Series editor
Dionysios Stathakopoulos, University of Cyprus

Advisory board
Kostis Smyrlis, New York University (NYU)
Vlada Stanković, University of Belgrade
Claudia Sode, University of Cologne

New and forthcoming titles:
Politics and Government in Byzantium: The Rise and Fall of the Bureaucrat Class, Jonathan Shea
From Byzantine to Norman Italy: Mediterranean Art and Architecture in Medieval Bari, Clare Vernon
Byzantium in the Popular Imagination: The Modern Reception of the Byzantine Empire, edited by Markéta Kulhánková and Przemysław Marciniak
Theodore Metochites: Patterns of Self-Representation in Fourteenth-Century Byzantium, Ioannis Polemis
Byzantine Spain: A History of Spania, Jamie Wood
Byzantine Sardinia: A History, Salvatore Cosentino

THEODORE METOCHITES

Patterns of Self-Representation in Fourteenth-Century Byzantium

Ioannis Polemis

I.B. TAURIS
LONDON • NEW YORK • OXFORD • NEW DELHI • SYDNEY

I.B. TAURIS
Bloomsbury Publishing Plc, 50 Bedford Square, London, WC1B 3DP, UK
Bloomsbury Publishing Inc, 1385 Broadway, New York, NY 10018, USA
Bloomsbury Publishing Ireland, 29 Earlsfort Terrace, Dublin 2, D02 AY28, Ireland

BLOOMSBURY, I.B. TAURIS and the I.B. Tauris logo
are trademarks of Bloomsbury Publishing Plc

First published in Great Britain 2024
This paperback edition published in 2025

Copyright © Ioannis Polemis, 2024

Ioannis Polemis has asserted his rights under the Copyright, Designs and
Patents Act, 1988, to be identified as Author of this work.

For legal purposes the Acknowledgements on p. vii constitute
an extension of this copyright page.

Series design by Rebecca Heselton
Cover image: Mosaic of Theodore Metochites in the Byzantine Church of the
Holy Saviour, Istanbul, Turkey. (© Paul Williams / Alamy Stock Photo)

All rights reserved. No part of this publication may be: i) reproduced or
transmitted in any form, electronic or mechanical, including photocopying,
recording or by means of any information storage or retrieval system without
prior permission in writing from the publishers; or ii) used or reproduced in any
way for the training, development or operation of artificial intelligence (AI)
technologies, including generative AI technologies. The rights holders expressly
reserve this publication from the text and data mining exception as per
Article 4(3) of the Digital Single Market Directive (EU) 2019/790.

Bloomsbury Publishing Inc does not have any control over, or responsibility for,
any third-party websites referred to or in this book. All internet addresses
given in this book were correct at the time of going to press. The author and
publisher regret any inconvenience caused if addresses have changed or sites
have ceased to exist, but can accept no responsibility for any such changes.

A catalogue record for this book is available from the British Library.

Library of Congress Cataloging-in-Publication Data
Names: Gaitanidis, Ioannis, author.
Title: Theodore Metochites : patterns of self-representation in fourteenth
century Byzantium / Ioannis Gaitanidis.
Description: London : I.B. Tauris, 2023. | Series: New Directions in
Byzantine Studies | Includes bibliographical references and index.
Identifiers: LCCN 2023020524 (print) | LCCN 2023020525 (ebook) | ISBN
9780755651429 (hardback) | ISBN 9780755651399 (paperback) | ISBN
9780755651412 (pdf) | ISBN 9780755651405 (epub) | ISBN 9780755651382
Subjects: LCSH: Metochites, Theodoros, 1270-1332–Criticism and
interpretation. | Philosophy–Byzantine Empire. | Byzantine
Empire–History. | Byzantine Empire–Civilization.
Classification: LCC PA5319.M4 Z44 2023 (print) | LCC PA5319.M4 (ebook) |
DDC 888/.02–dc23/eng/20231019
LC record available at https://lccn.loc.gov/2023020524
LC ebook record available at https://lccn.loc.gov/2023020525

ISBN: HB: 978-0-7556-5142-9
PB: 978-0-7556-5139-9
ePDF: 978-0-7556-5141-2
eBook: 978-0-7556-5140-5

Typeset by RefineCatch Limited, Bungay, Suffolk

For product safety related questions contact productsafety@bloomsbury.com.

To find out more about our authors and books visit www.bloomsbury.com
and sign up for our newsletters.

CONTENTS

Acknowledgements	vii
Introduction: Life and work at the end of Empire	1

Part I
METOCHITES' REPRESENTATIONS OF HIMSELF AND OTHERS

Chapter 1 METOCHITES ON HIMSELF: INNER AMBIGUITY	25
Chapter 2 METOCHITES ON OTHERS: MIRROR IMAGES OF HIMSELF	45
Chapter 3 CODA – DISPOSING OF ONESELF: A NEW WAY OF BEING?	57

Part II
THE QUEST FOR NOVELTY: INNOVATION VERSUS TRADITION IN METOCHITES' REPRESENTATIONS

Chapter 4 NOT EVERYTHING OLD IS TO BE REVERED	63
Chapter 5 ORATION 6, ON GREGORY OF NAZIANZUS: A RESPONSE TO MEN LIKE CHOUMNOS?	73
Chapter 6 CODA – METOCHITES ON RHETORIC: VEILED CRITICISM OF LATE BYZANTIUM DISCURSIVE CULTURE	89

Part III
VITA CONTEMPLATIVA VERSUS VITA ACTIVA: THEIR AMBIGUOUS RELATIONSHIP AND THE INNER AMBIGUITIES OF METOCHITES' SELF-IMAGE AS AN INTELLECTUAL

Chapter 7
'THE GREEKS SEEK WISDOM': POEM 6, FOR THE THREE GREAT PRELATES, AND POEM 5, FOR ST ATHANASIOS: THEOLOGY, GREEK LEARNING AND THE QUEST FOR A HUMANISTIC MONASTERY   95

Chapter 8
ORATION 11, *BYZANTIOS*: THE SECULAR BODY OF THE CITY AND A SECULAR WORLD CONTEMPLATED   131

Chapter 9
CODA – NATURE AND BEING: ELUSIVE CONCEPTS   147

CONCLUSION: METOCHITES, A PHILOSOPHER OF HIS TIME   153

Appendix: Works by Theodore Metochites   159
Notes   165
Bibliography   191
Index   201

ACKNOWLEDGEMENTS

I wish to thank Dr Dionysios Stathakopoulos for kindly accepting my book for publication and for his pertinent remarks which have greatly improved and enhanced my argumentation, as well as the two anonymous readers for their helpful advice. Many thanks are also due to my friends and colleagues, Professors Sophia Kotzabassi, Sophia Xenophontos and Eleni Kaltsogianni, for generously sharing with me their thoughts on Metochites and his intellectual background.

INTRODUCTION: LIFE AND WORK AT THE END OF EMPIRE

Theodore Metochites admits in some of his works that the period in which he lives is one of utter decline.[1] As a powerful minister under Emperor Andronikos II Palaiologos (r. 1282–1328), he could not ignore that the affairs of the Byzantine Empire had gone from bad to worse and that he had inherited and was obliged to govern a state that had been left powerless, failing and almost totally ruined by his predecessors. Metochites tries to justify taking the position by repeatedly invoking the Athenian orator Demades, who had felt obliged to act in administering a totally bankrupt state (e.g. Poem 1, 808). Such self-justification is valid in part. Although not evident when Metochites came to Andronikos' attention, the Byzantine realm was indeed in a state of ruin.

'Byzantine Empire' denotes the place where Metochites grew up and began his career, but the term 'empire' is not wholly appropriate. Metochites' state hardly resembled the one the Crusaders destroyed in 1204 and, despite its weaknesses, controlled a considerable part of the Balkans and Asia Minor and almost all the Aegean, including the great islands of Cyprus and Crete. The Byzantine state as restored in 1261 – after Emperor Michael VIII Palaiologos (r. 1259–82) reoccupied Constantinople – was tiny and fragile, no longer reminiscent of the empire of the past. It more closely resembled the small Frankish states that had been created as a result of the Fourth Crusade, like the principate of Achaea. Thanks to the efforts of the emperors of Nicaea, who tried to salvage what could still be saved from the former empire, the state of Michael VIII controlled part of the Balkan Peninsula centred on Thessalonike and the region west of the Sangarios River and north of the Meander River in Asia Minor.

Metochites, amid the decline visible to him, sought nonetheless to leave his mark on the political and intellectual life of the era. A prolific writer, he authored works on various subjects, and being ambitious as well, did not miss the opportunity to speak about himself, crafting various images of himself. In these works, he employed various patterns of self-representation that he adapted depending on the circumstances. Inevitably Metochites' self-portraits are closely intertwined with the history of the late Byzantine period.

Last throes of empire

Metochites' life begins in Constantinople a few years after the city's liberation from Latin rule by Michael VIII, founder of the last dynasty of the Byzantine Empire and father of Andronikos II. Michael had managed to retake several regions of the Balkans from the Latins while emperor of the Kingdom of Nicaea, the Greek rump state established in Asia Minor after Constantinople fell to the Crusaders in 1204. Though appearing to be resurrecting the former Byzantine Empire, that was not the case. The Latins still held strong positions in the Peloponnese and the Aegean Islands, and a new danger had appeared on the empire's eastern frontier: the small Ottoman beylik in eastern Bithynia had amassed considerable strength, and by the time of Michael's death in 1282, it was menacing the Byzantine frontier in Asia Minor.

Michael, aware of the dangers threatening his reconstituted empire, sought to avert the danger of a new crusade against Byzantium by offering the submission of the Orthodox Church to the Roman Catholic Church, a move formally promulgated by the Second Council of Lyons (1274) with dramatic repercussions in Byzantium. The Byzantine clergy responded violently against Michael, rendering the union with Rome a dead letter. When Michael died, Andronikos II ascended the throne, immediately rescinded his father's policy, and persecuted members of the clergy who had supported the union with the Latins. Among those who fell into imperial disfavour was Metochites' father.

The first decade of Andronikos' rule passed rather peacefully. The young emperor took care to heal the schism his father's pro-unionist policy had caused within the Byzantine church. The Council of Blachernai (1285) put an official end to related discussions concerning the procession of the Holy Spirit, and the canonical prelates were restored to their ecclesiastical thrones. In secular matters, Andronikos, having visited Asia Minor around 1290 to inspect its fortifications, was aware of the danger the Ottomans posed to his small and powerless domain. By 1300, major parts of the former kingdom of Nicaea had fallen to the Ottomans. The Turks defeated Michael IX Palaiologos (r. 1294–1320), Andronikos' son who had become co-emperor in 1294, and ultimately, Andronikos, seeing no other option, called on the mercenary Catalan Company and its leader, Roger de Flor, for assistance. The Catalans initially met with successes against the Ottomans, liberating the city of Philadelphia in Asia Minor in 1303, but they soon revolted against Andronikos, crossed over to the European part of the empire in 1304, and created their own state in Athens after plundering through the southern Balkans.

In the late 1290s, Andronikos had also attempted to curb the power of the independent Greek states in central Greece, the so-called Despotate of Epiros and the rump state of John Sebastokrator in Thessaly. After some initial successes, Andronikos was forced to divert his forces to the Serbian front. The Serbs had occupied several positions near their frontier with Byzantium and threatened Thessalonike, the empire's second most important city. Andronikos was forced to conclude a treaty in 1299, ceding all the territories his forces had occupied to the Serbian king, Stefan Uroš Milutin, ostensibly as a dowry for his young daughter

Simonis, who was given to Milutin as a bride that year. Metochites was involved in the sordid affair and negotiations. In the end, the only part of Andronikos' already small state left intact was the semi-autonomous area of Morea, which hung on despite attempts by the Franks of Achaea to destroy it.

The Ottomans progressed steadily. When Prousa fell to the Turks in 1326, toward the end of Andronikos II's reign, the north-western part of Asia Minor, which until then had been under Byzantine control, became an Ottoman province. The situation deteriorated further after civil war broke out: Andronikos III Palaiologos – encouraged by the death of his father, Michael IX, in 1320, and spurred on by his ambitious and vengeful mother, Maria (formerly Rita of Armenia) – revolted against his grandfather Andronikos II in 1321. The younger Andronikos had the support of some of the most important state actors, among them John Kantakouzenos, who would succeed him. The Serbs and the Bulgarians joined in the conflict, trying to seize as much as they could for themselves.

The civil war dragged on intermittently for seven years, until 1328, ultimately destroying what had been left of the might of the once glorious Byzantine Empire. That year, Andronikos III (r. 1328–41) entered Constantinople, seemingly in triumph, and forced his grandfather to concede the throne of a state that had almost ceased to exist. Some coastal areas in the southern Balkans and a tiny area around the city of Nicaea remained under its control, but they soon fell to the Ottomans as well, in 1331.

Georg Ostrogorsky argued that Andronikos II should not be blamed for the decline of the small state he inherited from his father, Michael VIII. On the contrary, Ostrogorsky praised Andronikos II for his efforts to raise the intellectual level of the learned class, surrounding himself with such high-calibre figures as Metochites and Nikephoros Gregoras. He created the college of the twelve judges, the highest judicial organ of the state. He also tried to tame widespread corruption among Byzantine officials. The reasons for the decline of the state ran much deeper, however, making the efforts of a single man insufficient to trigger a radical shift in a rather desperate situation.

The Byzantine political and economic magnates grew stronger under the rule of the Palaiologoi. Largely enjoying financial immunity, they increased their holdings to the detriment of the poor and middle classes, who became steadily poorer over time, and with the diminution of the number of free peasants. Most ploughmen became *paroikoi* on large estates. The landed aristocracy received tracts from the emperor as reward for their services (*pronoia*) but were no longer obliged to provide the state military assistance in return. In addition, rather than such land reverting to the state upon the beneficiary's death, it was passed on to his children. The decline of the *pronoia* system weakened the army to the extent that, under Andronikos II, the state was obliged to employ the services of mercenaries, who were untrustworthy and a great financial burden on the public treasury. Andronikos made a crucial misstep in his total neglect of the empire's fleet and in its stead relying on his stronger Genoese allies to provide maritime assistance when needed. Thus, it became inevitable that the Byzantine state would at some point fail to muster serious resistance to the Ottoman threat.

Andronikos II made efforts to heal the financial affairs of the state, but the decline he inherited was too steep to overcome. The price of the Byzantine gold coin decreased rapidly during his reign, reflecting the severity of the financial crisis. In this case, Ostrogorsky was right: Andronikos was not to be blamed for the sorry state of the empire, as the state was bankrupt even before he rose to power.

Metochites' life among the ruins

The main primary source on the career and early life of Theodore Metochites (1270–1332) is his Poem 1. In it, he offers an account of his advancement in the Byzantine court, underscoring how much he owed his rise to Emperor Andronikos II Palaiologos, his protector, and to God, who always provided for him (Poem 1, 302–756).[2]

Metochites had been born in Constantinople the son of George Metochites, an archdeacon of Hagia Sophia. The senior Metochites was a close collaborator of the pro-unionist patriarch John Bekkos, who at the instigation of Emperor Michael VIII Palaiologos had initiated a unification process to ostensibly heal the schism between the Orthodox and the Roman Catholic Churches, a move culminating in the Second Council of Lyons. The pro-unionist agenda ultimately failed, however, as the Byzantine clergy violently rebelled at the prospect of submitting their independent church to the Pope in Rome. Michael's death in 1282 delivered the final blow to the pro-Western policy. His son and successor, Andronikos II, reversed it immediately and deposed Bekkos, restoring the anti-unionist Joseph II to the patriarchal throne. He banished George Metochites and his family to Asia Minor.

Until that time, Theodore had enjoyed a quiet and rather privileged life in Constantinople. Educated like all the other children of the Byzantine literati, he had studied Greek grammar based on the Psalter and the relevant texts of George Choiroboskos, before proceeding to study Homer, the tragedians and the Greek orators. There is no doubt that Theodore continued his studies in Nicaea. After completing the so-called *enkyklios paideusis*, which emphasized learning grammar, Metochites pursued further knowledge. As he informs the reader in Poem 1, his first autobiographic verse, and in the preface to his introduction to astronomy, he studied the Greek orators attentively and composed several pieces of literature himself (Poem 1, 365–72). He likely did so through some sort of *progymnasmata*, Byzantine school exercises on various subjects or morality-themed examples drawn from Greek history and mythology. He also wrote praises of saints, but none of these early texts survive.

In 1290, Andronikos II had the opportunity to meet the young Theodore, at the time around 20 years old, when he travelled to the part of the former Kingdom of Nicaea that remained under Byzantine control, including the ancient city of Nicaea, the capital of the region. In all probability, Metochites delivered his first surviving oration, *Nicaeus*, during Andronikos' visit; the oration directly addresses the emperor. Andronikos was apparently not offended by Theodore being the son of a prominent opponent of his ecclesiastical policy who, in defence of his beloved patriarch, John Bekkos, had composed an extensive treatise on the causes of the schism between the Roman and Orthodox Churches. In fact, as Metochites proudly asserts in Poem 1, Andronikos, greatly impressed by his new acquaintance, decided to keep Theodore by his side (Poem 1, 399–423). As a cruel twist of fate would later have it, George Metochites, still persona non grata, probably died in prison in 1327, while his son served as megas logothetes.

Metochites notes that he was soon elevated to the Senate and was exceptionally acknowledged by the emperor, who appreciated his gifts and his total devotion to him (Poem 1, 424–9). He became logothete of the herds (*ton agelon*) sometime before 1295, and logothete of the emperor's private estates (*ton oikeiakon*) at some point after 1296. Andronikos also entrusted him with certain rather delicate tasks. In 1295, he participated in the emperor's embassy to the Latin kingdoms of Cyprus and Cilician Armenia (Poem 1, 446–93). While there, the ambassadors settled on Rita of Armenia as a suitable bride for Michael IX, Andronikos' co-emperor and son; the couple married in 1296. Metochites also notes in Poem 1 how the emperor entrusted him to arrange the marriage of his daughter Simonis to King Milutin of Serbia (Poem 1, 522–59). Making numerous trips to Serbia, Metochites eventually arrived at a mutually acceptable arrangement. Not without some pride, Metochites describes the warm reception he was accorded by Milutin, who treated him lavishly. Metochites had become a man with whom foreign kings and other rulers had to reckon.

Metochites also describes how Andronikos decided to keep him at the palace after the successful conclusion of the Serbian affair, unwilling to let the talents of his faithful servant go to waste (Poem 1, 704–49). Andronikos tasked him with monitoring the affairs of his rebellious wife, Eirene, who had settled in Thessalonike and governed the city as a personal fiefdom (Poem 1, 684–703). In this regard, Metochites served as the main intermediary between the emperor and his estranged wife, his ambition being to satisfy both parties, or so he implies in the poem. He travelled to Thessalonike but stayed only briefly, as Andronikos soon recalled him to Constantinople. Metochites describes this as a turning point in his career, and indeed, things took a turn for the better (Poem 1, 719–56).

Metochites was appointed logothete of the treasury (*tou genikou*) and became the most prominent collaborator of Andronikos. At this time, encouraged by the emperor, he developed a great interest in astronomy, which he notes in Poem 1. Metochites took private lessons with the contemporary astronomer Manuel Bryennios, and during 1316–17 he wrote an extensive, detailed introduction to the science, which had been until then treated with indifference (Poem 1, 565–649). Metochites also established royal familial ties when his daughter married John Palaiologos, nephew of Andronikos II (Poem 1, 750–3).

Metochites also took on the restoration of the Chora monastery, then in a rather sorry state. The work was completed in 1321 (or even earlier), after Metochites had become megas logothetes. It represented the culmination of a notably successful and unimpeded career. At around this time, Metochites became involved in a bitter controversy with Nikephoros Choumnos, an old friend and rival who in his oratory disputed both Metochites' literary talents and his achievements in astronomy. Metochites responded bitterly and uncompromisingly in two orations, accusing his adversary of ignorance of the most elementary laws of rhetoric and astronomy.

Unfortunately for Metochites, 1321 marked the end of relative peace and quiet, as that was the year that Andronikos III Palaiologos revolted against his grandfather, Metochites' protector, and started the seven-year civil war that would force Andronikos II to abdicate in favour of him. The toppling of Andronikos II meant the downfall of Metochites; the leading backers of Andronikos III and the people detested the megas logothetes. Thus, his splendid career came to a horrid end, with his house sacked and he himself stripped of his offices and banished to Didymoteichon, in Thrace. In 1330, he was permitted to return to Constantinople to reside at the Chora monastery. Metochites died a broken man in 1332, a few days after Andronikos II had taken his last breath.

Metochites' works and audiences: A chronology

Despite being constantly occupied with affairs of state, Metochites still found time to become a prolific author. He frequently bemoaned the inability of a scholar to devote himself to the contemplative life if involved in public affairs, but he never lost his appetite for writing. His works may be divided into orations, poems, the *Stoikheiosis Astronomike*, paraphrases of works of Aristotle and the *Miscellanea*. His letters, once preserved in a manuscript at the library of the monastery of Escorial, were lost in the fire of 1671. For a list of his works, see the appendices.

Ihor Ševčenko long ago established the chronology of Metochites' prose orations, noting that they had been copied in chronological order in the main manuscript preserving them, Vindobonensis phil. gr. 95.[3] Even if some doubts concerning the date of individual orations have been raised,[4] the order of most of them in the manuscript corresponds, more or less, to their relative date. This is not the case with the poems, preserved in Parisinus gr. 1776. The earliest poem, a monody for Empress Eirene, wife of Andronikos II, was written in 1317, the year of her death, while the first two poems, referring to the restoration of Chora, which was completed in 1321, were obviously later compositions.[5] Kostis Smyrlis has put forward a new date for Metochites' promotion to megas logothetes, citing a recently published document from the monastery of Prodromos, near Serres, in which Metochites is clearly referred to as megas logothetes as early as 1317 – provided the chronology from part of the document that has almost vanished has been read correctly.[6] If this new chronology is correct, Poems 1 and 2 of the compilation might have been written first, around 1315. One might even suggest that Poems 1 through 6 were written before 1317, the year of Irene's death; Poem 7 refers to her. The *Miscellanea*, a compilation of essays on various subjects, was written over a long period of time, although there are certain indications that the work assumed its final form near the end of Metochites' career.[7]

Whatever issues there may be regarding the chronology of Metochites' works, it has been established beyond a reasonable doubt that his works form a coherent whole; no development of his thought can be discerned. By contrast, certain themes, among them the instability of fortune and the value of the contemplative life, versus a life of action, appear repeatedly in his works throughout his life. Metochites is proud of this consistency, although one might be tempted to believe that it resulted from his reworking his original texts at the time of their collection to project his literary identity.[8] In any case, in his later poems he reminds the reader that his consistency may be proved by his earlier poems, which present the same attitude towards life and his manifest mistrust of the favours of fortune.[9]

This does not mean that Metochites' works are free of inconsistencies. On the contrary, there are several instances where he undermines assertions that he had made in earlier works. For example, he, the most vehement critic of those placing their faith in fortune, nevertheless praised the constancy of human fortune in the case of Empress Theodora, mother of Andronikos II,[10] and the gifts of fortune that had been generously bestowed on Constantinople since its founding.[11] These are deliberate contradictions, which Metochites expected his observant readers to detect. This was a common practice employed by both ancient and medieval authors, who sought to conceal their actual views and challenge the competent reader to explore the true meaning and discover their intentions.[12] Psellos was the most prominent Byzantine author to employ this approach.[13]

This dichotomy observable in most of Metochites' production also has to do with the audience addressed by the work. Some of the orations are clearly addressed to a broad audience, such as Orations 5 and 7 (the two *basilikoi logoi*, for Andronikos II Palaiologos) and Oration 9 (the monody for the emperor's mother). It was not proper to reference the empire's changes of fortune in front of the emperor, as it risked undermining his and his subjects' faith in the future of the empire and the emperor's own fate. It is not so easy to distinguish between the works of Metochites that he addressed to the general public and those aimed at a more limited audience (e.g. the *theatre* of his time) because all his orations and poems were most likely revised for public consumption in preparation for publication, under his own supervision, after their original recitation. One can, however, make a distinction between the audience to which a work was initially addressed (*Gebrauchskontext*, 'context of use') and the general public, to which all his works were addressed after being collected by him for publication (*Sekundärkontext*, 'secondary context').[14] Many Byzantine authors tried to control the publication and circulation of their works by producing editions, which they usually supervised themselves.[15] Metochites constantly intervened in the production of the manuscripts containing his literary output, inserting corrections here and there.

Certain indicators lend credence to the distinction between the limited audience of Metochites' friends and the general audience he addressed at the time of the collection and publication of his entire literary output. Metochites himself admits that Oration 10 (*Ethikos*) contains certain messages to be understood only by those who would carefully study the text.[16] This is not, however, equivalent to saying that *Ethikos* is an esoteric oration, at least initially. Poems 14 through 20, titled 'To Himself', are evidently addressed to friends and relatives who had been interested in Metochites' views after his fall from power, an apparently not insignificant number. One might then make a distinction between orations and speeches that were probably meant to be read publicly at special feasts – for example, the two *basilikoi logoi*, (Orations 5 and 7), the monody for the Empress Theodora (Oration 9), the speeches for St Marina (Oration 2), St Michael the Archangel (Oration 3), St Demetrius (Oration 4), St Michael the New Martyr of Egypt (Oration 12) and St John of Didymoteichon – and certain other orations addressed to the more limited circle of his intellectual friends and dealing with subjects of no interest to the general public – like his two speeches against Choumnos (Orations 13 and 14) and the one comparing Demosthenes and Aelius Aristeides (Oration 18). In these last orations, Metochites could give free rein to his thoughts. The same applies to his poems. Poems 1, 2, 5, 6, 7 and 8 – referring to the author's public activity, praising certain saints or mourning members of the imperial family – were certainly addressed to larger audiences, while the others – Poems 3, 4, 9 and 11 through 20 – dealt with his private affairs or addressed his close friends. This does not mean that in the orations and the poems of the first category Metochites refrained from expressing his views on the perennial issues that occupied his thoughts. Rather, he did so in a more restrained manner, adopting certain masks, that enabled him to speak through other persons without being identified with them.

One cannot exclude the possibility that Metochites reworked his writings like his opponent Choumnos, although no considerable traces of such activity have been found, except for some minor corrections by Metochites himself in the margins of his manuscripts.[17] In any case, when assembling his works, Metochites, like Choumnos, must have taken care to present them as coherent wholes, if necessary repositioning them in a new context appropriate for presenting his literary image to a larger audience.[18]

Methodology and purpose

The purpose of the present study is to examine the ways in which Metochites self-represents in his poems and orations and to a lesser extent in *Semeioseis Gnomikai*. The study is focused on Metochites' texts,[19] which are read critically, so that we may see the way the author tries to justify himself, employing his various rhetorical skills and uphold his reputation.[20] In other words, we shall try to investigate the discursive frame employed by Metochites in order both to understand himself and make himself understood by others.[21] The paraphrases of Aristotle are omitted here because most of them remain unpublished, and in any case, as mere paraphrases of Aristotle' works, are not usually indicative of Metochites' own views. It is certainly true as Paul Magdalino states that 'Metochites makes his own self-identification with the monastery [of Chora] very clear', and one should not neglect the great achievement of Metochites' restoration of it.[22] I am rather reluctant, however, to seek insights into the moral, aesthetic and philosophical values of Metochites by studying Chora's art and employ those insights to re-create the image of himself that Metochites wanted to project.[23] In a sense, I share the assessment by Robert Ousterhout, who appears to find in the architectural patterns and the iconographic programmes of Chora the same complexity and conscious contradictions so characteristic of Metochites' written works,[24] but my limited knowledge of Byzantine art does not permit me to follow his path. I have therefore limited myself to the study of Metochites' writings.

This is more easily said than done. Anyone wishing to explore the views of a Byzantine author on any given subject should be aware that Byzantium was a world of fictions. Although one may be tempted to read Metochites' poems or orations as true and accurate reflections of his turbulent inner self, as a true expression of his thoughts and anxieties, the temptation should be resisted. Like most Byzantine authors, Metochites, referring to himself, employs self-fashioning strategies, which are rather fictional.[25] These fictions were formed over centuries and maintained through the endeavours of Byzantine scholars eager to propagate official views and through time-honoured literary conventions.[26] Rhetoric promoted a series of devices that helped Byzantine authors form literary 'personae'.[27] As Ingela Nilsson asserts, the historical person who authors a work is not to be identified with the 'persona', in reality an authorial mask, the work might project.[28] The original audience for the work did not expect to learn the truth by reading it or hearing it recited.[29] In some cases, Byzantine authors re-created fictitious, yet credible situations, thus reproducing the views of a fictitious self hardly reflective of their own opinions.[30] Therefore, no oration or poem by Metochites should be regarded as an altogether true expression of his views or as a true reflection of his personality. Instead, his works should be viewed as a representation of his rhetorical character, as an expression of his rhetorical ethos.[31]

One type of *progymnasmata* were the so-called *ethopoiiai*. These were fictional speeches written by Byzantine students but supposedly delivered by historical or imaginary persons under circumstances defined by the teacher, who expected the students through the speeches to re-create the traits that constituted the 'ethos' (character) of that particular personality. For instance, a student might write a speech supposedly delivered by the Virgin Mary around the time of her son's crucifixion. The student should, through a vivid re-creation of the dramatic situation, convey to readers of his speech an accurate picture of the Virgin's sentiments and her way of handling them. In this way, from a tender age students were exposed to an educational practice of creating specific personae. The term 'personae' derives from the Latin verb *persono* (to sound through), referencing the masks worn in the ancient theatre that helped project an actor's voice so the audience could hear it. Metaphorically, the term may be applied to the masks authors employ to fashion an image of themselves, limiting the audience's access to their inner world. Modern authors make ample use of such masks, simultaneously revealing and hiding certain traits of their own personality, and the approach was not unknown to ancient and medieval writers either.

It was likely inevitable that Byzantine authors would continue to practise what they had learned in their youth. In their writing as adults, they created images both of other people and of themselves resembling those that they had learned to fashion in their compositions for *progymnasmata*. They did this mainly in their rhetorical writing, which conveyed impressions of others and themselves by social necessity, based on medieval society's demand for conformity in terms of stereotypes, dogmas and beliefs. This rhetorical 'ethos' was in some ways a restrictive function, compelling authors to efface themselves, maintaining a certain distance from their true self, but at the same time it provided them with the opportunity to play with the expectations of their audience, creating different or even contradictory images of themselves, or rather masks, behind which they remained hidden.

It is an axiom of modern analytic psychology that masks are a human necessity. Carl Jung adopted the word *persona* to identify the outer personality, outer attitude or outward face of man.[32] The persona can lead to the deduction of the character of a man's anima: 'Everything that should normally be in the outer attitude, but is conspicuously absent, will be invariably found in the inner attitude.'[33] Without psychologizing too much, that axiom is useful to the investigations here, not so much in discovering what hides beneath the mask of the contemplative intellectual often worn by Metochites, but in understanding the way masks function in his writings. The concept of the mask in literary studies has been around since the 1950s. It was introduced in response to the biographical-historical approach of the previous generation of scholars by those postulating the existence of an intermediary between authors and the audience in works of literature, helping authors formulate their views, adapting them to the needs and expectations of the audience.

In any case, the use of masks in addition to establishing a certain distance between the one wearing the mask and the audience also serves to create an elusiveness: the person wearing the mask is unapproachable and enigmatic. Elusiveness has been an important characteristic of serious literature since Homer. Supramundane figures in ancient epics and dramas possess many traits that distance them from the public, which is often puzzled by their contradictory actions and behaviours. In some cases, elusiveness in literature is a device for drawing the reader into the plot and its characters. There is also elusiveness on the part of the author. For example, the true beliefs of anonymous or pseudonymous authors of ancient or medieval works who, intentionally or unintentionally discarded objectivity, are undiscernible. At the same time, there are some authors whose self is problematic despite their identity being easily recognizable. This certainly applies to the religious or mystical authors of Byzantium whose self, or being, is radically transformed and sometimes totally effaced at the time of their union with God.

In other words, elusiveness, like masks, is part of the essence of the self; every person, including writers, is elusive to an extent. Metochites was no exception. What is striking, however, is his tendency to bolster his natural elusiveness as an author by adopting different personae more often than most other Byzantine authors. He did this in a way reminiscent of Michael Psellos, the Byzantine polymath of the eleventh century who did not hesitate to express his contradictory views on important issues publicly. Metochites does not go that far, but in a more subtle way he undermines images of himself that he had previously projected by later presenting portraits in sharp contrast to the earlier ones. Is that Metochites simply challenging his imagination? Is he trying to hide his personal views under an elusiveness, slyly communicating them to a close circle of his friends capable of discerning his true purpose hidden under constantly changing masks? Alternatively, is he at a loss to find the right voice, even a fictional one, for giving expression to his inner thoughts? There may be a degree of truth in each hypothesis. The purpose of *Patterns of Self-Representation in Fourteenth-Century Byzantium* is not to provide a definitive answer to those questions – itself an impossibility – but to share my view of that aspect of Metochites' literary activity. It is my view, however, that despite the masks Metochites employed throughout his literary carrier, he held certain philosophical convictions about the state, society and life that can be discerned despite those masks.

The Byzantine rhetorical practice of creating a fictitious image was facilitated through a particular 'sociolect' – that is, a set of certain communicative practices common among intellectuals that helped them create individual identities to distinguish themselves from the others. The sociolect of the Byzantine intellectuals was shaped through the centuries. It was in part determined and shaped through the practice of mimesis of ancient authors, who offered their Byzantine counterparts various rhetorically imagined worlds and personalities (*Identifikationfiguren*),[34] through which they might address their audience. In the case of Metochites, such rhetorical figures functioned like masks and were drawn mainly from the works of Roman-period authors – among them, Philo Judaeus, Gregory of Nazianzus and Synesius.[35] Metochites and other Byzantines adapted them to their needs, speaking through their voices, concealing their own true identity, their own beliefs, behind their masks.[36] Metochites shared with his audience the predilection for this rhetorical practice, which presupposed a common rhetorical 'ethos'.[37] One finds him speaking under the mantle of Philo Judaeus, Gregory of Nazianzus and Synesius. Using authoritative figures and models through which to speak to the audience is a prominent characteristic of Metochites' works.[38]

This tendency of Metochites and his fellow intellectuals during the early Palaiologan period has been reinterpreted as a way for them to promote their own interests, acting as 'lobbyists', to gain accession to the higher levels of power. The approach is certainly sound, but it should not be exaggerated to the extreme. All of Metochites' works were not lobbyist in nature, devoid of any real philosophical interest; he was not an author who changed masks solely for the purpose of self-promotion.[39] Alongside his aptitude in the sociolect of his time and manipulating images of himself in various writings, Metochites was a serious intellectual not averse to discussing the perennial problems of humanity and proposing solutions to them, at certain times also not bothering to conceal his real views behind a mask of someone else. His real views, or the mask of himself corresponding to his inner necessities and anxieties, must be somehow extracted from his writings. One has to draw closer to the individual behind his discourses, not taking at face value the data of literary self-presentations, as Pizzone puts it.[40] Despite the best efforts of theorists to deconstruct texts in the 1960s, denying any value or presence to the author, the author remains at centre stage; even Byzantinists must be aware of this.[41] In a sense, researchers must rediscover the author behind the masks. No author can write without a part of his or her personality showing through any mask and therefore being visible to his literary public. I am not unaware of the possibilities offered by Metochites' texts, full of inconsistencies and contradictions, both in their vocabulary and their meaning, for a deconstructionist analysis of the type suggested by Derrida and his followers, but I will refrain from making such an attempt here. Instead, I prefer to offer an overall explanation of those contradictions as deliberate attempts by the author to manipulate his image in the way he wished and to conceal his real self and his own views.

All medieval authors repeatedly employed certain patterns in their writing that helped mould a self-image that helped them reach their audience. Decipherment and examination of them aid in discovering and revealing an author's purposes. One such pattern is the opposing nature of novelty and tradition – here illustrated in discussion of Orations 4 (for St Demetrius) and 13 and 14 (against Nikephoros Choumnos) – but the main pattern Metochites employs to represent both himself and others is the opposition between the contemplative life and the active life. Men are judged and differentiated according to which way of life they adopt. Metochites insists on the value of the contemplative life and praises those who devote themselves to it. Expressing such sentiment was not unusual in the autobiographical writings of Byzantine scholars, who were eager to stress their reverence for education in general (*logoi*),[42] and at the same time, to justify themselves and their own intellectual pursuits.[43] Metochites is no exception to the rule, a fact well known to any scholar who has dealt with his works. It is a pattern Metochites superbly manipulates. Despite his insistence on the superiority of the contemplative life, in some instances, he distances himself from those who condemn a life of action as worthless. Such is the case with Oration 10 (*Ethikos*), where Metochites condemns Plato for his total rejection of a life of action,[44] and with Oration 11 (*Byzantios*), which is in praise of life in Constantinople – that is, of a public life. The shifting choice between the two ways of life is a hallmark of Metochites' elusiveness.

Examining the various ways Metochites represents himself and others performing roles in the theatre of life, as he often calls it, and looking more closely at his views on the problems of the contemplative life and its relationship to the active life can shed light on answers to some fundamental questions about the man: what was the true image of himself, if any, that Metochites sought to project and share with his audience? Which of the images of himself over the course of his career as an author came closest to his own heart? Was it a coherent image? The matter of a mask's internal coherence and inclusiveness is a criterion that may help us to hear the real voice of an author under his mask, without exposing ourselves to the danger of relapsing into the old biographical-historical approach.[45] This is a complex and multifaceted issue that deserves close examination.

Previous research on Metochites

No special treatment of Metochites' self-representation is to be found in any of the earlier or more recent studies of his works, but some of them offer important insights into Metochites' thought. A few examples are indicative of the different approaches to interpreting Metochites' writings.

The most important examination of Metochites' world view is the one undertaken by Hans-Georg Beck in his *Habilitationsschrift*, which takes a close look at *Gnomikai Semeioseis*. Though neglected by most recent scholars, it is a magisterial achievement. Beck explains Metochites' views in connection to the decline of the Byzantine state, highlighting the author's innovative approach, which challenged several time-honoured Byzantine perceptions about the eternity and ecumenical significance of the Byzantine state as well as some religious preconceptions of his contemporaries, which he viewed as no longer valid due to the particular circumstances of the turbulent times. Despite Beck's attempt to explain Metochites' peculiar theories as a result and an expression of the historical circumstances of the early fourteenth century, he does not close his eyes to the unique aspects of Metochites himself, who reacted to the changing and troubled times of late Byzantium in his own, unique way. Some of the most beautiful pages of Beck's book on Metochites are those describing the way the author tries to clarify his views on the divine providence, asserting that his thinking is free from any theological or dogmatic considerations,[46] being instead the expression of his personal anguished self. Beck does not ask whether the agonizing self of Metochites is but one mask hiding his true views behind it, but in any case, his approach is indicative of his way of seeing things, which is far removed from the mechanical, historicistic consideration of things that characterize the works of younger scholars. For Beck, Metochites is a true intellectual directly coping with the problems of his time, offering important and innovative insights into the social and spiritual climate. Beck's book has many merits but is not devoid of a certain deficiency: apparently taking Metochites' statements about himself at face value and thus succumbing to the fallacy of the biographical approach common among the researchers of the past generation. For example, Beck, taking seriously the frequently stated negative position towards the active life, not suspecting them to be a mask, believes that Metochites really suffered from 'einer allgemeiner Überdruß gegenüber dem Dasein (a general weariness towards existence)', which handicapped Metochites in his attempt to find a proper balance between the two ways of life. This interpretation needs revision.[47]

Other scholars also adopted the biographical approach. Herbert Hunger considers *Ethikos* 'autobiographisch nich uninteressant (not uninteresting autobiographically)',[48] believing that Metochites' attempt to combine contemplative and active life is clearly a humanistic trait.[49] Ihor Ševčenko speaks about a dichotomy in his own existence and takes at face value Metochites' assertion that he had tried to combine both lives but failed at it.[50] On the other hand, Eva de Vries-Van der Velden, attempting to refute those scholars who in her eyes glorified Metochites, believes that he drew an autoportrait of a malicious man who prefers the active life to promote his personal materialistic interests.[51] Hers is an extreme case of trying to extract biographic or psychological information about an author on the basis of supposedly autobiographic passages of his works.

A recent book on Metochites by Markos Kermanidis is characteristic of another tendency that some might view as a novel contribution to the interpretation of Byzantine texts. Despite the author's laudable attempt to offer new insights into the world of Metochites by employing new theories like indexicality in a rather ambitious manner, one must be cautious about his achievement. Kermanidis attempts to deny the value of both *Ethikos* and *Byzantios* as sources for reconstructing Metochites' philosophy – that is, as treatises that reflected his views on the contemplative life. He prefers to interpret the texts, especially those referring to the problem of pleasure, through the perspective of narratology,[52] insisting on their aesthetic aspects. This is not a bad idea in and of itself, but it seems that such an approach does not do full justice to the contemplative side of Metochites' personality; it is a denial of Metochites' value as a philosopher. Insisting on the validity of this approach, Kermanidis goes so far as to interpret the architectural structure of the monastery of Chora on the basis of the supposed aesthetic principles governing *Ethikos* and *Byzantios* in addition to the *Miscellanea*.[53] He even denies the existence of theological considerations both in Metochites' works and in the theological programme for the reconstruction of Chora.[54] Kermanidis' theory is an example, albeit a somewhat extreme one, of a recent, quite widespread paradigm among Byzantinists: the desire of certain scholars to secularize Byzantine culture and sideline its theological aspects.

Kermanidis tries to discern narrative models on the basis of the modern theories of digrammatology and indexicality, using obscure terminology understandable only to the initiated, but the reader is unable to ascertain the veracity of these interpretations; the models the author proposes may simply not exist. He even uses these theories to interpret the order of the Orations of Metochites in Vindobonensis phil. gr. 95 as being divided into three parts – that is, texts with theological content (Orations 2, 3, 4 and 6), texts with political content (Orations 5, 7, 8 and 9) and texts with epistemological content (Orations 10, 13–18).[55] Alongside grievously failing to mention three crucial hagiographic texts (Orations 2, 12 and 19), his insistence on the existence of an organizing principle governing the disposition of the texts in the manuscript is hardly convincing: the texts are scattered throughout the manuscript, and their relative chronology is the only recognizable organizing principle. The monody for Loukas, abbot of Chora (Oration 16), is certainly not an epistemological text, even if we accept that Metochites knew what epistemology was. This is a small but telling example of Kermanidis' method of identifying organizing principles and structures. His handling of modern terms, using them without offering the slightest explanation or definition, is a great impediment to anyone wishing to comprehend his work, which in any case is obscure and difficult to understand.

Kermanidis offers a broad picture of Metochites and his works but fails to do justice to the real content and purpose of the works. A historicist perspective is prominent in Kermanidis' approach. He goes so far as to inform the reader that any attempt at interpreting Metochites through the prism of Heidegger, as I had undertaken in the past, is wrong.[56] In all probability, Kermanidis considers such an approach ahistorical. He may be right, that there is an ahistorical core in all historical phenomena. The denial of it is tantamount to neglecting the value of individuality, especially in the case of literature, and explaining everything in a deterministic and mechanical, supposedly historical way. Any work of literature poses questions of transhistorical significance, of which both past and present thinkers were acutely aware.

Relativizing the views of a medieval author like Metochites as a mere product of the historical circumstances of his time is not a proper way of analysing his multifaceted work. Metochites had a peculiar spirituality of his own, which should not be trivialized and reduced to a mere 'aesthetic' approach to things, as Kermanidis seems to maintain. Metochites certainly took into account the situation around him in order to make his teachings understandable to his contemporaries, but he also held strong views on virtue, contemplation and politics, subjects that are not mere products of historical circumstances and have to be taken into consideration in their own right. In other words, when Metochites employs masks of himself, speaking through them to his audience, he does so to make his views more feasible or intelligible based on the opinions of his audience, which varied.[57] He did not employ masks for their own sake.

Of course, some contemporary studies on Metochites are valuable and illuminating. An exceptional example is a study by Sophia Xenophontos devoted to Metochites' treatment of emotions in his writings. Xenophontos correctly points out that Metochites gives prominent place to his emotions, allowing them to surface and giving them freer rein than other contemporary or earlier Byzantine intellectuals did. The literary genre of some of Metochites' writings no doubt facilitates this to some extent. It holds true for most of his poems, which were not addressed to the public, at least originally, but were intended to be read privately by Metochites' close friends or students. This permitted the author to give expression to his inner thoughts or sentiments in a way not appropriate in some of his more solemn works (like the *basilikoi logoi*), allowing him to create his own self-portrait.[58] The same applied to another study by Xenophontos, who demonstrated how Metochites, appropriating for himself the term *hellanodikes*, drew a careful self-portrait that was to influence his student Nikephoros Gregoras.[59] Xenophontos' articles pave the way for a proper treatment of Metochites' self-representation through his writings, clarifying some of the conditions that enabled Metochites to create a picture of himself.

As a true Byzantine intellectual, Metochites employs several masks in his works, hiding his true self behind them. This is not, however, a sign of his being a superficial writer, caring only about the aesthetic aspects of his works, or a mere lobbyist trying to promote his interests through the manipulations of certain views and themes to which he did not feel an inner affinity. These masks were a way of adapting to the conditions imposed by his social environment, which was not particularly receptive to his message. That message had to be communicated to a close circle of his fellow intellectuals, who could appreciate his use of those masks and discern behind them his true self and convictions.

Metochites, like others, formulated his views on the limited capacities of human speech to express the truth and on the theatre of the world, which forces everyone to adopt certain modes of behaviour, concealing their true self. These views are the theoretical foundation upon which Metochites creates his own multifaced and elusive image. Anyone examining Metochites' self-image must take them into account.

On the capacities of speech: A case of medieval esotericism?

Metochites was rather pessimistic about the capacity of human speech to provide an exact accounting of the truth:

> All men have this in common, both the most uneducated and those most accomplished in the art of rhetoric, that they cannot easily express what they think in the way they think and wish to express it. And to begin with all the other, external things that hinder the [free] flow of speech, what can one say? There may be fear and suspicion on the part of those who wish to speak that it will not be to their advantage if they actually utter their thoughts and choose to express them on a given occasion, because of the brutality, wilfulness and cruelty of depraved rulers, who would like everybody to join them in depravity or licentiousness in their judgements, thoughts and speech, and hold the same opinions as they do, and think and want the same perverse things. If not, those will come to grief who seem to understand better and do not follow them quite imprudently or unhesitatingly or heedlessly of all things and unwaveringly, in the way that shadows [follow] bodies.[60]

Metochites goes on to cite other reasons people are unable to express their true views: consideration for their friends, who might be hurt by a speaker's frankness, or fondness for certain relatives, whom the speaker does not wish to offend. The desire of anyone who speaks to obtain a benevolent audience may persuade someone to desist from clearly and sincerely stating his true views on a subject. The human mind is unable to report the cogitations within, however accurate and wise they might be. Metochites deplores this situation, citing his own example: 'When I do not know what to do when I attempt to speak, or how to behave [to achieve] what I want, I immediately fall silent and refrain from speaking.'[61] It is one of the rare cases in ancient and medieval Greek literature where an author expressly states that his works may contain views that do not correspond to his true opinions because of his fear or consideration of his audience, who always want to hear what pleases them.

Metochites also goes a step further. Presenting the case of Aristotle, he asserts that the philosopher's contradictions and difficult style were deliberate:

> [H]e tries to be as ambiguous as possible and tries to conceal what he thinks about these things. When he has decided to speak and gives the impression of saying something, whatever it is he is not at all easy to understand, nor is he clear as to what he is saying, escaping through the obscurity of his words the criticism which he suspects will be levelled against him.[62]

Metochites stresses Aristotle's willingness to evade the comprehension of his audience 'in order to secretly evade those who are examining him'.[63] This was a widespread view in antiquity. Plutarch and most Neoplatonic commentators believed that Aristotle employed a multilevel form of esotericism, hiding his true views under a veil of artful obscurity.[64] Metochites appears to agree with this traditional interpretation of Aristotle's obscurity.

Metochites does not, however, limit his remarks to Aristotle. Rather, he points out that ancient authors who contradict themselves constituted a widespread phenomenon, since most philosophers, not being able to obtain stable criteria for defining the essence of beings, expounded views that contradicted their previous ones:

> This is quite obvious with regard to those who engage in philosophy and spend a lot of energy on doing research on and contemplating the nature of reality: about most things they do not only maintain views totally opposite to those of their opponents (and abundant argument is used on both sides), but also in some cases views in opposition to their own, and they stumble on what they have said before and on another occasion.[65]

Having concluded that contradictions were quite common in the writings of all philosophers, Metochites did not consider himself an exception. One must, however, heed a distinction. In the passage just quoted, Metochites clearly did not have in mind those writers who in some of their works conceal their true views because they feared a ruler's response – and reserved the right to express their true views in other, esoteric treatises – but seems to imply that contradictions are due to the natural inability of philosophers to reach a consensus on the criterion of the truth. This is a clear case of Metochites' scepticism, but it is also a clear admission by him that authors who deal with serious subjects are quite prone to contradictions.

The works of Metochites are full of contradictions in the way he presents himself, in the way he depicts other people, and in the way he deals with the most important problem of life – the choice between contemplation and action. Having been trained as a young man to compose *progymnasmata*, short essays examining a subject from different, even contradictory, angles, Metochites, like many other Byzantine authors, is a master at crafting a thesis in different ways, providing opposing, or contradictory, answers to the same question. This is evident, for example, in Sententious Notes 73–6 and 79–81, which present different answers to the fundamental question of whether men should engage in public affairs.[66] Dimitar Angelov has pointed out that in the Sententious Notes concerning the emperor's will, which could not be decreed as law, Metochites expounds a position that differs from the one he takes in his imperial orations, where he expressly calls the emperor law incarnate.[67] These contradictions, far from being accidental or due to a lack of care, are intentional and appear to adhere to a certain rationale. Like Psellos in the eleventh century,[68] Metochites tries to strike a balance between different conventions and sets of standards that depend upon various factors, such as the audience, the occasion, the genre and so on. His self-image is far from uniform. His 'persona' is multisided. In other words, it is a mask behind which the author's true self hides.

Metochites thought that the difficulty of human speech to adequately express the truth forced men to say things that did not comport with what they really believed. His theory of the world as a stage and all men as performers of a role assigned to them by the circumstances of their lives may be a consequence of this belief. Metochites depicts himself and others in portraits that are often contradictory and multifaced. Thus, verification of the function of masks for Metochites can be found in the actual words of Metochites himself.

On the theatre of the world: Life as performance

Comparing Basil of Caesarea and Gregory of Nazianzus in his oration for the latter, Metochites states how the two church fathers led totally different lives: '[C]ircumstances brought a different drama of life to each one of them, or rather each one adopted a different mask and performed a different role, as if human life was one and the same stage.'[69] In antiquity, the Greek word πρόσωπον, employed by Metochites in this passage, meant a mask. The author does not appear to be implying that fundamental differences existed between the two friends. Rather, they adapted themselves according to the differing circumstances they faced. Being archbishop of the illustrious city of Caesarea required that Basil be an energetic church leader, while Gregory led a quiet life devoted to his studies. The former led an active life, while the latter adopted a life of contemplation. Of significance here is that Metochites describes these two ways of life as different masks adopted by the two great fathers in accordance with the requirements of their path of life.

'All the world is a stage.' This expression of Shakespeare, which is a modern theoretical proposition as well,[70] could have been uttered by Metochites, for whom the theatrical aspect of life was a deeply felt experience.[71] Commenting on the bitter experiences of his own life, Metochites reaches the following conclusion: 'The truly wise man also knows that the person who only yesterday or the day before or even today is soaring exceedingly high is very soon destined to put aside the performance and this stage, although this will be extremely painful to him and result in great ridicule by his enemies and those who envy him.'[72]

Metochites, throughout his life, engaged in role-playing, in constructing and staging his multiple identities. Even in the extensive Poem 1, his official autobiography so to speak, where he tries to define his role in society as a public figure, he presents his life as a stage performance: 'Our true Lord who is goodness itself, from whom all good things, all gifts which are perfect come to mankind, has made me most prominent in the theatre of this life.'[73] Speaking as a prominent member of the governing elite, Metochites is more or less forced to put on the mask of an official who is satisfied with his life, being most grateful to his benefactor, Emperor Andronikos II, who bestowed ever more gifts upon him. Metochites presents himself as a poor, destitute young man devoted to his studies until the age of twenty, when his life took a turn for the better, when Andronikos decided to bring the talented young man to his court. It is noteworthy that Metochites describes this change in positive terms:

However, after reaching the age of twenty (or slightly more), my life took a radical turn. I abandoned the path I considered the most pleasant until then: Fate changed the austere, unpleasant Dorian tune of my life, transforming it into the Lydian one which is much more pleasant; it opened the door leading to a new way of life, full of hopes, for until then my future had looked gloomy. In the past I did not expect at all such a change for the better coming from the emperor.[74]

Metochites is rather careful here, employing the somewhat ambiguous adjective 'more pleasant' (ἥδιον), rather than, say, 'good'. On the surface, Metochites does not express any disappointment with this turn of his life. On the contrary, his gratitude towards his benefactor, the emperor, knows no limits. When he states that his disappointment with the affairs of the state is great, it is simply an expression of the disappointment shared by all thoughtful citizens who had eyes and had witnessed the decline of their state.

It is not a surprise that even Metochites' 'biographies of himself', written at various stages of his career, are presented as performances on a stage. This is not unusual for a Byzantine intellectual. Several examples may be seen in the case of hagiography. References to 'theatres' – that is, 'audiences of faithful people ardently wishing to listen to the stories of the saints' – are commonplace in many Byzantine hagiographic texts,[75] and Metochites' hagiographic works offer clear examples of this style. St Marina, who is led to her persecutor, Agrikolaos, is presented as a young girl who enters a theatre.[76] Metochites is amazed at the spectacle of a tender girl who dares to resist the pressure put on her by the idolaters. He even calls on his audience to imagine her as she takes the stage full of confidence in God, disdaining her savage persecutors.[77] In other words, he urges his readers to themselves become part of the public viewing Marina's interrogation.

St Demetrius is also presented as an actor on stage – that is, the great office entrusted to him by Emperor Maximianus.[78] Of note is the explicit statement that St Demetrius needed both a space (τόπος) as well as a theatre. In other words, there was a need for a physical space properly organized so that Demetrius could perform in front of a large audience.[79] There is also another stage, however: the one imagined by every man in Demetrius' times, the stage onto which everyone expected Demetrius to enter and prove his value.[80] The stage, therefore, functions on two levels, one real and one metaphorical.

The same dichotomy appears in Metochites' oration for St Michael the New Martyr of Egypt. The saint, deciding to suffer martyrdom for the sake of his faith, enters the stage prepared for him by Christ,[81] but Metochites unfailingly admonishes his audience to also share that experience, preparing and opening the stage of their mind.[82] Joseph Rhakendytes (Joseph the Philosopher) acts upon the stage of the entire world,[83] but his whole life is also considered a stage,[84] which gloriously concludes with the end of his life. John of Didymoteichon enters a new stage in his career by deciding to embrace the monastic life.[85] Thus, Metochites concedes that life consists of a constant changing of the mask adopted by men according to ever-changing circumstances. The life of John, who hides from his fellow men, is a 'most blessed stage'.[86] Metochites does not present the death of John as entering into a new stage, but this is what he means when he says that John had an ardent desire to change and transform his life.[87] He seems to imply that this transformation is the entrance into a new (and eternal) stage.

Particularly noteworthy is the image of the world as a stage in Oration 11, the so-called *Byzantios*. The picture is twofold. Constantinople is personified, presented as an actor in the theatre of the world, but the city is itself also a stage, a theatre, in which her citizens are acting. Metochites wonders how it is possible for so many plays to be performed on such a small stage.[88] He also compares the city to a theatre of science and knowledge,[89] and he refers to the theatre of the whole world, in which Constantinople is destined to play a prominent role, competing with other prominent cities.[90] Constantinople is an actor on the stage of an international theatre, but it is also an international theatre itself.[91]

Uncovering the sources of this conception of the theatre in Metochites' works requires going back to ancient philosophy. Plato discussed the theatre and comedy of life, and Democritus argued that 'all the world's a stage', *totus mundus agit histrionem*.[92] The referencing of theatre was widespread among the Stoics, and Panaetius of Rhodes and Epictetus later developed the theory of a man's 'persona', his mask, the role he had to play in human society, adapting himself to the various circumstances. As Anthony Arthur Long puts it, '[T]he term *prosopon*, "role", had become a way of designating a person's character and the performance expected of one.'[93] Metochites, obliging himself of this theory, like the ancient Stoics, saw his life as a self-conscious choice of a determinate role, a symptom of his turbulent times. Like the ancient Stoics, Metochites faced a reality that was hostile to him and his true beliefs. Therefore, like Seneca in the past, Metochites insists on the theatrical or illusory character of the reality around him; instead, he lives in the world of his mind, fashioning it in his own way. In this respect, existence for Metochites was a realm fashioned according to his own rules, in defiance of the laws of reality.[94]

In presenting both himself and his main heroes as men consciously choosing a particular role, Metochites wanted to stress that they performed the role, which in some cases implied doing so consistently, under all circumstances, however threatening they might have been; such was the case of the martyrs and the saints. He also implied, however, that the role adopted by people did not always correspond to their inner needs, to their true convictions. This gave him the opportunity to undermine that role or to try to change it.[95] For example, as Metochites himself clearly states at the beginning of Poem 1, after he entered the stage of this life, he experienced a drastic change in his lifestyle, which initially appeared quite felicitous. In *Ethikos*, which may have been written before Poem 1, he castigates himself for having made such a choice. He also employs another technique. Like Psellos, Metochites becomes a stage director, allowing his heroes to perform on the stage of this world; it is he himself who hides behind the masks of the heroes. This is confirmed by most of Psellos' heroes exhibiting certain of his own distinct characteristics. His works are thus imbued with a high degree of allusiveness. Metochites also displays an elusiveness. One can easily suspect that

Metochites himself is hidden behind a person referred to in his works. This gives an autobiographic tone to some of Metochites' orations and poems.

To see how Metochites' masks of himself function in his writings, one must make a basic distinction between those works in which he speaks clearly about himself and those in which he speaks about other people whose personalities and career present a certain (in most cases close) affinity with his own. In many cases, Metochites does not hesitate to amalgamate his own personality with the personalities of the people (friends and others) he speaks about, inserting his own autobiographical traits into the lives of others. Therefore, the investigation here begins with an examination of the way Metochites presents himself and the way he treats other people.

Part I

METOCHITES' REPRESENTATIONS OF HIMSELF AND OTHERS

Chapter 1

METOCHITES ON HIMSELF: INNER AMBIGUITY

Metochites speaks about himself in his works quite frequently, a phenomenon widespread in Byzantine literature from the eleventh century onwards. Various authors adopted it as a self-fashioning strategy to communicate their message in an effective manner and promote an image of themselves with a high degree of persuasive, communicative value.[1]

A public servant and servant of god

The most important of Metochites' works revealing the multiple traits of his complex personality is beyond a doubt Poem 1, 'A glorification of the Lord together with an account of the author's life (περὶ τῶν κατ'αὐτὸν)[2] and a description of the monastery of Chora'.[3] It is certain that Metochites, who considered himself the new 'founder' of Chora, took advantage of monastic typika containing autobiographies of their founders, with Athanasios of Athos, Christodoulos of Patmos, and to a certain extent, Nikephoros Blemmydes, being prominent examples.[4] This is, so to speak, the broader narrative Metochites used to construct his autobiography, as Poem 1 may justifiably be considered his autobiography. In some respects, however, this autobiography is more reminiscent, *mutatis mutandis*, of a modern curriculum vitae written by somebody applying for a job than an honest accounting of one's inner life full of passions, doubts and inner struggles. Metochites discusses his career, omitting many significant details, such as his decision to abandon the contemplative life and his quarrels with Nikephoros Choumnos.[5] It is not a philosophical biography that reveals the ethos of the man describing his life. This is not unusual for the literary tradition to which poem 1 belongs.[6] At least this is the initial impression one gets by reading the poem.

At the beginning of Poem 1, Metochites speaks in the first person singular, presenting himself as a humble human being devastated before the Almighty Lord.[7] He presents himself as a herald of the magnificent works of God. He also does not hesitate to characterize himself as 'foolish',[8] not so much a self-accusation as an expression of his being a representative of fallen humanity. His tone changes somewhat when he shifts from the glorification of God to the account of his own life. His self-confidence appears greater. Employing the sociolect of his particular social class – that of the Byzantine courtiers – he considers himself in the theatre of this life the 'most prominent' (ἀρίζηλον),[9] expressing his gratitude to the emperor, who appointed him, 'preferring him over many others',[10] while at the same time noting that he has been successful in his tasks, fulfilling his duties properly and quickly (τελεσφόρον).[11] He speaks about his 'sincere goodwill' towards the emperor (εἰλικρινέος εὐνοίης).[12] Metochites, as a good courtier, views himself as the sovereign's collaborator, with 'a natural aptitude for the affairs' (δόκιμον) of the state.[13] He accomplishes his tasks 'most willingly' (πρόφρονι θυμῷ).[14] His love for his emperor is described as an ardent desire (πόθος).[15] When Metochites gets to the third part of the poem, describing Chora, his self-confidence disappears when addressing God and the Virgin Mary. He refers to himself as a 'wretched' creature,[16] humbly prostrating himself before God.

There can be no doubt that in Poem 1 Metochites does not try to present an accurate account of his life. Instead, he interprets it in a way that befits his audience,[17] which in all probability included Emperor Andronikos II Palaiologos himself. Otherwise, it is impossible to explain the perspective Metochites takes, presenting himself as a passive tool in the hands of his emperor. It is the emperor who appointed Metochites to a prestigious job in the Byzantine court, who entrusted him with the most delicate diplomatic missions, who ordered him to study astronomy, and who encouraged him to rebuild Chora. It is evident that Metochites deliberately chose the perspective of depicting his career, not his life. His career fits the pattern of the conscientious Byzantine public servant, the bureaucrat of the court who is faithful to his master, which dominates his narrative, allowing him to interpret his career as a providential act of God and of his emperor. Metochites presents himself as the ideal Byzantine courtier of the Palaiologan period who owed his promotion to his intellectual skills and to his education.[18] The ideals of the social environment in which Metochites lived drastically influenced his autobiographic representation.[19]

Poem 1 also contains a religious dimension. True to the Byzantine typological interpretation of the events unfolding in this world, Metochites presents his own life, or rather that of his emperor, Andronikos II, to whom his life is bound, as a reflection of the perennial battle between God and the Evil One. The struggles of the emperor against the enemies of the empire, in which Metochites, as a close collaborator of the monarch, plays a prominent part, are explained as an extension of the struggle of God against the Evil One.[20] There is, however, a distinct difference from other autobiographic accounts of the same period in their tendency to extol the authors as almost saintly figures. Despite Metochites' involvement in the reconstruction of Chora, he does not dare to present himself as a saint like Nikephoros Blemmydes;[21] rather, he considers himself a sinner, who needs God's compassion and nothing more. He glorifies God for the benefactions bestowed on him like other authors of the period,[22] but he stops there.

Metochites probably sought to purposely distance himself from those authors who extolled themselves as potential saints. His vision of life was more secular. He preferred to identify himself as a successful scholar and a conscientious public servant, with little interest in presenting himself as a holy figure. The monastic ideal that shaped the narratives in the autobiographies of many Byzantine authors gave way in Metochites' case to ancient Greek thought on the opposition between a life of contemplation and a life of action. Poem 1 offers only hints of this dimension of Metochites' life, but he fully develops the theme in Poem 2, the continuation and logical conclusion of Poem 1.

In Poem 2, addressing the Virgin Mary and Chora, Metochites adopts the humble attitude evident in the third part of Poem 1. Chora is his refuge from all worldly cares, safeguarding his inner tranquillity, and he implores the Virgin to receive him as a refugee in her sanctuary.[23] He addresses the monastery itself as his 'love'.[24] Of particular note, Metochites takes a perspective opposite from that in Poem 1: 'I wish I had no children, no wife, enjoying my prosperity however, people consider me lucky especially because of my children, since they have made prestigious marriages, which brings me great honour.'[25] Here he employs the terms ἀριδείκετος and περικλέϊστος, which brings to mind the term ἀρίζηλον, which he used in Poem 1. Thus, in Poem 2, Metochites projects an image of himself quite different from the one projected in Poem 1, when he speaks about his relations with the emperor; rejecting worldly glory, he is now a humble servant of God who needs his protection. He projects this same image in Poems 14–20, written after his fall from power.

Poems 1 and 2 are connected, it appears, in a certain way to make a point. In Poem 1, Metochites speaks as a servant of the emperor before turning in the third and final part of the poem to the account of the reconstruction of Chora. After providing a long description of the renovated monastery and the many material possessions he offered to the monks to cover their material needs, Metochites, stressing once more that all the gifts had been given to him by the emperor, invokes Christ in a beseeching prayer, asking him to forgive his trespasses and save him from the torments of hell. Metochites introduces Poem 2 with the Greek particle *de*, which connects it with Poem 1, indicating its continuation. Poem 2, however, makes no reference to Andronikos. Metochites presents himself as a poor refugee, who requests the Virgin's protection. One gets the impression that the transition from Poem 1 to Poem 2 signifies an inner transition in Metochites' life and a rather radical change in perspective: the image of the emperor's self-confident courtier gives way to that of the humble sinner, who asks for divine mercy and the Virgin's protection. In short, Poem 2 is not just a continuation of Poem 1, but its reversal. Reading the two poems together, one can conclude that Metochites willingly abandoned the palace for the monastery in his mind before physically doing so. It was an inner journey towards seclusion, his personal version of a monastic *anachoresis*, which he experiences before his fall from power in 1328. This seems to be the image he wants to project.

Therefore, Poems 1 and 2 must be read together, as two parts of a single poetic composition that constitutes Metochites' autobiography. The initial impression one gets from reading Poem 1 in isolation from Poem 2 is then countered by a different perspective. Both Poems testify to Metochites' emancipation from the external, social environment and his internal, conscious sovereignty over himself. As Misch points out, this transformation is the essence of an autobiography and the necessary precondition for the creation of a corresponding literary genre.[26] This turning of man inward is a phenomenon difficult to explain, but when it happens, there is not only a philosophical but also oftentimes a religious dimension to it.[27]

One may say that the autobiography of Metochites as presented in Poems 1 and 2 is the story of an inner conversion. By reconstructing Chora, Metochites passes from one way of life to the other (in a sense, changing one mask for another); he begins the journeys from the active life of a public servant to the contemplative life of a monk; he had not yet become a monk at the time he composed the two poems. In these pieces, Metochites self-consciously created and interpreted a picture of his own life that helped him to understand its inner dynamics. It is an 'authentic' interpretation of his life that Metochites expected his audience to believe and adopt. Although personal, it is also, more or less, a traditional Byzantine portrait, that of a layman who embraces the monastic life. Metochites became a monk at the end of his life, and his poetic autobiography stands as a testimony to his inner estrangement from the worldly life and his desire to live in solitude. It is not a full description of the inner aspects of his life, which would give his autobiography a psychological depth comparable, say, to that of St Augustine, but it is an eloquent testimony to his struggle to find the deeper meaning behind the trials of his life.

An intellectual and servant

Metochites' scattered other passages on his life throughout his works. Essay 28 of his *Gnomikai Semeioseis* presents a summary of sorts of Poem 1. In it, Metochites, far from offering unqualified praise of the contemplative life, goes as far as maintaining that when he was young, he occupied himself with the *logoi* willy-nilly: 'I struggled hard with education and learning until my twentieth year and longer, partly voluntarily – my desire was a strong driving force – and partly involuntarily, not knowing what else to do.'[28] He makes a somewhat different point in his introduction to the *Stoikheiosis Astronomike*, where he combines his intellectual preoccupations with the handling of the affairs of the state in a most successful manner.[29] Both accounts, however, like Poem 1, present Metochites as gratefully accepting the emperor's decision to occupy him with state's affairs. It's a far cry from Oration 10, *Ethikos*, where Metochites deplores his decision to combine a contemplative life with an active life as a totally futile venture.[30] One passage from this treatise is crucial in this respect: '[O]n the other hand, however, they are beguiled and diverted by the distractions and pleasures of public life, as well as by the attractions – I do not know which, exactly – stemming from it and the mode of conduct, and are then led to change direction from the Dorian mode to the Lydian, as they say.'[31]

One of those beguiled by the charms of the active life is Metochites himself.[32] This seems a retraction of sorts of the views he expressed in Poem 1. Since Poem 1 was written after *Ethikos*, one must assume that Metochites, in the latter, addressing his close circle of friends instead of the audience of the imperial court, as with the former, had by then put on another mask, that of the intellectual, who was disappointed because he had abandoned his studies (the Dorian mode) in order to embrace another way of life (the Lydian mode) that failed to satisfy his inner self. He employs the terms that he had used in Poem 1, but does so in a negative way. As if wanting to leave no doubt about what he had in mind when speaking about a change of musical mode, in chapter 45 of *Ethikos,* Metochites explicitly references his own case:

> This has accordingly gnawed away at the core of my heart, and I cannot bear to recall how I somehow suddenly backed water, changed direction, and followed a completely different route, while I was in the midst of my voyage towards wisdom and was sailing with favourable winds. That was a pleasant journey, and I desired to locate the purpose of my life around education itself. Then suddenly it was as if I encountered an adverse wind, which I myself welcomed and engendered. I chose to sink, and I am now still wandering around and suffering hardships as I seek to find my old love again – for I am not so insane as to completely forget my youthful passion. And yet, I do not know who I should be, I cannot find any kind of security, nor I can return to the point from which I started initially.[33]

One can hardly doubt the sincerity of Metochites' feelings, but one must keep in mind that the difference of perspective between Poem 1 and *Ethikos* has to do with the different audiences addressed by the two texts. Metochites is conscious that each text is a stage on which he must present a performance suitable for his audience; he could not address both or all of them in the same way. This is why the word *theoria* does not appear in Poem 1. The term, prominent in *Ethikos,* and suitable for discussion within the closed circle of intellectuals in Constantinople, is inappropriate for an official autobiography of the megas logothetes to be read by the emperor.

An author

Metochites does not speak about himself as a writer as frequently as other authors do, including Michael Psellos. One does, however, encounter the hallmark tension between modesty and exhibitionism in Byzantine texts in the prefaces to Metochites' orations.[34] He seems at first unable to properly praise several saints (e.g. Marina, Demetrius) or the emperor, Andronikos II, but he eventually undertakes the laborious task because he realizes that orators even more competent than himself are not in a position to perform it. Thus, his own incompetence might not be apparent.

In Poem 1, Metochites, employing fake modesty, describes his early writings as follows:

> I managed to compose a few writings which are perhaps worthy of some praise; I published some texts which have an accomplished style, and those texts

brought me fame disproportionate to any age. I exercised myself vigorously, writing some pieces of fiction; I chose some Greek stories of the past, as was the custom, so that, labouring very hard, I could become an effective fighter in those rhetorical contests I entered willingly. With some others I expressed my veneration towards several saints, servants of the Lord, as occasion served.[35]

Metochites is probably referring to *progymnasmata* that have since been lost and possibly to some of his early works, like Orations 2 (for St Marina), 3 (for the archangel Michael and the angels) and 4 (for St Demetrius). Metochites continues to describe his success in both rhetoric and philosophy. After referring to his triumphs as a servant of the emperor, he returns to his literary achievements when he speaks about the utility of his treatise on astronomy: 'I composed and brought out new writings on astronomy, so that a student of that science might understand whatever was necessary in each particular case better than previously.'[36]

One of the most important expressions of Metochites' self-confidence as a writer is Poem 4, addressed to his student Nikephoros Gregoras. In it, he stresses that he was able to prove his competence in all branches of human knowledge: 'Being most willing to win glory, I have written books dealing with many different branches of human wisdom, which demonstrate amply my deep knowledge; no one who knows the selfishness of our common human nature would blame such a desire: all men enjoy to be or to look glorious.'[37] Metochites reminds Gregoras of his abilities as both an accomplished orator and a philosopher: 'So I wrote several pieces of rhetoric, demonstrating my rhetorical skill and good style, which I cultivated always. In addition to them, I composed several philosophical treatises, the style of which is simple and unstudied.'[38] He also praises his achievements in astronomy.

The way he describes his own works in Poem 4 is far from modest. He admits he did not care to compose his philosophical works in an elaborate, adorned and rhetorical style, but instead preferred to write them in a simple manner,[39] in contrast to Psellos, who valued his ability to adorn his philosophical writings with the proper, elevated rhetorical style. He confidently asserts that they will be very useful both to Gregoras himself and to other men in the future.[40]

In the introduction to his paraphrases of Aristotle, Metochites adopts a more reserved tone than he takes in Poem 4, but he remains similarly confident as conveyed there.[41] His most important account of his literary activity is to be found in Poem 12, which is addressed to Nikephoros Xanthopoulos, another important scholar of the Palaiologan period. Once more Metochites refers to a dimension of scholarly activity encountered in Poem 4 – that is, glory: '[W]henever you read them, you praise them, believing that they are very useful for our fellow men and that they may bring me great glory in this life, a sort of glory admired by most people.' Metochites does not indicate whether he feels the same about Xanthopoulos' work as he proclaims the scholar feels about his. He then distinguishes between his philosophical works, which caused him great difficulty in finding the most proper way to express his thoughts, and his rhetorical works, which have an adorned and elevated style.[42] In this case, he makes no comment on the style of the former. He states the following about his rhetorical production: 'My writings are preserved in various copybooks in my private lodgings; each of them was a product of a different occasion. They or they may not be appreciated as adequate writings. In my view, of all these works the following seem to have accomplished the task for which I composed them in a most satisfactory way.'[43]

Metochites expresses his views on his own writings in a somewhat more discreet tone than Psellos, who boasts unreservedly about his own literary activities. He singles out three of his own rhetorical works, *Ethikos*, Oration 11, *Byzantios*, and Oration 6, for Gregory of Nazianzus. *Ethikos* borders on the esoteric, understandable only to those initiated in the thought of its author: '[I]t is the herald of my mind, bringing forward all my inner thoughts; some of them can be easily comprehended, some others are hidden deep within, waiting for the man who could penetrate my mind in order to understand them. It is also beautifully written, and its style is not devoid of some grace.'[44] It is significant that in this case, Metochites seems to approve of the combination of a proper philosophical investigation with the employment of an elevated rhetorical style. *Byzantios*, he states,

> is modelled on those ancient patterns composed by illustrious authors, the fame of which is great; it follows the example of those ancient prestigious writers, who fought in the contest of speech, on account of its whole structure, its following of the laws of rhetoric, its content, its beautiful vocabulary and its eloquent style: I refer you to the shining and pure Attic diction and the beauty of language.[45]

Metochites seems to be referring to the well-known *Panathenaikos*, by Aelius Aristeides, which was his main source of inspiration in composing *Byzantios*. He does not refer to any innovative aspects of *Byzantios*; rather, its main value lies in its imitation of the illustrious authors of the past. Metochites refrains from evaluating his oration for Gregory the Theologian, making only a passing reference to it.

Metochites then mentions his *Miscellanea*:

> Examples of all the things I have just mentioned, dressed in a proper style, may be found in it; they gush out of my mind as if from a treasury, various theories shaped by the subcategories of manifold wisdom, both old and new, being most prestigious. The book may be considered a testimony to the strength of my mind and to my erudition.[46]

Further on, Metochites notes: 'I consider that book an image of my mind, or rather a statue of myself for the sake of future generations.'[47] He also mentions his astronomical works and his commentary on Aristotle's *Physics*: 'Anyone who studies that book of mine will be able to understand whatever he wishes or needs to learn from those difficult and greatly desired doctrines of Aristotle, readily and easily.'[48]

Metochites also refers to his poems in Poem 12, for Michael the New Martyr:

> But I also hold in esteem the poems I composed recently, which have the grace of poetry, trying to refresh a little my heart which is constantly tormented by my

sorrows, and to relieve it from my mischievous cares. Thus, I bring a refreshing breath to my heart inside, which comes from the spring-time flowers of the evergreen meadows of poetry; I am playing in a situation which is quite serious.[49]

Metochites presents himself as a player, although he is surrounded by the most adverse circumstances of life. Poetry is presented as a meadow full of flowers, the notion of a poem as a collection of flowers being an ancient concept,[50] and the imagery of a meadow of literature being widespread in late antique literature.[51] In other images of literary activity, for example, in Oration 3, dealing with the archangel Michael, who is of an immaterial substance, Metochites offers up the traditional comparison of the writer, able to create a multifaceted representation of his object, with the painter (or any other artist), unable to craft a full representation of an object due to the inferiority of the visual arts, which are limited to depicting the external characteristics of it.[52] In Oration 4, for St Demetrius, Metochites also compares the writer to an athlete or a musician, who takes part in competitions.[53] He even compares himself to a bird mourning for the misfortunes that befell it.[54]

In *Ethikos*, Metochites states that the gift of speech is most important because through it someone may benefit his friends and harm his enemies:

> Whatever you might need on any occasion, you can accomplish this via the gift of wisdom or use it as an item of exchange, you can enjoy the rewards of wisdom and the graces of reasoning and offer them as a compensation for anything, and if anything were to happen to you, you would not face any difficulty in paying it back; and whatever you might love and partake in can be substituted, offering instead the gifts of reason. This could happen also to human beings, of course, because no one can be so miserable and ignorant as not to be eager to buy fine rhetorical speeches and the weighty fame that comes with them, offering whatever he can in exchange. But it is also possible to use these speeches especially for divine purposes, in our relations with the merciful common Master of us all, as well as with his own friends and servants. In this area, the gifts of reason are particularly beloved, since these are the only gifts one can offer, and the tributes of reason on our own part are welcome like nothing else I can think of, in fact more welcome than anything else. If you need someone among the friends of God who can for his part protect you in a troublesome situation, for example when you are in danger, sickness, or in any other difficulty, you can easily rid yourself of the affliction that troubles you by promising to contribute somehow a laudatory thanksgiving Oration.[55]

This passage is key in highlighting Metochites' conception of his literary output. In Byzantium, rhetoric provided a way to promote oneself and ascend the social ladder. Metochites was well aware that it was thanks to his literary charisma that Emperor Andronikos II Palaiologos decided to promote him; he had employed him for his renowned wisdom.[56] This was typical. Most Byzantine authors were cognizant of this dimension of their literary achievements, but mere lobbyism should not be considered the primary aim of their literary activity.[57] What astonishes about

Metochites is that he projects the writers' situation to the level of the supernatural reality: he considers his literary output as his true property, which he can offer to God and the saints and in return receive material advantages as a reward.

The quintessential medieval man, Metochites discerns hidden connections between the realities of the earth and the supernatural world of the heavenly realm. God, the supreme ruler, stands ready to accept the gifts of men and reward them accordingly. It is a view far removed from the theology of the Orthodox Church, which discouraged the idea that man's relationship to God is transactional in nature, including providing for the material needs of man. In any case, the way Metochites regards his own literary output indicates the strong feelings he had for it. His writings are his children and his property at the same time.[58] He can present and distribute them as he wishes. It is an attitude not frequently encountered among the intellectual elite of Byzantium, although the term 'tribute' is frequently encountered as a designation of an author's own writings in the Palaiologan period.[59] Few intellectuals were willing to admit that their literary output represented nothing more than a materialistic bargain between themselves and their powerful patrons, who made use of their abilities to promote themselves and immortalize their achievements. Even fewer of them would have dared speak about a bargain with God, implying that men who lacked the gift of speech were at a disadvantage if they wanted to approach God and ask for his intervention.

The introduction to *Stoikkheiosis Astronomike* constitutes a short autobiography. Since most of the information in it also appears in Poem 1 and Essay 28 of the *Miscellanea* and has been exhaustively studied by Martin Hinterberger,[60] there is only a need here to underline that there, too, Metochites insists that glory comes to man as a result of the individual's literary achievements. Metochites points out that he took care to study properly all the glorious orators of the past and to avoid the rhetorical excesses of his contemporaries.[61]

Metochites' views on his own literary activity leave the impression that he evaluates it as a safeguard for his future glory. One might be inclined to believe in the sincerity of this expression of concern for his own legacy were it not for a passage in *Ethikos* where he expressly criticizes those authors who have a disproportionately high view of the value of education and learnedness as sources of post-mortem glory while ignoring other aspects of human activity, such as art, that may be sources of glory as well:

> It is also wholly true, and this is what I have argued, that the occupations of the wise man are not the cause of a more enduring afterlife for him than are those of other craftsmen, due to the essential nature of the commemoration that is left behind, as some people want to believe. For what we were now seeking to find, I think, was not which of the occupations with which different people are engaged is the best and most profitable for human life, but whether it is only literary compositions that secure eternal memory for their author and do not allow him to die. I have observed that other occupations leave their creators unforgotten or immortal to the same extent, because of this memory. Still, apart from this, what is the value of such fame? In what way are the works that endure

significant for the learned man, or what benefit does he get from the writings he left behind, even if subsequent generations study and honour them? Or what greater pleasure and satisfaction could he receive when his works are studied compared to other people who now lie dead along with him, having spent their whole life as rustic peasants and artisans?[62]

Metochites does not deny the supreme value of education. What he does question is whether a learned man can attain more glory than an artisan who creates significant works of art or edifices that immortalize their fame. Such a confession comes as a surprise to those familiar with Metochites' poems, where the glory attained by authors through the dissemination of their writings is considered the most desirable thing in life. This particular glory was praised by many intellectuals in both antiquity and Byzantium. Thomas Magistros, a contemporary and friend of Metochites, extolled the glory attained by writers in some of his works, which Metochites certainly read. It is possible that Metochites wanted to mitigate the enthusiasm of his contemporaries, like Magistros, who were eager to attain glory and fame by composing works that would be immortalized.[63] In *Ethikos*, Metochites seems to dismiss the utility and value of such glory. His main concern in the treatise is to prove the value of education per se and to persuade his audience that education is something desirable for any man and valuable for his own spiritual and moral improvement, regardless of the fame he might or might not attain through his literary endeavours. This was a somewhat novel conception of education and culture and ran counter to the dominant preconceptions in Byzantine society, which considered attaining a good education as equivalent to fame and promotion in society. Metochites, who appeared sensitive to the matter in his poems, bluntly denies such a conception, which he views as contrary to his inner, perhaps humanistic, convictions. One would certainly be right to have some doubts about the sincerity of such a harsh rejection of the social function of education by Metochites, who like Michael Choniates in the late twelfth century presents himself as a scholar who refuses to 'sell out' by abandoning his life of studying.[64] Metochites' elusiveness is evident once more.

This is another case of Metochites – when clearly speaking about himself, employing the first person – projecting ambiguous and multifaceted images of himself. Metochites as the self-confident public servant devoted to his emperor appears side by side with Metochites the sinner, who humbly asks God and the Virgin Mary for the remittance of his sins. The mask of the self-confident author proud of his literary output, which he considers a safeguard for his future glory, gives way to that of a sceptic with serious doubts about the glory attained by any writer. It is evident that Metochites employs different masks before his audience.

Soliloquy: Image creation through dialogue with the soul

Metochites employed another strategy to create and promote certain images of himself. It neither involved presenting himself as a protagonist nor hiding himself behind the masks of others. Instead, he intentionally conceals his true self from the

1. Metochites on Himself

audience by creating two images of himself in dialogue with each other – that is, through soliloquy.

Soliloquy is 'an internal dialogue between two speaking voices within the same mind or soul'.[65] It is neither a monologue nor a dialogue. The trail of this literary genre, if one may use that term, can be traced back to late antiquity, most particularly to St Gregory of Nazianzus and St Augustine. Soliloquy usually takes the form of self-questioning,[66] like a soul engaging in conversation with itself. This is a realization of none other than Plato, who described such thought in a passage of the *Sophist*, which Metochites quotes in Oration 3.[67] Metochites employs soliloquy in Poems 19 and 20, the last two in his collection. In fact, all the poems written after his fall from power – that is, Poems 14–20 – are titled 'To Himself' (Εἰς ἑαυτὸν). In Poems 14–18, the author's engagement with his soul takes the form of a monologue, with no evidence of a discussion between opposing voices. In the first verse of both Poems 19 and 20, Metochites directly addresses his soul.

The poet addressing his soul has a long history in Greek literature.[68] Homer (*Odyssey* 20.18) has Ulysses do so when he realizes the suitors have been having sex with the maidens of his palace. Byzantine authors also had access to the Psalms of David, several of which are soliloquies. Byzantine hymnographers maintained the tradition of the soliloquies of David, addressing their souls quite frequently and lamenting their sinful pasts.[69] Some poems of John Mauropous may be considered soliloquies.[70] Thus, Metochites follows in a well-established tradition of soliloquy, probably not as complex as that of the Latin West, which dates back to Augustine.[71] Regardless, it was sufficiently rich to provide Metochites with certain patterns for manipulating his thoughts and creating images of himself appropriate to the ever-changing conditions of his life.

Poems 19 and 20 resemble some of the autobiographic poems of Gregory of Nazianzus. Prayers alternate with dialogues between Metochites and his soul to discuss the misery and instability of life.[72] Metochites' inner tensions are resolved by his realization that his attitude has remained unchanged amid the turmoil. Poem 19 (vv. 1–5) begins with Metochites asking his soul what it thinks about the losses inflicted on him by adverse fortune.[73] One might be tempted to consider what comes next (vv. 6–45) as his soul's extensive answer to the question,[74] but this is far from certain. In any case, Metochites addresses his soul once more (v. 46), urging it not to be exceedingly upset by the disasters that had befallen him. He continues with a rather long account of the reasons for his soul to remain calm in the face of his adverse fortune, into which he inserts a laborious description of his house in Constantinople.[75] Metochites had a habit of repeating the opening phrase of a section of his poems after completing it, and he follows this pattern in Poem 19 (v. 252), where he encourages his soul once more, advising it not to be exceedingly sad because of his misfortunes.[76] He again repeats the same advice later on.[77] In fact, Metochites repeats the arguments he had employed in the introductory section of his poem. A new section is introduced in v. 279: Metochites considers himself lucky, since he had enjoyed the gifts of God for many years without interruption. In this section, the dialogue of the author with his soul intensifies, becoming more vivid through frequent exchanges between his two selves.[78] In vv. 320-6, Metochites cites in indirect speech a possible objection his soul might raise to his arguments: his success might be considered his own personal achievement.[79] Metochites denies this, asserting to his soul that whatever he possesses is in fact a gift from God.[80] The author addresses his soul one last time near the end of the poem,[81] advising it to remain calm, turning towards God.

With this soliloquy, Metochites is trying to project an image somewhat different from the ones he had painted in his earlier works. As noted, in the autobiographical Poem 1 – probably addressed to and in praise of Emperor Andronikos II – Metochites projected the image of a self-confident young bureaucrat who had taken every step to the peak of career success. He abandoned his scholarly pursuits, adopting a more plum way of life, that of a bureaucrat with close ties to the emperor, who was impressed by his merits and made him his chief adviser; there is no trace of self-doubt or regret for abandoning his studies for the sake of worldly glory. The picture Metochites presents of himself in *Ethikos*, however, is quite different: there, the image of the self-confident public servant gives way to that of an almost broken man disappointed by his decision to abandon the contemplative life for an active life.

Thus, in Poem 19, one of Metochites' last works, he forged a new image of himself equally distant from both the gloomy picture of *Ethikos*, though somehow related to it, and the more positive one of Poem 1: Metochites projects the image of the self-confident and self-sufficient scholar who has finally learned his lesson. The adversities of life cannot distract him from the goal he has pursued all his life – the attainment of virtue and education. His serenity resembles that of late antique scholars, like Epictetus and Marcus Aurelius, who remained untroubled by adversity. Indeed, the period after 1328 was the appropriate moment for Metochites to project such an image of himself. He had lost everything. He no longer needed to flatter the emperor, as had been the case of Poem 1. He had no need to reaffirm his friends of his devotion to scholarship despite his earlier decision to abandon the contemplative life, as pertained to *Ethikos*. Metochites is totally alone and speaking to a very limited audience. Feeling the need to address himself solemnly, probably for one last time, he settled on the soliloquy at this phase of his life to present an account of his endeavours and his shattered plans to himself. The soliloquy provided Metochites with a principle of organization, as evident in Poem 19. An instance of self-questioning marks each transition to a new section of the poem. Combining soliloquy with a narrative section, the one describing his house, Metochites projects a convincing picture of himself, remaining calm and stable amid his misfortune.

Poem 20 offers a somewhat different perspective. Metochites does not urge his soul to remain calm, but instead asks why it's disturbed. The soul with which he engages in discussion is probably his previous self, that of the industrious and ambitious politician unable to accept the reversal of his luck. Reminding his soul that many people have suffered similar misfortune in the past, Metochites argues that no one is immune to attacks on fortune, which are malicious and fickle.[82] Metochites then turns his soliloquy into an address to an imaginary audience.[83] In it, he admonishes his fellow men to stop wandering aimlessly in life and to cease placing confidence in capricious fortune, which can overturn man's happiness in an instant. The same advice could have been given to his own soul; it is in fact an address to himself, which takes the form of a more general address to an imaginary audience. In v. 61, Metochites chides his soul not to be immoderate in its grief, for other people have suffered much more in the past.[84] In v. 90, he expresses an objection his soul might raise in the form of a question, which he immediately answers: 'Did you endure more pain than those people? Remember that you have enjoyed many more goods for a long time.'[85] Later on, Metochites repeats his advice to his soul to keep those considerations in mind to avoid being covered by the cloud of distress, adding that it would be shameful for it to behave in a manner unbefitting his various works, which constantly advised men to keep their serenity in the midst of misfortune.[86] In vv. 206–7, Metochites, in his usual fashion, marks the end of this section, urging his soul to remain faithful to its principles, reminding it of the story of the Rhodian captain who retained his serenity in the face of a menacing storm.[87] The poem ends abruptly due to the loss of some of the manuscript folios preserving it. It is noteworthy that, in the last preserved verses of the poem,[88] Metochites urges both himself (ἑαυτὸν) and his mind to maintain this disposition (θυμὸν). Metochites does not make a philosophical distinction between the various parts of the human soul; he uses the soul as a way to distinguish his inner self (mind) from the disposition that it had to keep in the face of the calamities of life.

This distinction may have another function in Metochites' soliloquies: it serves as an appropriate way for Metochites to keep his distance from himself, affording him the opportunity to create various self-images, each different from the other. Take, for instance, his use of soliloquy in Poem 13, addressed to his close friend and kinsman Leon Bardales. Here, Metochites urges his soul to remain calm and keep its composure when remembering the felicitous previous years, during which the author was occupied with his studies and had no other concern.[89] Then the soliloquy takes a turn, with Metochites addressing the church of Hagia Sophia, to him heaven on earth, the place of his past spiritual achievements, the place that safeguarded his serenity and composure.[90] The address is in fact a soliloquy, but with his soul having been replaced by a personification of Hagia Sophia. In fact, the church is an image of Metochites' other self, of his soul, or rather, as Metochites himself puts it, the 'light and breath of his soul'.[91] Hagia Sophia becomes in fact a heterotopy, which Metochites manipulates in such a way as to express his inner doubts concerning the fateful choice he made early on in his life to abandon his literary studies and focus his attention on the affairs of the Byzantine state. Poem 13 creates an atmosphere similar to that in *Ethikos*. Metochites is at the peak of his career, and his doubts concerning his choices in life torture him. He expresses them through a soliloquy. Then, Hagia Sophia becomes a mirror of himself, which reflects all his disappointments after a long and laborious life.

Heterotopies: Struggles with realities of the times

Michel Foucault's concept of heterotopy is useful in discussing this basic aspect of Metochites' literary output. A heterotopy is a realized utopia, so to speak, a specific place where people throughout the ages have tried to realize their dreams. It is, in essence, a social, political or sometimes psychological laboratory where the laws of life that the people have come to know are replaced by different laws introduced by those who control the utopia, mildly or possibly radically transforming those who live in it.[92] For Metochites, the Byzantine capital, Constantinople, which he describes in *Byzantios*, is such a heterotopy.

The capital depicted in *Byzantios* is the combination of all the differences in this world which are led towards their reconciliation through Constantinople and because of it.[93] Being a harbour, Constantinople is the only place on earth where, according to Metochites, all men of various races are able to communicate with each other without fear.[94] This is obviously wishful thinking. Metochites, the all-powerful megas logothetes of the emperor, creates his own heterotopy out of Constantinople. In short, what he presents is an expression of his own dream of the ideal city. One should not, however, interpret this image of Constantinople as a pure utopia. Metochites is deeply attached to the city, and his admiration for its achievements and its civilizing mission seems genuine. He tries to extract the city from its real environment to create a heterotopy, which for him is a place where the ideals of the contemplative life and the active life are combined.

Metochites' somewhat impassioned extraction of Constantinople from its environs is quite powerful. He establishes the geographical location of the city with the natural environment surrounding it, especially the Black Sea, a rough and frightening body of water, and comes to the conclusion that the city tames the Black Sea through the Bosporus Straits, transforming it into an obedient tool.[95] Crucially however, the city manages to make the Black Sea, which descends upon it like a frightening river that destroys everything in its path, its most faithful lover.[96] The symbolic function of the Black Sea in the text is quite evident. For Metochites, it represents the external or internal forces that threatened what was left of the Byzantine Empire, which according to him remained the cradle of civilization. Metochites' image of the city taming and subjugating these forces has a triumphant tone, but the imperial city becomes a site of crisis threatening its very existence and disrupting the author's life[97]. In moments of sobriety, Metochites surely would have had doubts about the reality of this image. It must have been obvious to him that the city might not be able to survive the attacks by its enemies, who became increasingly powerful with time. Nonetheless, the image he wishes to convey is clear: Constantinople is the last remnant of civilization, a mighty and constant bulwark against the forces of darkness that threaten to overcome it. This seems to be the real vision of Metochites' heterotopy.

The Byzantine state, or what remained of it, was another heterotopy dear to Metochites. The way he describes the part of Asia Minor still controlled by Constantinople in Oration 7 is indicative of his perspective. He presents Asia Minor – more precisely the area between the Sangarios and Maeandros Rivers – as an area of civilization, compared to the forces of barbarity and darkness that surround it,[98] clearly referring to the Turkoman tribes that had gained the upper hand after the fall of the Sultanate of Rum in the late thirteenth century. Adopting the ancient philosophical distinction between *limit* and *limitless*, Metochites applies these terms to the two respective areas of Asia Minor, Byzantine and

Turkish. He contrasts the Greek area, with well-defined limits, and the vast expanse of lands across Anatolia, which are limitless in both the literal and metaphorical sense. This limitlessness is, in fact, equivalent to lawlessness and barbarity. On the other hand, the Greek area resembles a treasury, exhibiting everything valuable in Byzantine culture.

There are heterotopies in many other works of Metochites. He addresses Poem 3 to Gregory of Bulgaria, the former archbishop of Bulgaria who settled in the monastery of the archangel Michael in the suburbs of Constantinople. Metochites stresses that Gregory has deliberately cut himself off from all contact with worldly affairs. The imagery drawn by Metochites is telling: Gregory has built a wall around himself, protecting himself from all of his enemies' attacks.[99] He has detached his soul from all the adversity of this world.[100] Of note, the image of the rough sea, also found in *Byzantios*, appears in Poem 3: Gregory, observing the waves of the Bosporus from his commanding post, realizes that the world is pounded by the ever-shifting waves of fortune.[101] Metochites writes that Gregory, in a monastery near the Bosporus, sees the tides of the sea changing directions all day and compares them with the ups and downs of human life, a state of constant flux.[102]

Of importance here is that Metochites contrasts the tides of the Bosporus with the calmness of Gregory's small hermitage. Therefore, the waves of the Bosporus help Metochites accurately and concretely delineate the heterotopy of Gregory. The rough and threatening Black Sea contrasts with the city of Constantinople similarly to the portrayal in *Byzantios*; there, the threatening and unstable Black Sea, probably symbolic of the uncivilized part of the world, had helped Metochites to establish Constantinople as a safe haven through which the values of civilization could be sent to the four corners of the earth. In the poem to Gregory, the tides of the Bosporus do not appear to be tamed by anything, in contrast to *Byzantios*. The Bosporus reminds Gregory 'of the tides of the sea of our life, which is unreliable'.[103] It resists placation by anything, unlike in *Byzantios*, where the civilizing influence of Constantinople prevails. Through this heterotopy, one sees how Metochites manipulates images as if they were successive stages of a theatrical drama. A heterotopy used by the author in a positive sense in one of work can be used in a less positive sense in another. Heterotopies are an expression of the constant change that dominates the theatre of human life.

One also finds smaller heterotopies within the larger heterotopy of Constantinople in the works of Metochites, among them the church of Hagia Sophia, which Metochites describes in some detail in *Byzantios*. According to him the Great Church is the apex of the city, akin to the acropolis of the cities of the past.[104] It is the abode of the divinity. As a heterotopy, Hagia Sophia plays an important role in Poems 11 and 13, addressed to Theodore Xanthopoulos and Leon Bardales, respectively. In both poems, Metochites describes the church as a haven,[105] which safeguarded his serenity in the past. In Poem 11, he juxtaposes Hagia Sophia to another heterotopy, the imperial palace, at the time the site of Metochites' service and the source of his anxiety and grief.[106] As noted above, in Poem 13 Metochites addresses Hagia Sophia directly.[107] It is in fact a soliloquy, in which Metochites seems to identify the church with the contemplative life. In other words, Hagia Sophia becomes a *figura* of the ideal life as described by Metochites in many of his works, a *figura* here being a concrete, historical reality that prefigures another reality, concrete and historical.[108] The use of these juxtaposed heterotopies imbues them with symbolic meaning, whose opposition Metochites further developed in describing the monastery of Chora, his most important heterotopy.

Metochites' effort to restore Chora represents the culmination of his efforts to leave his mark on his beloved city as well as an attempt to placate God for his transgressions. Chora was to stand as his most enduring achievement, safeguarding his glory in the future. It is particularly in his poems that Metochites applies the safe haven image to Chora. The restored monastery became a heterotopy inside the larger heterotopy of the Constantinople described in *Byzantios*. With the restoration, Metochites also took care to install a monastic group in Chora with an eye towards transforming the place into a spiritual abode and sanctuary for himself. In this regard, he transferred all his books, his most important possessions, to the monastery, urging the monks to keep them safe. He describes his restorative work at length in Poem 2, which is for the most part a traditional *ekphrasis* on the buildings of Chora, and speaks about Chora in language characteristic of him, calling it his κρησφύγετον,[109] keeping him safe from the attacks of his enemies.

Poem 19 deals with Metochites' misfortunes after he fell from power in 1328. The angry mob of Constantinople, at the instigation of the supporters of the new emperor, Andronikos III Palaiologos, pillaged Metochites' house, destroying everything inside it. This gives the author the opportunity to share a detailed description, *ekphrasis*, of his house that closely resembles the one of Chora in Poem 2. He presents the house as a treasury of all manner of valuable and luxurious things.[110] One would surmise that Metochites sees this description as an opportunity to exhibit his glory and wealth, except that he then rushes to conclude that all these were destroyed when the house was sacked. At the end of the poem, he remarks that his only consolation is that Chora was left intact and undamaged amid the turmoil.[111]

The poem is highly allusive, almost symbolic. Metochites' house, which represents certain aspects of earthly life – luxury, wealth, glory – is one of the heterotopies in the work, Chora being the other one. The monastery represents the absence or rejection of worldly and material values in the form of self-denial, asceticism and spirituality. The house as heterotopy is ephemeral; its destruction symbolizes the futility of materialistic values. On the other hand, the survival of Chora indicates that only what pertains to the soul is of real value, being stable and unperishable. Poem 19, on the basis of these two juxtaposed heterotopies, offers a graphic representation of the theme permeating the corpus of Metochites' works: whatever is given to the material self by human fortune is unstable and elusive; only treasures of the soul are stable, providing an opportunity for salvation and access to the ineffable riches of the unperishable and eternal kingdom of the Lord.

Some of the heterotopies in the works of Metochites have a clear political symbolism, serving as another means of concealing his real political views. These heterotopies cannot, however, be considered proper symbols since they are concrete realities. The term *figura* is preferable for those kinds of heterotopies. For example, Jesus of Naue prefigures Jesus Christ; Hagar is a figure of the Old Testament, Sarah is a figure of the New Testament; Noah's ark is a figure of the church. One may also employ the Greek term τύπος, often used by the church fathers to mean images or figures under which other realities are hidden; the adherents try to uncover those realities. A figure is not the same as a symbol. Whiteness is a symbol, not a figure of chastity; Moses is a figure, not a symbol of Christ. Figures were closely connected with the allegorical interpretation of the Holy Scripture and were an integral component of both Eastern and Western medieval spirituality.[112] The medieval man detected such connections, between appearances (persons, objects, etc.) and the realities that lay underneath them.

Figurae: Elements of self-referentiality

Metochites used another type of figure – actual personalities from ancient history – in his last seven poems, written after his fall from power in 1328. He stresses that this turn of events in his life did not come to him unexpectedly, since as a good philosopher he had long ago contemplated the instability of human fortune and prepared himself for such an eventuality. His last poems are full of generalizations concerning the value of human goods and the futility of man's efforts to attain happiness in this world, but he refrains from stating his views on the concrete causes of his fall from power. He mentions neither his patron and protector, Andronikos II, nor the usurper, Andronikos III, who persecuted Metochites, banishing him to Didymoteichon and stripping him of all vestiges of power. One gets the impression that Metochites thereafter lost interest in the affairs of the state and ultimately turned inwards, following the precepts of the ancient Stoic philosophers. Such an impression is in all probability false, as attested by the historical examples he chose to illustrate his case, two of which are particularly revealing.

In Poem 17, Metochites invokes the examples of Polycrates of Samos and Philip II of Macedon in discussing the inevitability of eventual bad fortune for men like himself, who enjoy a provisional happiness. Polycrates was famous for his good fortune, which incurred the envy of the gods, who destroyed him. Metochites reproduces the story of the tyrant of Samos based on Herodotus' well-known account.[113] Can the arrogant tyrant of Samos be identified with the unlucky Andronikos II, deposed by his own grandson? While there is no definitive answer to this question, the case of Philip of Macedon shares even more similarities with Andronikos II. When a string of fortuitous events visited Philip in a single day, he anxiously asked Zeus to send him a misfortune as well, being aware that excessive fortune was impermissible for human beings. Sometime later, Philip, the most illustrious and worthy king, fell victim to Pausanias, a nonentity who assassinated him. Metochites adds that he, too, had been prepared for the reversal of his fortune long before it occurred. Thus, Metochites clearly identifies himself with Philip,[114] but the question remains whether Philip might also be identified with Andronikos

II and Pausanias with Andronikos III, the arrogant, young usurper. The obvious answer is that Metochites employs the case of Pausanias as a symbol of Andronikos III. Metochites presents Pausanias as a victim of wine, employing a Homeric phrase ἀτάσθαλα ἐοργότος, to underline his moral depravity and ignorance.[115] Therefore, Philip may be a *figura* of the wise and experienced emperor Andronikos II, who lost his throne despite not deserving such a fate.

In Poem 19, Metochites employs another example that can be interpreted as veiled criticism of the new lords of the empire. Urging his soul not to be excessively saddened by the loss of his material wealth, Metochites states that man's only true wealth is wisdom and the other ornaments of his soul. He reminds himself of the story of Stilpo of Megara, who was asked by Demetrius Poliorketes, after his soldiers had sacked the city, whether they had taken anything belonging to him. Stilpo calmly answered that he had not seen any of Demetrius' soldiers carrying wisdom on their shoulders.[116] It is evident that Metochites identifies himself with Stilpo the philosopher. Could he be depicting Andronikos III as a new Demetrius Poliorketes? Possibly. Demetrius was infamous for his depravity, erotic adventures and lack of moral principles. Although Metochites refrains from describing Demetrius' character traits in Poem 19, his readers must have been familiar with the Macedonian king's proclivities. Andronikos III was guilty of a certain moral laxity. Demetrius would have been an excellent choice behind which to hide criticism of the new emperor.

Demetrius Poliorcetes, Polycrates and Philip of Macedon are not symbols, but *figurae* – that is, real people who point towards concrete realities but have no other connections with them except for those invented by the author who employs them. The inclusion of those figures in the poems after Metochites' fall from power is not accidental. Metochites used them in a political context, while alluding to contemporary events. Therefore, Metochites' elusiveness is once again present, in the last case of Demetrius and Andronikos III in the way he manipulates the figures to criticize the new political elite in an allusive, concealed manner. Metochites, who had nothing but praise for the emperor as long as he remained in power, goes to the other extreme, criticizing the new emperor as soon as he removes Metochites from the all-powerful position of megas logothetes. Even near the end of Metochites' life, stripped of his illustrious insigniae of power, he remained elusive, never clearly and unequivocally taking sides. Metochites used heterotopies and figures as tools for creating new masks, enhancing his renowned elusiveness exactly as he did in planning and carrying out the reconstruction of the monastery of Chora, a complex and innovative structure, as Robert Ousterhout pointed out long ago.[117]

Speaking of Chora, in Poems 1 and 2, Metochites included long descriptions of the monastery, leading one to wonder whether there are hidden *figurae* in them. Can the realities he describes be considered allegories of his texts or even of his own persona? Metochites describes the world as a harmonious whole in Poems 1 and 10. Despite all the rhetorical force of his argumentation, there is nothing special in his assertion that God put the harmonic laws governing the world inside it at the Creation. What is noteworthy is his insistence on describing his own text, praising the laws of harmony – for example, noting that Poem 10 obeys the same laws of harmony governing the world.[118] Thus, his text seems to be an image of the world, of the cosmos. A similar picture is painted in Poem 1, where Metochites seems to once more compare his own text with the world, when affirming that his text is a herald of his own thoughts immediately after asserting that the world is a herald of the majestic plans of God.[119] Although the connection between the world and his text, Poem 1, praising it, is not as clear as the connection established between the other text, Poem 10, and the harmonious world, one cannot fail to see the connection established when taking into account another fact: in Poem 1 Metochites clearly connects the world and a restored Chora to his former glory. Chora is not just a harmonious whole constructed according to the laws of harmony and symmetry;[120] what astonishes is that its contemplation creates inside the soul of the spectator the same feeling generated by the contemplation of the world according to the many texts of Metochites: serenity mixed with joy.[121] Therefore, Metochites seems to try to establish an intertextual discourse, in which his text makes a commentary, although hidden and allusive, on itself.

This is not an arbitrary conclusion. At the end of Oration 10 (*Ethikos*), Metochites speaks in almost identical terms as those employed in the case of Chora about his own text: it is an offering pure and clean, most proper for God.[122] Therefore, his offering of the monastery of the Virgin to God, as a most immaculate and proper gift,[123] is tantamount to the offering of his text to God as well. This may be interpreted in connection with the description of Chora in Poem 1: both his text and his monastery are his most valuable offerings to his Creator. It is also remarkable that Metochites offers himself to God or to the Virgin Mary as well.[124] Both Chora and the world may be interpreted as *figurae* of Metochites' own written discourse or even of himself as an author. It seems to me that the cosmos, Chora, Metochites' text, and even Metochites himself, reflect each other in a subtle way, a metatextual element that gives Poem 1 its coherence and persuasiveness. This is hardly surprising: in medieval thought, both Eastern and Western, the world was seen as a great book, a text written by God. Did Metochites consider himself as such a text? In Poem 12, he characterizes *Gnomikai Semeioseis* as a πίναξ of his own mind,[125] while *Ethikos* is described as a herald (κῆρυξ) of it.[126] The words would not have been unfamiliar to his audience. Most orators did not fail to describe their writings as pictures, images or icons of the persons who were praised by them; it was an old topos employed by most orators who wanted to stress the moral aspect of their art; a rhetorical speech, being an image of a certain most virtuous person, may be used as an archetype of proper behaviour by its audience. In Poem 12, πίναξ may well retain its usual meaning – in which case one has to assume that the identification of the author with his own text is almost complete – but πίναξ also can mean 'inventory' or a 'table', as in a book's contents (like the ones at the front of manuscripts containing Metochites' works). Does Metochites regard his *Gnomikai Semeioseis*, a miscellaneous work, as an inventory of the various branches of knowledge stored inside his mind? It is possible.

In any case one must conclude that Metochites did not hesitate to employ various *figurae* to function as allegories, including of himself and his own texts. This served as a way for him to view his persona from a certain distance as an author. At the same time, it provided him space for introspection.[127]

Chapter 2

METOCHITES ON OTHERS: MIRROR IMAGES OF HIMSELF

In addition to first-person discourses in Metochites' works, one also finds numerous idealized portraits of men from his near and distant past. Of particular interest, these men appear strikingly familiar, 'mirror figures' as it were, in that they exhibit most of the characteristics the author attributes to himself in the self-portraits he created in his works.[1]

Metochites in his orations describes his relationship with Emperor Andronikos II Palaiologos as one of 'ardent desire' (πόθος),[2] which seems to denote the feeling of subjects towards their sovereign. He also speaks about the 'benevolence' (εὔνοια) the citizens of Thessalonike feel towards the emperor.[3] Citizens' attitude towards Andronikos' mother, Empress Theodora, is also described as πόθος.[4] He speaks about the εὔνοια that Loukas, the abbot of the monastery of Chora, felt towards him.[5] Loukas was subordinate to Metochites in being his 'employee' at Chora. His relationships with Joseph Rhakendytes, the brothers Xanthopouloi, Nikephoros Gregoras and Leon Bardales were different: Metochites considered Joseph a 'friend' (φίλος). He enjoyed his relationship with Joseph as an equal. On the other hand, addressing St Demetrius of Thessalonike, Metochites does not hesitate to call himself 'miserable';[6] he takes refuge in the saint as his last anchor of hope.[7] His feelings of superiority disappear. Thus, his relations with his contemporaries are determined by the sociolect. This should be expected from a man so well versed in the intricacies of the stratified society of his times.

In discussing the texts of Metochites speaking about other people, one may begin with Metochites' longest speech, Oration 6, for Gregory of Nazianzus, the Byzantine intellectual par excellence. The two men travelled a broadly similar path. An ambitious young intellectual devoted to his studies, Gregory was forced by the circumstances of life to abandon his intellectual endeavours and take up the affairs of the church. Gregory's struggle between the realities of life and striving for the freedom of the contemplative life is vividly portrayed by Metochites, who was himself well aware of this tension. Metochites' Oration 17, for his close friend Joseph Rhakendytes, confers on his subject traits similar to Gregory's, but with one major difference: Joseph remained adamant in his pursuit of the contemplative life, which he zealously maintained until his death. The oration for Joseph borders on hagiography. Metochites idealizes the philosopher par excellence of his times and presents him as a new saint who deserves such characterization because of his devotion both to philosophy and to virtue. Joseph is the opposing counterpart to both Metochites and Gregory of Nazianzus, who were forced to yield to the necessities of this world, sacrificing themselves for the sake of their fellow Byzantines. The case of Gregory, the archbishop of Bulgaria whom Metochites addresses in Poem 3, is similar to Joseph's. Archbishop Gregory is a hero of the contemplative life. He abandoned all worldly cares, retiring to a hermitage on the shores of the Bosporus, contemplating the world and its marvels. Gregory of Bulgaria represents the type of scholar Metochites exudes great praise for in *Ethikos*.

Nikephoros Gregoras is something of a mirror of the young Metochites – a young scholar eager to learn everything and devote himself to the life of contemplation. In Poem 4, Metochites describes the educational curriculum for the sake of the young scholar, urging him to devote himself to his studies and become his intellectual heir. Oration 4, for St Demetrius, deals once more with a young man. Demetrius is not, however, an intellectual, but someone wanting to serve his country as a public official. Like the young Metochites, he attracts the attention of the emperor, in his case Maximianus, who appoints him to the highest office of the Roman Empire, but unlike Metochites, he goes on to become a saint. He does not appear to seek the fruits of secular contemplation, consistently training his mind and his thoughts on the realm of God.

The Oration 19, for St John of Didymoteichon, is one of Metochites' last writings. The forgotten saint of the early eleventh century had founded a monastery in Thrace, his only similarity with Metochites, who restored Chora. John is a humble and illiterate man with the single-minded ambition of avoiding any worldly glory. The same applies to Loukas, the abbot of Chora, whom Metochites praises in Oration 16. Loukas was an ascetic from Asia Minor, who strove for monastic perfection throughout his life. Learning was far from his ideal. Metochites, despite his enthusiasm for secular studies, seems to have a fondness for such simple men, who strove for union with God. This affinity is the also case with two other hagiographic speeches – Oration 3, for St Marina, and Oration 12, for Michael the New Martyr of Egypt.

Two success stories: Oration 4, on St Demetrius, and poem 1

Metochites dedicated Oration 4 to St Demetrius of Thessalonike, a great saint of the Byzantine church who had healed the author from an illness while in Asia Minor. The oration is a typical encomium of an illustrious saint. After a brief praise of the saint's native city, Thessalonike, and a passing reference to his aristocratic lineage, Metochites praises Demetrius' decision to embrace Christianity despite being a high-ranking Roman official. He describes with obvious self-satisfaction the glorious career of the saint, which was abruptly interrupted after Emperor Maximianus learned of his Christianity. Metochites reproduces the dialogue between the saint and his persecutor, describes the miracles that took place afterwards – Demetrius' fight with a scorpion in prison and the struggle between Nestor and Lyaios – and then arrives at the saint's execution. What comes next is very interesting: Metochites summarily recounts the saint's career, speaking about his four politeiai, or πολιτεῖαι (*politeiai*), a term of art in Byzantine hagiographic literature referring to a saint's conduct of his or her life:

> We see four politeiai in the case of the great martyr. He paid serious attention to all of them in a perfect manner. Proceeding further, he became prominent and reached the peak, from which he could not go any higher as the philosophical proverb says. Let us make a distinction between them, if you wish. The first politeia was that he offered himself to his native country to deal with him in the way it wished. But very soon he jumped up and nothing was able to contain his nature: he moved out of his city and advanced forward. His fame also spread as far as the emperor, who administered all the affairs of the Roman state, almost the entire earth. The emperor decided to summon Demetrius after he learned about him and did so. He gave Demetrius a trial, wishing to know if he could administer the imperial politeia, or rather to administer all the city. He became a senator and became engaged in various affairs immediately. Then an election of magistrates was held, and Demetrius was appointed to the governorship of the best province. It was the best allotment. He went to his province, got a taste of the whole affair, and settled the affairs of that province. But he was not satisfied with that. He did not want to stay idle there but was game for any venture. He summoned great courage and altered his course a third time: he turned his eyes to the whole world and became involved in the common politeia of all men. The most important thing was this: he did not join this community as a simple member, like any other man, but became their leader. He helped human nature recover, leading it towards the truth. He furnished it with the laws of Christ openly, wishing to link all men to each other if possible. He subdued them through certain confessions of piety. But all these were just preparation for the final politeia, which had been his goal since the beginning: he wanted to migrate and become a citizen of heaven, giving everything else in exchange. Therefore, he entertained high thoughts in his heart and abandoned vain material things and the whole world. In the end he abandoned his body as well. The scripture says that Israel went up with all his servants in a glorious way. What a harmonious and orderly procedure! How admirable was this gradual progress: he proceeded from his city to the whole Roman state, and then moved towards the whole world. Finally, he moved out of the world and sprang to heaven. He joined the heavenly orders and shares the politeia of the angels, standing in front of our common Lord together with them.[8]

The origin of the word πολιτεία may be found in the *Republic* of Plato, who distinguishes between the internal state of man, its internal politeia and its external reflection – that is, society, which is organized and governed by laws. Metochites describes a similar procedure in *Byzantios*: Constantinople is described from three perspectives – its relationships to the natural environment, the Roman state and

God.⁹ Metochites seems to purposely create a correspondence between these three angles and at least three of the politeia in the oration for St Demetrius. They are, so to speak, the general aspects under which any phenomenon of our world may be examined. In the four politeia of St Demetrius, however, Metochites seems to be referring to the four levels of society the saint gradually and progressively joined: the small society of his own native city, the larger society of the Roman state, the whole world and the society of heaven.

The career path of the saint described in Oration 4 could have been that of any Byzantine provincial nobleman ambitious enough to seek public office. Hailing from a noble family, the young nobleman sought to join the imperial service and become involved in the administration of the affairs of the Roman state. What about the ambitious nobleman who wished to enter the broader society of the world? The way Metochites speaks of this is typically Byzantine, asserting that a man may enter the commonwealth of the world by becoming a Christian herald.¹⁰ In short, one could imitate St Demetrius, who taught the faith to his brethren and suffered martyrdom, thus managing to join the huge commonwealth of the world by becoming a saint. There are many examples of such a saintly career in Byzantium, of provincial noblemen becoming public officials in Constantinople before turning their attention to God. One should bear in mind that sainthood came in many varieties in Byzantium. A person could become a saint by choosing martyrdom, but the opportunities for martyrdom were rather limited in Metochites' days. One could also become a saint by embracing monasticism or by devoting oneself to works of charity, or even by restoring a monastery, like Metochites.

Revisiting Metochites' autobiographical Poem 1 in light of his oration for Demetrius, one notices that the story resembles the same basic narrative of St Demetrius' life – that of a successful public servant of the Roman state. Metochites adopts the narrative found in the Life of St Demetrius by Symeon Metaphrastes, probably his main source, but also in other saints' lives resembling that of St Demetrius. Metochites was a promising young man who grew up in the Byzantine province of Bithynia. He provides no information on his duties towards the city in which he was educated, but it is certain that he felt an attachment to it, as evidenced by Oration 1, *Nikaeus*, an encomium for the city of Nicaea. Metochites explains in the oration how Emperor Andronikos II took an interest in him as a young man. The way he describes his entry into the Byzantine court is reminiscent of what he wrote about St Demetrius:

> After a short time, rather prematurely, although I was so young and not many years had passed since my birth, and a year had not yet passed since I had joined the other courtiers at his palace, my sovereign honoured me with one of those titles the emperors used to bestow upon whomever of their subjects they wished; this may be given to someone as a gift, although he has achieved or offered nothing in advance through his labours; sometimes the recipient is a kinsman of the emperor, or somebody may receive it as a reward for his services to him, or after he has been subjected to an examination. People address these men with their honorific title, according to the custom of the royal court, and their number

is limited. In any case, as I said, our sovereign emperor honored me in this way, though I was very young, and he appointed me a senator. Afterwards he decided to try me in several political or royal affairs. He did that in various cases in which it was fitting for the emperor to do so, both in some affairs in which learning is not useless, and in those diplomatic missions in which he was especially interested, preferring me over many others and sending me abroad. And this decision was proved right, since I fulfilled my duties properly and quickly, and then came back to my dear country after executing all my lord's orders successfully. O Christ my Lord, how much you honoured me, when I was still a young man.[11]

This passage is rather illuminating regarding the employment of courtiers and the bestowing of offices upon them. Noble birth, a kinship with the emperor, meritorious service to the state and even just imperial favour were the main routes to success and privilege as a servant of the Roman state. Metochites, like Demetrius, was subjected to a test by the emperor. He was neither a kinsman nor a man of noble birth, and lacking connections in the imperial court, he managed nonetheless to soon become a senator, like Demetrius, after splendidly fulfilling his public duties.

Metochites continues enumerating his services to the state – his missions to foreign countries, his diplomatic settlement of the dispute with the Serbs, etc. – and then he speaks about the culmination of his career:

But the emperor did not cease glorifying me and his love for me increased, since, to say the truth, he thought that I made a contribution to the conduct of public affairs and all other affairs far more important than anyone else, helping him both in the administration, in his decision-making and in the implementation of those decisions in a way that satisfied him.[12]

This corresponds to the second politeia of St Demetrius: the conduct of the affairs of the Roman state. Metochites is proud of achieving great prominence next to the emperor. The last of his achievements, the restoration of the monastery of Chora, he mentions in Poem 1. The description of the monastery occupies the greatest part of the Poem 1, suggesting that he considers it his greatest service to humanity. The third politeia of Demetrius was the saint's benefactions to the whole of humanity, and in Poem 1, Metochites presents the Chora restoration as a benefaction to humanity, especially the endowment of his library to the monastery:

It is a fountain of all good things, a common benefaction to all men, being open to everyone like the gift of air or water, with which God has supplied every man living on earth, both rich and poor or needy; all can enjoy them without pain. The same applies to my library: everyone can use it; it is the product of my own efforts; the library is full of books, dealing with both our holy wisdom and with the alien, Greek learning, which is useful to all mortal men of all times; they are most useful to those who bear the name of Christ, for many other reasons, and because they offer them the opportunity to make a comparative study of their own religion and the Greek one and understand its superiority; thus they will be steadfast, and they will know how to fight their enemies with their weapons.[13]

Thus, Metochites, with his restoration of the monastery, enters his third politeia, his attempt to enter the great commonwealth of mankind, through his benefactions. When read in light of what Metochites says about St Demetrius, he had entered the final phase of his life. If this is so, one may go a step further and conclude that Metochites' final prayer to God to enter the eternal kingdom expresses his wish to follow St Demetrius to the fourth politeia, heaven, to stand with the angels in front of the eternal Lord. One can only attain the fourth politeia after death.

There is another noteworthy aspect of the oration for St Demetrius. Demetrius, having reached the peak of a successful career, ponders the meaning of it in a soliloquy:

> What is the point of this hard toil? What is the reward of all this? What is the meaning of an empty ambition concerning things worldly? What is the grace of things that are so unstable? Is there any profit to my blood, if I come down to the destruction, as the Holy Scripture has it? Why do I remain among those things that are not stable because of their nature? Why do you give those things that do not belong to you? Why do you keep those things that you do not possess? Why do you try to keep under your control those things that are fluid? As somebody has said, why do you join the like with the like? Why do you twine ropes out of sand, trying to keep together things that run away? Why do you entertain ambitions concerning things that do not exist? You have to turn to the inner world, to turn to yourself, abandoning everything else, and to take care only of your immaterial and indestructible soul, as far as you can, leaving aside everything else and letting them shift up and down together with the ever-changing times; let the toys of matter run always.[14]

This is a harsh criticism by Demetrius himself of his previous life. It is a turning point in his life, when he sets his attention on the fourth politeia, entrance into the kingdom of God. His decision follows his realization that all earthly things, especially his worldly glory, are futile. Is this a subtle self-criticism by Metochites? Probably, bearing in mind that almost the exact words appear in Poem 19, one of his last poems:

> If you say that all these glories and a better way of life were given to you as a reward for your approval after much scrutiny, for your wisdom or for your great capacity to accomplish the great tasks entrusted to you by the emperor, who is always in need of such things, while other people less competent as you did not enjoy such a prestigious, glorious life, consider this. The word of the apostle Paul, wise in the things of God, who walked in heaven and knows everything perfectly, says: is there something you have, which is not a gift of God, but you gained it yourself? If everything you have is a gift, why are you so proud, as if you did not receive it as a gift (I Cor. 4,7).[15]

Even if Metochites did not have in mind the verse from the first Letter to the Corinthians in writing his oration for St Demetrius, the meaning would be the same: man has nothing on this earth that can be properly called his own. Therefore, at an early stage of his career – keeping in mind that the oration for St Demetrius is one of his earliest works – Metochites entertained certain doubts about the validity of the mask he had adopted in Poem 1.

The different path of a brilliant young nobleman: Oration 17, funeral speech for Joseph the Philosopher

Metochites in his final years wrote Oration 17, a text devoted to his recently deceased friend Joseph the Philosopher, or Joseph Rhakendytes, the famous scholar of the early fourteenth century. Metochites had already fallen from power and had been banished to Didymoteichon. The years of glory were just a sad reminiscence for him. His anxious attempt to proceed through the Byzantine cursus honorum and gain recognition among the members of the Byzantine elite had proven futile and meaningless. Indeed, in the end it brought disaster and calamity. The idyllic description of the four politeiai of St Demetrius and his own account of his glorious career in Poem 1 were things of the past. In Oration 17, Metochites took the opportunity to reverse the image he had drawn in his previous works. By describing the life of another promising young provincial nobleman who was similar to himself, but who chose a completely different path, Metochites was probably criticizing his own way of life, distancing himself from what he had said in the past.

Joseph strove for virtue and learning.[16] This is the true content of the contemplative life, the way of life adopted by the cultured elites of late antiquity. The contemplative life had not lost its appeal in Byzantium but had to be combined with the ascetic struggle towards union with God through maintaining the commandments of Christ and living according to his will. Joseph was a lover of that life and struggled uncompromisingly to achieve it until his death.

Joseph was born in Ithaca, under Latin rule at the time. As a scion of a Roman noble family, he obtained a good education. Very soon Joseph, like St Demetrius and Metochites himself, attracted the attention of the Latin rulers of his island. Metochites stresses this fact: '[I]t is a habit for the rulers of each place to bring near them those men who are able and distinguished among their fellows; therefore, the rulers of his country hired him. That thing was most desirable and welcome to them: Joseph was placed among those who were close to the rulers and competed with them.'[17] I do not doubt the veracity of what Metochites says, but his phrasing is indicative of the prevailing mood in the contemporary Byzantine court. The same is affirmed in Oration 4, for St Demetrius: promising young men are hired by the rulers, who are impressed by their exceptional qualities. In this regard, Joseph did not disappoint his masters. Metochites states, '[H]e proved himself a highly successful servant in every respect, and his masters were aware of this. He was lavished with honours by them and participated in their good fortune, giving them proof of his abilities.'[18] In the end they appointed him master of all their house, whatever that might mean. Thus, Joseph reached the peak of his career, having managed to prove himself a worthy citizen of the first politeia of Demetrius.

At this point, Joseph decided to abandon everything, even his native soil, the most pleasant of all things, and begin a journey towards his first fatherland (ch. 8), the heavenly kingdom of Christ. He had no wish to become a citizen of the second politeia (the Roman Empire) or the third politeia (the whole world) of Oration 4. His only concern was to become a citizen of the fourth politeia, the kingdom of heaven. The way to the kingdom demanded constant flight from all things that link man to this world. Joseph did, however, travel to the Roman Empire – first to Thessalonike, then to Mount Athos, and last but not least, to Constantinople – but these were not turning points in his career. The only purpose for these journeys was to find new opportunities to educate himself and become more virtuous. Is it accidental that Thessalonike was an important place in Joseph's life, as it was for Metochites? If not, then the life of Joseph may be considered the complete opposite of Metochites'.

According to Poem 1, Metochites moved from glory to glory – Serbia, Thessalonike, Constantinople – while Joseph moved from (self-)humiliation to (self-) humiliation and always concealed his virtue and education, whether in Thessalonike, on Mount Athos or in Constantinople. The result was always the same: those around Joseph recognized his virtue, as with Metochites, despite himself. In the end, Joseph emerged as the favourite of Constantinople's intellectual elite. He became close to the imperial family, and the bishops considered appointing him ecumenical patriarch. A consensus was formed: '[A] noble opinion prevailed about him; all were in agreement and deemed him worthy of all honours and appointments.'[19] The word 'examination' (δοκιμασία),[20] a technical term encountered in Poem 1 and Oration 4,[21] also appears in Oration 17. Joseph is considered βιωφελέστατος, 'most useful for life'.[22] Contrary to the (young) Metochites, however, Joseph held all Byzantine bureaucratic procedures in contempt. He chose to escape once more. His final place of residence was a mountain near Thessalonike, where he lived with a faithful companion in a hermitage. Both Joseph and Metochites died at a cloister: '[T]hey shared the time of their exile here on earth, which had such a long duration because their ardent desire was to leave, administering it perfectly. They were always ready to leave and finally they managed to escape and reach their heavenly fatherland: although they were still here, they behaved as citizens (ἐπολιτεύοντο) of that heavenly fatherland.'[23] The verb ἐπολιτεύοντο is prominent. It recalls the fourth politeia of St Demetrius. At the end of Metochites' life, he realized that there was no need for a man to ascend all the steps of the ladder he described in his Oration 4 while an ambitious young man. There was another, more successful way to reach the top: the road of Joseph Rhakendytes.

Joseph the philosopher and elusiveness as the essence of human life

Joseph Rhakendytes, whom Metochites considered one of the most admired men of his time, emphasized transformation of the individual through personal contact combined with the Socratic method. Though he left no written works of any note, many thought of Joseph as the philosopher par excellence. The death of such a close friend as Joseph must have been a terrible blow for Metochites, a man already shattered by the capriciousness of vicious, adverse fortune, as he constantly complains in his poems.

As noted, Metochites provides a rather long account of Joseph's life. He describes his educational curriculum at length, emphasizing Joseph's exceptional ability in all branches of human knowledge, particularly his efforts to profit spiritually from his philosophical studies – of Aristotle and the Neoplatonists Plotinus and Proclus – to better defend the doctrines of the Christian faith. It is clear from the above summary of Oration 17 that the main motif of the funeral oration is Joseph's elusiveness. Joseph abandons Ithaca, like his mythological compatriot Ulysses, choosing an itinerant life, constantly moving from one place to another in his pursuit of knowledge and his desire to reach higher, spiritual goals. He does not hesitate to disguise himself behind different masks at each stop. There is one significant difference, however, and Metochites does not fail to point out: whereas Ulysses returned to his home island, Joseph never did.[24]

Joseph took care to remain unnoticed (λανθάνων ἅπαντας) even during his sojourn in Thessalonike.[25] He exhibited this behaviour during his time on Mount Athos. Metochites employs the verb λανθάνει (to escape someone's notice) in both instances.[26] Metochites also employs the noun σκηνή (scene), drawn from the technical vocabulary of Greek theatre.[27] He considers Joseph an actor in the theatre of the world, rather than the stage, a metaphor frequently encountered in many of his works. Metochites stresses Joseph's lack of any possessions, noting that he maintained a monastic virtue until the end of his life. A nobleman on his native island, Joseph consciously forsakes everything for the sake of Christ, preferring a state of extreme poverty.[28]

Metochites highlights the extreme nature of Joseph's self-effacement in a brief story he relays in his speech. Once while returning from Thessalonike to Mount Athos on foot, Joseph spent the night in a small, abandoned chapel in a deserted area, because he suddenly developed a fever. During the night, some robbers came upon him and demanded money, but Joseph was unable to comply. The robbers were ready to rough him up, but Joseph persuaded them to carry him somewhere close to civilization so that he might be spared. The robbers did so and left. From this encounter, Metochites stresses the willingness of the thieves to help a fellow man; it was proof of their humanity, which came to the surface through Joseph.[29]

Metochites compares the story of the robbers, which he masterfully narrates, to other stories from the Holy Scripture where wild beasts are compelled to offer food to the men of God.[30] The story reveals the deep meaning behind Joseph's abandonment of all material goods and his endorsement and acceptance of the most extreme poverty for the sake of Christ. It is noteworthy that Joseph, the scholar's scholar, addresses the robbers in their own 'barbaric' language, depriving himself of the most important sign of his cultural superiority.[31] It is through his self-abasement that Joseph brings out the humanity hidden inside these 'barbarians', what is really true in an individual. Without being explicit, Metochites presents the deeper meaning of Christian humility, which has the power to transform not only those who possess it, but even those who come into contact with it. The robbers are forced to abandon the mask of their cruelty and thus reveal their true selves, thanks to the mask hiding Joseph's true face.

The monks of Athos ultimately recognize Joseph's true identity; he was unable to remain hidden forever, despite his efforts.[32] The same had occurred in Constantinople, where Joseph had adopted another mask, that of a humble servant of the ailing monk Makarios. In Metochites' telling, many of his friends pressure him to abandon his 'play-acting' (σκηνή),[33] employing a term common throughout his works. In the end, Joseph, the man who made himself humble, became recognized by everybody, prompting him to abandon everything one last time and migrate to Thessalonike to lead a solitary life. The end came soon thereafter. Through death, Joseph abandons the false life of the present to enjoy the true, heavenly life of the saints, bringing the play-acting of life on earth to a joyous conclusion.[34] Metochites deplores that Joseph has done so at such a critical juncture in his own life; he no longer has anyone to comfort him.[35] Here, Joseph's elusiveness becomes apparent once more. As he had left his kinsmen on the island of Ithaca many years prior, so he leaves Metochites, a close friend, to finally enjoy the fruits of his struggles, in heaven.

Metochites discerned traits of his own personality in both St Demetrius and Joseph the Philosopher. He was both a successful public servant, like Demetrius, and a philosopher, like Joseph, who was always striving for those circumstances that would enable him to realize the ideal of the contemplative life. That said, he did not identify himself with any of these men since his differences with them were considerable. Rather, Metochites tried to focus on certain of their characteristics to highlight some of his own, enabling his audience to recognize the author himself behind the mask of Demetrius or Joseph. In this way Metochites both reveals and hides himself through these two people. The orations for them are eloquent testimony to Metochites' elusiveness.

In Metochites' eyes, elusiveness – the use of a mask or even several masks to hide an individual's true identify or self – was a vital component of sanctity. This perspective is supported by another hagiographic text, Metochites' last prose work preserved in Vindobonensis phil. gr. 95, which deals with the life of St John of Didymoteichon. According to Metochites, John lived during the reign of Emperor Basil II (r. 976–1025). Metochites' attention was drawn to him by inhabitants of Didymoteichon after Metochites' banishment there in 1328. The details of the saint's life, and even his very existence, remain in doubt. Metochites' text reproduces the Byzantine hagiographic motif of the accidental encounter between a saint isolating in the desert (or forest) and a hunter (or monk) who subsequently reveals the former's spiritual achievements to others. The Life of St Mary of Egypt by Sophronios of Jerusalem is the most famous example of this motif. Of interest in the case here is how Metochites utilizes it in his text.

Unlike Joseph the Philosopher, John of Didymoteichon was a man of humble origins, his parents being simple farmers whose only virtue was their faith in Christ, which Metochites notes is the only real value man possesses in this life.[36] Like Joseph, John was eager to shed the skene of this life as soon as possible and became a monk.[37] This is the only instance in which Metochites employs the motif of the theatre – used abundantly in the funeral oration for Joseph – in the Life of John of Didymoteichon. The similarities between John and Joseph are, however, obvious: both men abandoned all worldly comforts (in the case of John, if he ever had any), stripping themselves naked of everything for the sake of Christ. Nature itself became John's adversary,[38] a motif Metochites made heavy use of in Oration 4, for St Demetrius.[39] Like Joseph, John was finally revealed to his fellow men, because God did not wish such a treasure to remain hidden any longer,[40] although also like Joseph, John wished to escape the attention of men.[41] Finally, John was pressed into assuming the burden of leading a monastic community, although he took care not to become completely estranged from his previous, solitary way of life.[42] John's end is presented as his final victory over the limitations of human nature.[43]

John's case is simpler than that of Joseph. John was not an elusive philosopher like Joseph, who was forced to constantly change his masks in an attempt to hide his true self. John was a simple, probably completely illiterate monk lacking a complex character like Joseph, the urban intellectual. This highlights the particularity of Joseph's case as presented by Metochites. John dropped his mask once and for all to see when he embraced the monastic life. Joseph was forced to do so constantly. In all probability, if one were to ask Metochites for an explanation, he would say that Joseph's superb education attracted the attention of others and thus forced him to constantly don various masks to escape said attention. In other words, his wisdom might have been the cause of his elusiveness; *mutatis mutandis*, the same applied as well to Metochites himself. On the other hand, it was enough for John to change his mask only once, tossing aside the mask of secular life to become a monk.

While reading the works of Metochites, one must keep in mind the concept of the mask, which seems to be central to his outlook. In the ancient theatre, it was compulsory for the performers to wear a mask, but behind a mask hides reality. So, too, in Metochites' world. To him, life is a constant performance in the theatre of this world, where everyone – not only simple men, but even a saint – must consider the proper mask to wear at any given time. For the saint in the theatre of this world, playing his role safeguards his sanctity. In regard to Metochites, one must conclude that everything in this life must have been elusive for him. Joseph the Philosopher abandoned his last mask only in death, implying that the true identity of man is not to be revealed in this life. Elusiveness is a fundamental law of life, a basic component of human nature.

Chapter 3

CODA – DISPOSING OF ONESELF: A NEW WAY OF BEING?

Sometimes Theodore Metochites imagined himself a man pursuing a solitary existence, a distance that kept him safe and undisturbed by the turbulence and misery of life among society – or, at least, that was the life he desired. A passage from Poem 2, addressing the monks of the monastery of Chora, makes this clear:

> I wish I lived with them. I wish I was a monk like them in your beautiful monastery of Chora, O pure mother of God, being your servant relieved of all my troubles, that keep me their prisoner, willy-nilly, oppressing me because of the numerous misfortunes they bring on me; I wish I could escape these fearsome unbreakable fetters, which keep me bound, twisted as they are around my whole body, head, hands, feet; oh miserable I, I am leading a horrible life indeed, although people consider me happy; my hardships are far more numerous than my privileges, but people think that these privileges are numerous indeed. I wish I had no children, no wife, enjoying my prosperity; however, people consider me lucky especially because of my children, since they have made prestigious marriages, which brings me great honour. But I wish I enjoyed no such things, so that I might return to myself absolutely free, released from those many troubles, which are as numerous as my children.[1]

It is difficult to translate the phrase ἐμαυτῷ κεχρῆσθαι that Metochites used, but one may render it 'so that I might dispose of myself absolutely free'. The rendering 'so that I might return to myself', though not as literal as the former, is also acceptable. The translation settled on here is an expression common in late antique writing denoting man's abandonment of worldly cares and the turning of attention to the needs of the soul, which is the real self. Metochites employs different terms to denote such a return. Take, for instance, a passage in Poem 3, addressed to Gregory, archbishop of Bulgaria: 'You kept yourself away from all these, being like a master of your own destiny. You live in this graceful, holy, beautiful hermitage, which is inaccessible.'[2]

Michel Foucault has observed the growth of individualism as a phenomenon that occurs in various societies at different times. It gives more importance 'to the private aspects of existence, to the values of personal conduct, and to the interest that people focused on themselves'.³ Metochites focuses on his own self, viewing himself as an object of knowledge and a field of action so as to transform and right himself and find salvation.⁴ Individualism in the form of man's self-determination was a burning issue in Metochites' time.⁵ Χρῆσθαι ἑαυτῷ, the term Metochites employed, seems to be identical to the term ἑαυτοῦ ἐπιμελεῖσθαι. One may also speak of a 'return towards himself', like a conversion, which signifies turning away from the preoccupations of daily life, interpreting one's life in a new way, rediscovering its true purpose and significance.⁶ That said, this was not a widespread phenomenon. Only members of the upper classes, like Metochites, had the luxury of actually contemplating such issues as self-determination and the prospects of an inner life.

Although the tendency of the privileged classes to retreat inwards may have been a consequence of the loss of privileges that came with the decline of the Byzantine state, it can only be considered one among other driving factors; the phenomenon was quite complex. Although Metochites constantly feared losing his prestigious position in the state, he was one of the luckiest among his contemporaries, and had no real justification for eventually looking down with contempt on all those privileges he had acquired through many years of patience and hard work while striving for retirement.

In any case, Metochites had managed throughout his public life to formulate a certain pattern of ethical behaviour,⁷ allowing him to create an image of a public servant somehow estranged from his social environment and in a constant dialogue with himself. This privatization goes hand in hand with Metochites' tendency to find new ways of appreciating the values of literature and his willingness to recognize pleasure as an integral part of human nature. Oration 10, *Ethikos*, deals extensively with the latter issue. In one passage on pleasure, he asserts the following:

> Apart from the above, if the issue of pleasure is not entirely trivial and blameworthy, as I think it is not, but rather there are some contrary instances in which it is permitted, used customarily, and not forbidden, in what other circumstances could this mostly occur, or in what other case could a person opt for it, except for the case we are now examining – that is, that of education? In this latter case, the pleasure is both great and extremely beautiful.⁸

This passage is indicative of Metochites' outlook on life: education and learning are man's most prized possessions, and one must constantly cultivate them. Their pursuit satisfies man's soul; such cultivation is a pleasure that is true, unblemished and most useful for the soul. One may better understand the meaning of ἑαυτῷ χρῆσθαι by keeping in mind that the scholar melds striving to learn with an elusiveness and a marked tendency to avoid revealing his true identity by hiding behind various masks, as observed in Oration 17; in short, it is the scholar's natural disposition to lead a solitary life, hidden from society. This is the true meaning of the contemplative life, according to Metochites. This is not all there is, however. One should not forget that Metochites also created a powerful image of himself as a successful politician and bureaucrat in Poem 1.

3. Coda – Disposing of Oneself

Taking into account the images Metochites painted of himself and others, one can safely conclude that he held the contemplative life in great esteem. He proclaims it the best refuge of man, who is oppressed by the trials of this world and thus seeks solace in an inner calmness and peace of mind. At the same time, however, some texts testify to his ardent desire, at least in his youth, to become a Byzantine bureaucrat, taking up affairs of state and drawing from it certain material benefits hardly compatible with the requirements of the contemplative life. Yet, in Metochites' self-portraits, a certain elusiveness is clearly discernible. That elusiveness stems from his declining to stake out an unequivocal position on the relative merit of the two ways of life – contemplative and active – and his insistence on the elusive aspects of Joseph the Philosopher's personality when describing it. One gets the impression that two selves are struggling inside Metochites for supremacy. This is most evident in the poems he wrote near the end of his life, where his contemplative self engages in discussion with his other, public servant self, who remembers his past glories and bemoans their loss.

The investigation has thus far produced a contradictory image of Metochites himself. He seems to have preferred the solitary life of the intellectual, devoted to his studies, but not so much that he was averse to enjoying the privileges of life as a rich Byzantine bureaucrat. Therefore, to solve the mystery of Metochites' elusiveness, one must turn to his two great treatises – Oration 10, *Ethikos*, and Oration 11, *Byzantios* – for their detailed discussion on the relationship between the contemplative life and the active life. But before embarking upon a more detailed investigation of his thoughts on the contemplative life as presented in *Ethikos* and *Byzantios*, we should first examine certain innovative aspects of his image, the understanding of which is indispensable for anyone who wishes to investigate the various images of himself Metochites created. I am referring to his mask as an innovative scholar breaking with the conventions of the past. After this digression we shall return to the investigation of Metochites' image as a contemplative scholar, focusing on *Ethikos* and *Byzantios*.

Part II

THE QUEST FOR NOVELTY: INNOVATION VERSUS
TRADITION IN METOCHITES' REPRESENTATIONS

Chapter 4

NOT EVERYTHING OLD IS TO BE REVERED

Despite some ambiguities, Metochites insisted on projecting himself as an intellectual; therefore, it seems to be the image of himself that probably lay closer to Metochites' heart than the others. Another aspect of that image was that of the innovative scholar who never hesitates to break prevailing conventions, presenting new visions to his fellow intellectuals. Innovation became an integral part of Metochites' self-image as a scholar, a concept encountered in Oration 6, for Gregory of Nazianzus; Orations 13 and 14, the treatises against Nikephoros Choumnos; and Oration 18, the treatise comparing Demosthenes and Aelius Aristeides.

Oration 4, on St Demetrius, revisited

In Oration 4, for St Demetrius, Metochites' speech seems at first glance to be a rather conventional Byzantine text. As Metochites explicitly notes, he wrote the oration as an expression of gratitude to the saint, who had cured him of disease during his sojourn in Asia Minor.[1] The text is a formal and conventional encomium for the saint. In the introduction, Metochites discusses the difficulties he has in dealing with the subject, the saint's origins and his native city of Thessalonike, taking the opportunity to write a short encomium for the city and its citizens. After that, he presents Demetrius as the perfect example of a Roman functionary, becoming a senator at a young age, a sign of his great virtue or an indication of his noble origin. Demetrius, however, paid no mind to the glory that accompanied his dignity. Instead, he used it as an instrument to spread the Christian faith to as many people as possible. When the emperor Maximianus learned of Demetrius' religious activity, he rushed to Thessalonike to investigate his rebellious subordinate.

Following earlier texts – most probably the Life of the saint, written by Symeon Metaphrastes in the late tenth century – Metochites reproduces the conversation between Demetrius and the emperor in Thessalonike, stressing the courageous attitude of the saint, who did not hesitate to publicly defend his faith. Maximianus asks Demetrius why he has rejected the old, safe doctrines of his forefathers for the sake of a totally unknown and new religion. Answering, the saint expounds the Christian argument that Christianity is the most ancient religion, having its origins in the faith of Moses and the prophets of Israel. Of particular note, before extolling the virtues of the Jewish faith, Demetrius presents a view that contradicts what comes afterwards, namely that one is not required to blindly accept every doctrine of the ancestors:

> Why is it necessary to bring forth these arguments and use the argument of time in our favour? Can we seriously maintain that the past may provide us with our gods or that we must move, think and live only inside the limits set by the men of previous times? Can we dabble in those things while we discuss a matter so important? We should not spare our ancestors in every respect; neither the laws of the state nor nature itself force us to do so. As far as other things are concerned, we do not follow the advice of our ancestors and we do not consider it necessary to believe them always; in some cases, we take things into our own hands and claim that we are wiser than they, although everything is in a constant movement and flux, changing always, and nothing human is stable and safe. Should we have blind confidence in our ancestors as far as the doctrines regarding the most important things are concerned? Should we agree to be enthusiastic over their views as coming from a supreme nature and utter them as if they were divinization? Should we be persuaded by those poets about those things which are most necessary, seduced by the metre, the rhythm and the plot? Should we, who are at the most advanced stage of the world's progress, remain idle, resembling statues, which are mute? Or should we bow in front of our ancestors as if they were holy statues, making offerings and worshipping them? Should we condemn that part of time which came after them, as if it were something unholy and unhealthy according to the proverb? Not at all, if we are healthy and prudent, o emperor. In my view time passed has no value at all. I do not consider it my duty to conform to the demands of time; pure reason and the search for the truth decide everything. That is what I persuade myself to follow. On the other hand, I will speak to you about this, although you are not ignorant. But even if time has any value for some people and one is willing to be persuaded by the argument of time, the privilege of seniority belongs more to the followers of Christ than to anybody else.[2]

Metochites is clearly presenting two different views on the same subject by making use of the Byzantine *progymnasmata* to simultaneously affirm and deny the thesis that tradition is to be honoured. As previously noted, there are several examples of this time-honoured Byzantine practice in his writings, but the case here is different. The author dares to challenge one of the most sacred axioms of Byzantium, a view shared by almost every intellectual of his time – that is, tradition is something not to be touched, because it is tradition that safeguards the Byzantine religion, which in turn bonds Byzantine society. If the views of the ancestors are not respected, the entire edifice of Byzantine ideology would crumble. Metochites clearly takes a position opposing the sanctity of tradition. Granted, after the above passage Metochites presents the arguments of those who believe in Christ, because Christianity is the most ancient faith in the world, but this is clearly a concession. The phrase introducing the argument for tradition – 'if time has any value for some people' – suggests Metochites' unwillingness to accept such an argument for himself.

Metochites' devaluation of seniority and tradition is quite innovative. In the medieval world, the past, whether classical or Christian, was idealized. The figures of the past functioned as archetypes of good behaviour, while their writings offered valuable instruction for all men and were not to be blithely disregarded. On occasion, someone might use the argument of time to support a view as an alternative when lacking any other real or rational arguments.

In Metochites' day, a different perspective on time and respect for tradition is to be observed among certain Byzantine intellectual circles: what is old is not necessarily valuable. Even before Metochites came of age, John Bekkos, the pro-Latin patriarch of Constantinople, had discussed the 'irrationality of time' in the treatise *On the Union of the Churches*,[3] wanting to disprove the anti-Latin claim that the Byzantines were now the guardians of their fathers' doctrine and to undermine respect for their primacy based on tradition.[4] To suggest that there is a direct line linking Metochites, the guardian of orthodoxy, to the heterodox John Bekkos would be hazardous, although one should not forget that Metochites' father, George Metochites, was a close collaborator of Bekkos. Some thirty years after Metochites' death, Demetrius Kydones, in his *Apology*, challenges his compatriots for their confidence in the argument for time past: '[T]herefore if we must yield to the long time and to the previous fathers, we must respect the status quo.'[5] In any case, the possibility that in the late thirteenth century there existed an intellectual milieu willing to question certain traditional premises of long-held ideology that favoured such opinions as those of Metochites cannot be rejected out of hand.

Attention should also be paid to the way Metochites tries to obscure his actual views. While he presents his argument against the absolute value of time in a rather succinct way, he also expounds at great length on the opposite argument, that for the validity of time. This indicates that Metochites was aware of the heterodox character of his argument against the validity of time; he is likely trying to leave readers uninitiated in his thought in the dark about his real intentions. He uses this technique in several cases. That aside, Metochites' views on the validity of time have a programmatic character: they open the door for him to dispute old-fashioned tenets of his compatriots' ideology.

The Metochites–Choumnos controversy: Novelty versus tradition and the Byzantine battle of the books

The controversy between Metochites and Nikephoros Choumnos is presented by both adversaries as a struggle between tradition and innovation. It is noteworthy that both authors offer themselves as champions of tradition, which the other supposedly threatened. Even Metochites, who in some of his other writings, especially in *Ethikos*, was so eager to present himself as an innovator,[6] insists in his treatises against Choumnos that he defended the teaching of the ancient authors against the ignorant attacks of Choumnos, who supposedly considered himself superior to the most revered writers of the past. This is the mask he wore at the time. The controversy itself shows that Metochites manipulated the image of himself as a champion of the Byantine literary tradition and at the same time undermined the tradition in a most subtle way.

Orations 13 and 14, against Choumnos: Content and chronology

In Oration 13 Metochites complains that his adversaries pretend to know nature better than Plato and Aristotle and are taking advantage of the ignorance of their fellow men in promoting themselves as exacting scholars.[7] Filled with an inexplicable envy of the great philosophers of the past, they ridicule the two of them while at the same time pretending to be their followers. Their particular target is the mathematical sciences, although the emperor Andronikos II Palaiologos trusted in the Greeks' theories.[8] By contrast, Metochites and his circle refrain from such shameful behaviour: they honour the philosophers of the past and extol their achievements, although they take care not to contaminate the purity of the true faith with their erroneous doctrines.[9] Another point of contention between Metochites and his opponents is the proper evaluation of the great Greek orators, who, if used as models of style, would benefit his contemporaries. Instead, his opponents prove themselves unable to appreciate the value of the ancients;[10] they go so far as to reject Thucydides and take Demosthenes as their sole model, disregarding his great admiration of Thucydides.[11] Metochites and his followers appreciate the value of Thucydides' style in spite of its difficulty, following the advice of Hermogenes and all the other teachers of rhetoric.[12] Concluding Oration 13, Metochites pleads with his opponents to stop condemning any long speech, reminding them of the assertion of Cicero, who, when asked which speech of Demosthenes was the best, answered, 'The longest one.'[13]

Oration 14 deals with roughly the same subjects as the previous one, but its tone is more aggressive.[14] Metochites castigates Choumnos and his followers for introducing a new mode of writing that is based on the total rejection of the teachings of classical rhetoric.[15] Choumnos aspires to promote himself as a new teacher of style, holding Hermogenes and all the ancient teachers of the art of speech in contempt. Choumnos proclaims the speeches of Metochites as totally unintelligible.[16] It is odd that Choumnos excludes Thucydides in his list of the great writers of the past, despite including Plato, Demosthenes and Aelius Aristeides.[17] Metochites begs Choumnos to calm down and to remember that Plato was a great admirer of the science of astronomy. In short, Choumnos should stop arguing against Plato, whom he supposedly admires.[18] Metochites affirms that he is not an opponent of Plato as Choumnos accuses him of being, but a faithful interpreter of the great teacher.[19] Metochites ridicules Choumnos, arguing that astronomy does not consist of mere epidermal knowledge of the science, but in the conscious and painstaking examination of all the phenomena of the sky and the interpretation of the laws governing them.[20] Choumnos is criticized for his ignorance of Claudius Ptolemaeus and his writings despite his assertion that he knows them well.[21]

Alexander Riehle has recently begun arguing for a different chronology of Orations 13 and 14, rejecting the judgement of Ševčenko, who dated them after 1324/5 and believed that the controversy took place between late 1322, early 1323 and 1324. Asserting that Metochites might not have been appointed the emperor's main adviser (μεσάζων) as early as 1305, as Sevcenko had maintained,[22] Riehle argues that the parting of the ways between Metochites and Choumnos did not take place as early as Ševčenko believed; he also notes that Choumnos' first treatise (Περὶ λόγων κρίσεως καὶ ἐργασίας) was not written as a pamphlet against Metochites, despite the latter's assertions, but was merely a theoretical work without any particular target, although later on Choumnos, enraged by Metochites' attacks, reworked the treatise, introducing a certain criticism of Metochites to it. In any case, Riehle, contrary to Ševčenko, who considered the controversy rather trivial, asserts that the discussion involved serious issues that the two men addressed in a serious and thoughtful manner: Choumnos was convinced that the literary discourse promoted social accessibility through clarity of diction, making it a commendable virtue, while Metochites considered it a means of social distinction, provided that it was obscure enough and inaccessible to most people, such that only a limited circle of initiated scholars would be able to appreciate it and gain from it. Metochites held that his vision could only be achieved through the lofty style (δεινότης).[23] Despite any objections to Riehle suggesting a later date for Metochites' promotion, one particular point likely warrants agreement with him: the controversy between Metochites and Choumnos involved serious intellectual issues. They did not quarrel just for the sake of quarrelling or because they wanted to settle personal scores. The opposition of social accessibility versus exclusivity was undoubtedly an issue at the time.

Predilections: Metochites' for Thucydides, Choumnos' for Demosthenes

Demosthenes was a recognized model of style for both Metochites and his opponents. The same applies to Plato and Aelius Aristeides. This is not out of the ordinary; the works of Demosthenes and Aristeides were intensively studied in all Byzantine periods. Meanwhile, Thucydides was considered difficult.[24] In light of this, Metochites sought to stress his opponents' denial of Thucydides' value as a model of style, pointing to their disapproval of the δεινότης (lofty) and complicated style considered characteristic of Thucydides by all the ancient teachers of rhetoric.[25] The reason for Metochites' predilection for Thucydides is revealed afterwards: Choumnos and his followers prefer to compose short speeches for fear that longer writings would reveal to everyone their inability to write properly; thus, they avoid the traps set by the art of grammar, which they are unable to comprehend in its entirety.[26] They prefer to keep to the path of their predecessors lest they lose their way. They are fond of the common word order and a habitual style (κατειθισμένης χρήσεως),[27] making no attempt to experiment or to deviate even slightly from the common path, fearing that they might fall into a trap of errors. Metochites then castigates his opponents for their tendency to avoid long, carefully structured and compact sentences, aiming for a terseness of style by compressing the speech and fortifying its meaning.[28] The accusation of not realizing the value of δεινότης is levelled against them once more. Choumnos and his followers strive for clarity of speech (τὸ σαφὲς);[29] therefore, they disapprove of the austerity and obscurity of Thucydides' style, confining themselves to imitating Demosthenes. Metochites states explicitly that he admires Thucydides' obscure style, following the example of the ancient teachers of rhetoric. Even time, which corrupts everything, maintained respect for Thucydides' work, while consigning to oblivion the works of writers fond of a simple style. Metochites claims that his opponents do not like the power of nature, which leads to actual literary achievements.[30]

Despite rendering lip service to the traditional literary values of Byzantium, Metochites, by promoting Thucydides as a writer to be imitated by his contemporaries, seems to be arguing for literary experimentation and innovation to some extent. He is not content to simply imitate writers of the past who were easier than Thucydides and contribute nothing to the development of the art of speech. Deviations from the norms of rhetoric are not only permissible but highly desirable. Attempts to write in a flat and lifeless style must be rejected. The author should dare to employ a style that challenges the audience with some difficulty; the text must go beyond simple syntax and well-worn vocabulary; the author must strive for δεινότης, like Thucydides. Metochites seems to have been cognizant of the innovative aspects of Thucydides' writing, which almost all subsequent authors extolled, and thus could not bear the faint, lifeless imitations of Demosthenes produced in abundance by his contemporaries.

Brief examination of Choumnos' treatises aimed against Metochites corroborates the findings here. In his first oration against Metochites, Choumnos stresses the absolute value of the ancient writers as models for style; they resemble priceless paintings, so a good author should be content to copy them as faithfully as possible. Such imitation provides a guarantee of success.[31] Choumnos holds that a good writer strives for clarity of speech (σαφὲς),[32] and he disapproves of long sentences (τὰ μακροτενῆ ταῦτα),[33] which, he claims, destroy the balance of the text and render it unintelligible. Short sentences and simple vocabulary are to be employed, if one does not wish to transform the garden of his speech into a field full of spines.[34]

In Choumnos' second oration against Metochites, he expounds the same approach to style. He also offers a rather interesting, if brief, historical explanation of the quarrelling over style from his own perspective. His own teacher, the patriarch and famous orator Gregory of Cyprus, had set the other orators on the correct path, orientating them towards the great authors of the past – Plato, Demosthenes and Aelius Aristeides. Though an admirer of Gregory of Nazianzus, Gregory of Cyprus neither attempted to imitate him nor suggested his style as a model for his students. He knew that Gregory of Nazianzus had been a church orator with an admirable but rather peculiar style. Those who tried to imitate him failed miserably; their texts look like an accidental mish-mash of words, without inner coherence.[35] Those who heeded his advice attained well-deserved glory, while the misled who neglected it composed totally obscure and unintelligible writings full of strange vocabulary and a style far removed from common Greek speech.[36] Choumnos admits that he avoids long and elaborate sentences, lest he fall into the traps of grammar.³⁷ He stresses that Demosthenes was a model of clarity and could not have been otherwise, since he delivered his speeches in front of the Athenian people. Demosthenes' situation required that he be clear, and the orator wished to address his audience directly.³⁸ Choumnos ridicules Metochites for daring to compare his own writings with the work of Thucydides.³⁹ Choumnos also tries to answer Metochites' accusations concerning the science of astronomy. He admits his lack of knowledge of the science, but vehemently and indignantly denies that he does not admire Plato's erudition and achievements in astronomy.⁴⁰

Choumnos' perspective is clear: a writer should strive to imitate the writers from antiquity renowned for their clarity of speech. For Choumnos, an unclear text was not Greek; anyone who employed such a horrible style (ἐπαχθοῦς γλώττης) should go to live with the Scythians.⁴¹ He admonishes those who employ the style he disapproves of for committing patricide.⁴² Time and again he urges his readers to keep close to the Greek authors whose reputation has been confirmed by the long centuries that have passed; no one is greater than those authors. Choumnos does not condemn Thucydides; rather, he disapproves of any attempts by inferior writers to imitate him: it is as if the hop of a frog is compared to the leap of a lion.⁴³ Choumnos also disapproves of the lack of structure he observes in the writing of his opponents, whom he compares to men running in circles on a rough road, unable to reach their destination and with speech that confuses their readers.⁴⁴ One cannot fail to see this as a criticism of Metochites' style, especially as employed in *Ethikos* and *Byzantios*, which, at least to the superficial reader, lack coherent structures. Here Metochites touches on the same subject again and again, leaving the impression that he is not proceeding in a linear fashion but is moving in circles. The same is true to an even greater extent for Metochites' poems. Even the modern reader is at a loss when trying to discern the structure of some of his texts.

Choumnos' approach is the quintessence of Byzantine stylistic conservatism. Metochites certainly looked down with contempt on the efforts of Choumnos and his followers to imitate certain authors of the past on the basis of the clarity and simplicity of their style. For Metochites, such attempts were tantamount to sacrificing real literature and rejecting real competence in writing for the sake of convenience. There is no doubt that Metochites believed the adoption of Choumnos' practices hindered the advancement of literature, instead producing faint imitations of past works and lacking any real substance.

Gregory of Nazianzus: To imitate, or not to imitate?

Another aspect of Choumnos' criticism of Metochites involved the evaluation, and rejection, of Gregory of Nazianzus as a model for style. As noted above, Choumnos spoke about the attitude of his teacher, Gregory of Cyprus, towards Gregory of Nazianzus. Here is the relevant passage:

> My leader and guide and teacher had been for as long as he was alive that great sage and writer Gregory, who came from Cyprus and became teacher and bishop of the whole earth afterwards, that great miracle of our life. I wish I were his

student for my whole life. I would have been very happy to study by him constantly. It so happened that he said in some respects the same things as his namesake, who was superior to all other writers, even those of the past, because of the power of his speech and his wisdom, both theological and secular, which examines all the depths and heights of the arcane mysteries of the supernatural nature and divinity. But he also happened to speak in a way that was totally opposed to that of his namesake. The older writer, like somebody who breathed fire, being inspired by the Holy Spirit, spoke before the whole church, burning and destroying whatever his opponents deceitfully expounded and introduced into the church. His tongue was full of grace and beauty, as the tongue of nobody else of those admirable men of past times, who boasted of their literary achievements. His speeches had also a perfect rhythm; some men of later times looked upon it and tried to compare their sound with his; they were unable either to discern any other good things in his writings, although these were beyond the natural measures, or to imitate them with zeal. Therefore, they failed completely: they spent all their effort in gathering certain ignoble and wretched words, unsuitable for describing the things they wished to describe. They looked like certain young birds that try to follow an eagle flying in the air, although they have no wings. This was their only profit from their zeal to follow that great man. As far as the contemporaries of my teacher are concerned, they were truly glorified because of their improper enthusiasm! However, my teacher paid no heed to those young and wretched orators but turned his attention towards the first foundations of the science and art of rhetoric, where it stands safely and firmly. He fixed his gaze on those ancient orators, Plato, Demosthenes and Aristeides, on whom he had focused his attention anyway, and tried to imitate their own writings in a proper manner. He opened a new road of speech writing and recommended it to the others.[45]

Choumnos, while not denying the literary value of the orations of Gregory of Nazianzus, rejects the attempts of lesser authors to imitate him. The comparison of those authors who mimic Gregory with young birds following an eagle is reminiscent of the image he employed in the case of Thucydides of a frog imitating a lion.[46] Choumnos observes that Gregory employs a difficult style that others cannot imitate. Unfortunately, little information exists on the contemporary literary environment of Gregory of Cyprus, but one can confidently argue that he attempted to set the Byzantine literati on a new path, helping them avoid excessive reliance on a model unsuitable for their time. We must also keep in mind the rhetorical texts composed during the late twelfth century. Long, elaborate sentences and a fondness for an unusual vocabulary characterize the works of some orators of the period, most of them being connected to the patriarchate of Constantinople. In all probability, Gregory of Cyprus tried to put an end to the use of such an extravagant style. There are no comprehensive studies on the development of Byzantine literature style(s), making it impossible to properly evaluate Choumnos' assertions. In any case, Metochites' style bears a certain resemblance to that of Gregory of Nazianzus. It is thus a bit strange that Metochites fails to mention him as a model of style in Orations 13 and 14. His taste for Thucydides, however, is likely connected to the predilection for Gregory of Nazianzus demonstrated by certain of his contemporaries, who were castigated so severely by Choumnos. Metochites extols Gregory's style in Oration 6. Thucydides' difficult and obscure style may have reminded Metochites of it.

The line dividing the two opposing style factions is thus clear. It was a Byzantine battle of the books. The conservatives, like Choumnos, advocated a simple and clear style, promoting Plato, Demosthenes and Aristeides as models for those looking to compose a proper, decent speech. The inclusion of Aristeides is a bit difficult to explain, since his style was far from simple and clear. Metochites had something to say about this in Oration 18, revealing that he did not consider Aristeides a pattern to be imitated for all time, but only as a paradigm suitable for his own period, a rather illiberal position. At the least, he did not consider Aristeides a model for truly innovative spirits, although he admired some of his literary accomplishments. The innovators like Metochites, fond of literary experiments, detested the servility towards the classical models of speech. For this reason, they tried to revive the interest of their contemporaries in Thucydides and Gregory of Nazianzus. Of course, it would be a mistake to argue that these two writers had been forgotten by Metochites' time. What Metochites wanted to teach his contemporaries was the possibility of creatively imitating Thucydides and Gregory, of breaking free of the limitations imposed by a rigid and scholastic tradition and instead employing a non-conventional style. It remains unknown whether such an attempt found popularity among his contemporaries. Even Nikephoros Gregoras, Metochites' most faithful student, avoids the excesses of his master in composing works. Metochites tried, however, to consistently apply his thinking on the matter to his own writings, explaining his views in Orations 6 and 18.

Chapter 5

ORATION 6, ON GREGORY OF NAZIANZUS: A RESPONSE TO MEN LIKE CHOUMNOS?

Content of the oration

Gregory of Nazianzus influenced almost every Byzantine author, which helps explain why Metochites felt compelled to compose a funeral speech for him.[1]

Metochites opens Oration 6 bemoaning that no orator alive was up to the task of praising Gregory of Nazianzus, echoing a similar assertion Gregory himself had made in Oration 43, his funeral speech for Basil the Great: Only the deceased was qualified to compose a competent praise of Basil![2] Metochites, who is equally indebted to that well-known oration and to Gregory's biography by Gregory the Presbyter, describes Gregory's career and intellectual development, from his modest beginnings in Caesarea to his lengthy stay in Athens to his establishment in Cappadocia and his subsequent flight to the desert with his friend Basil. Metochites sticks to the description of Gregory's achievements in Athens and presents a rather long appraisal of his exceptional literary qualities. He describes Gregory's life as a constant switching between attempts to avoid the burdens of public life and the forced abandonment of seclusion to help the church, an ongoing struggle between the contemplative life and the active life that so vexed Metochites himself and contributed to his elusiveness. Metochites refers to the estrangement between Basil and Gregory after Basil appointed Gregory bishop of Sasima, but he does not dwell on it. He focuses instead on Gregory's struggles against the heresy of Arius, the support he gave to his friend Basil until his death, and his own struggles after Basil's demise: his appointment to the Church of St Anastasia in Constantinople; his speeches against the Arians that attracted great crowds; and his subsequent appointment to the patriarchal throne of the imperial city by Theodosius I. He describes Gregory's struggle against Maximus the Cynic, who conspired with the bishops of Egypt against him, his opponents' attempt to assassinate him, the miracle that took place during his official instalment on the patriarchal throne, the convocation of the Second Ecumenical Council, and his resignation from the throne because of his disappointment with the intrigues of his fellow bishops. Metochites also speaks about the last doctrinal quarrel in which Gregory was involved, regarding the doctrinal positions of Apollinarius of Laodicea. Metochites also refers to Gregory's poems, to his speeches against the emperor Julian, and to his oration to his fellow bishops before departing from Constantinople.

Following the rules of composition for praises established by the late antique orators, Metochites attempts to compare Gregory with other famous men of the past. He first points out that Gregory's literary talent surpassed that of all other writers, because he exhibited evidence of his competence in all literary genres – that is, theology, moral exhortation, speeches against the opponents of the Christian faith, explication of the Holy Scripture, praises of the saints, libels against the evil, and hymns of the Christian mysteries. He also stresses Gregory's moral achievements, such as how he held all worldly glories in contempt, but also managed to lead the people of God to the right path whenever he reluctantly undertook certain public duties. His only equal is his friend Basil, who along with him managed to successfully combine the active life and the contemplative life. Thus, the two friends provided concrete proof that virtue was not an abstraction devoid of any real sense, but something real that could be achieved in this life, albeit rarely.

Purpose of the oration

Oration 6 poses a number of questions worth exploring. In the preface to the text, Metochites asserts that no one could appropriately praise Gregory of Nazianzus except for his friend Basil, and that he has undertaken the task himself because there is no one alive comparable to Basil.[3] He employs a commonplace of Byzantine rhetorical texts: when it is felt that anyone who dares to deal with a particular subject will most likely fail, it encourages the author to proceed with it given the certainty that his failure is not unexpected or due to his own general inadequacy. By proclaiming Basil the only person capable of praising Gregory, the author appears to go a bit further: in all probability, by deciding to write a speech for Gregory, Metochites is presenting himself, however unworthy, as a successor to the two great prelates of the fourth century. His decision to undertake the difficult task since there is no other writer good enough implies just that – and this despite so many speeches praising Gregory having been composed between his death, in 390, and Metochites' birth, in 1270. At last, an author of the early fourteenth century answers the call and fills the literary gap, so to speak.

The above helps explain Metochites' assertion in Poem 12 that the speech on Gregory is one of his three best orations, the other two being Oration 10, *Ethikos*, and Oration 11, *Byzantios*.[4] At the end of the oration, Metochites returns to the theme of his adequacy: if he fails in his effort to write a proper praise for Gregory, then Gregory's prophecy in his speech for Basil has come to pass. Of this, Metochites is certain! Since Basil is already dead, nobody will be able to praise Gregory in the future.[5] One must not take this at face value. Metochites almost explicitly states that his text seeks to confute Gregory's prophecy. This is the real sense of his insistence that only Basil – or Gregory himself, if that were possible – could praise Gregory competently. Michael Gabras, a lesser author of Metochites' times, seems to have caught the real sense with which Metochites employed this 'prophecy'. He refers specifically to this passage and praises the author for his success![6]

It seems clear that Metochites is presenting himself as a late-period Gregory of Nazianzus.[7] Metochites felt a special bond to Gregory through a shared fate: although their original wish was to devote themselves to the contemplative life, they were forced by circumstance to undertake certain public obligations, which led them astray. Metochites' public career was not always without turbulence, and Gregory was forced to abandon the patriarchal throne of Constantinople in disappointment because of the machinations of his fellow bishops. Thus, Metochites presented his own struggle to combine an active and a contemplative life in terms borrowed from the relevant works of Gregory of Nazianzus, with whom he perhaps felt a kinship.

Gregory of Nazianzus: Inventor of a new literary style

One should interpret Metochites' evaluation of Gregory's literary achievements in Oration 6, chapters 18–20, in light of his literary quarrel with Choumnos and his attempt to imitate Gregory, or rather, to act as a literary agent under Gregory's mantle.

In chapter 18, Metochites evaluates Gregory's writing style. The section belongs to a part of the text devoted to his education. Metochites duly dissects the relevant section of Gregory's funeral oration for Basil the Great but also includes a detailed appreciation of the saint's literary qualities.

According to Metochites, Gregory acquired flawless knowledge of the art of writing (γραμματική), surpassing even the technical wisdom of experts in the art. He composed technically exquisite poems and combined a majestic and solemn style with a rhythm most pleasant to his audience. In this way, the saint fulfilled his pastoral duties towards his readers by seducing them with his artful speech.[8] What Metochites admires most, however, is Gregory's use of the art of rhetoric. Gregory's is a true feast (ἑορτή) and a solemn exhibition of the hidden possibilities of human language.[9] Nobody before him had achieved such a combination of qualities of speech into one harmonious whole. Gregory's speech is both sweet and powerful.[10] Even those who experience it are unable to explain the workings of his art within them, the source of their inner delight, and instead appear as inundated initiates of the ancient god Dionysus.[11] Although most writers have a natural tendency to imitate this great author, they cannot explain how he managed to combine the various colours of speech so successfully. It is truly miraculous how he managed to achieve such loftiness of style (ὄγκος) with such beauty of expression (ὥρα).[12] Gregory is both majestic (σεμνόν) and pleasant (χάριεν), resembling spring weather, equally removed from winter's cold and the summer's heat.[13]

Metochites uses the term δεινόν, which he also employed in Orations 13 and 14 to describe Thucydides' style. He calls Gregory's style δεινόν but at the same time simple.[14] Only Gregory managed to so successfully combined these two different qualities of speech. This combination was Gregory's personal contribution to the development of the art of speech, eclipsing all other innovations of the past. Gregory managed to surpass both the majestic style of the classical orators and the licentious style of their successors.[15] Metochites references the opposing rhetorical practices of Atticism and Asianism in late antiquity. He surpassed the noble style of classical authors through his own outstanding nobility, and with the grace of his own compositions, he stood above the modern orators, who strove for a pleasant, palatable and extravagant style.

Gregory invented a new variety of rhetoric, combining loftiness and pleasantness, making him a benefactor of humankind in offering the true doctrines of faith in the soundest manner and also showing the way to achieving true nobility of speech.[16] Metochites insists that all Gregory's contemporaries ought to imitate him: 'He was the one who showed us the nobility of good speech and proper oration, provided that somebody has the possibility to realize and take advantage of it.'[17]

In reality, the combination of loftiness and grace, severity and simplicity, was not unfamiliar to Byzantine readers. Hermogenes, in the treatise *On Ideas*, had discussed in detail the characters, or virtues, of style. He identifies seven ideas – that is, general qualities of style – that when combined in various ways give each piece of writing its particular flavour: beauty, grace, grandeur, loftiness, pleasure, severity and simplicity.[18] Hermogenes stresses the importance of combining these ideas, focusing as an example on Demosthenes and his ability to masterfully combine different characters of style in a convincing and persuasive manner. For example, Hermogenes asserts that a proper panegyric should combine grandeur (μέγεθος or ὄγκος) with pleasure (ἡδονή).[19] For him, grandeur results from a combination of six of the seven ideas. Hermogenes also discusses the ideas that give a speech its beauty (κάλλος) followed by the combination of the various ideas with each other, which seems to be obligatory. He even appears to castigate Thucydides for striving only for grandeur, neglecting the other characters.[20] On the other hand, he seems to approve of the combination of grandeur and pleasure, which is characteristic of Herodotus.[21] Thus, the combination of loftiness with grace in the speeches of Gregory of Nazianzus was not a new invention, as Metochites wants his readers to believe. One could appreciate the dexterity with which Gregory combined the various characters of style, even those most opposed to each other, but this was his task as an orator. Metochites likely wanted to propose Gregory's style as a model by stressing a quality of it that Byzantine readers familiar with Hermogenes' teachings could have appreciated.

Metochites also evaluates Gregory's contribution to the study of philosophy. Gregory investigated all matters pertaining to nature and examined what his predecessors left unexplained.[22] He then studied the four mathematical sciences – that is, entities beyond matter, although they were studied on the basis of it. He avoided any dangerous paths that might lead astray those studying astronomy.[23] He employed the knowledge he gained from his studies as a useful weapon to defend the Orthodox faith. This passage by Metochites, inspired by a section of Gregory's funeral speech for Basil, exercised a considerable influence on all Byzantine orators who praised the education of saints or other prominent men. A similar passage is to be found in Oration 17, Metochites' funeral speech for Joseph Rhakendytes.[24]

In any case, it is evident that Metochites expounds views also found in Orations 13 and 14, countering Choumnos. For example, difficulty of style, or so-called *deinotes*, is something to be considered desirable. Far from condemning the attempts of his contemporaries to imitate the style of Gregory of Nazianzus, as Gregory of Cyprus and Choumnos did, he encourages them to do so, as he considers Gregory a benefactor of mankind thanks to his invention of a new rhetorical style. The loftiness of speech that Metochites admired in Thucydides' style could also be enjoyed while reading Gregory's texts. Metochites stresses the fact that Gregory is the most admirable creature of nature, being a supreme example of what man is able to achieve using his physical and innate abilities.[25] Thus, Metochites employs the case of Gregory of Nazianzus to explain his views on good writing through a tangible example known to all his contemporaries. If those contemporaries only superficially read Metochites' text, they would not detect the text's hidden polemic against his opponents. If, however, they were to compare what Metochites wrote in his oration on Gregory with the views of Choumnos in Orations 13 and 14, the real issue would become abundantly clear. In chapter 58, Metochites praises the way Gregory 'employed his speech' (τὴν τῶν λόγων χρῆσιν). One wonders whether Choumnos had used this very expression accidentally in the title of his first speech against Metochites, Περὶ λόγων χρήσεως καὶ ἐργασίας. In all likelihood, Oration 6, on Gregory, was composed before Orations 13 and 14, which dealt with Choumnos. It seems that the issues addressed in Orations 13 and 14 had been discussed before between the two adversaries, an echo of which may be found in Oration 6.

It is difficult to detect the real purpose, if any, of a Byzantine rhetorical text, especially in the case of the rhetorical praises for the great saints. Most Byzantine authors were content to employ rhetorical commonplaces, or at the least, attempt to hide their real interest in composing such texts behind them. The real purpose of Metochites' speech on Gregory of Nazianzus, however, may be clearer if one compares his text with a speech on Gregory composed by Thomas Magistros, a contemporary of Metochites who was almost certainly acquainted with Metochites' work. The two men both do the following in their texts on Gregory:

1. Hail Gregory as the utmost example of human nature;
2. Draw material seemingly from the Life of Gregory of Nazianzus written by Gregory the Presbyter;
3. Mention that only Gregory would be in a position to write a proper encomium for himself;
4. Quote Gregory's complaint in his funeral oration for Basil that no one will be found to write a proper funeral oration for him after he dies;
5. Praise the high quality of Gregory's style, insisting on his mastery of all literary genres as well as his ability to combine philosophy and rhetoric.

In addition, the description of the course of Gregory's studies in Athens is almost identical in both texts.

When quoting the epilogue of Gregory's funeral oration for Basil, Thomas knew that he was one among many others who had attempted to praise Gregory. He does not appear to be as ambitious as Metochites, who seemingly ignores all other orators who had praised the saint. Thomas notes how so many have tried to praise the saint in vain, and that this in a sense does them honour, because every man who loves literature must compose a praise for Gregory.[26] Thomas regards himself as just one member of the group of sages of the past who have praised Gregory; he does not try to distinguish himself in the way Metochites does.

Metochites is unaccepting of the honour that Thomas perceives. In his view, his praise is a matter of either absolute failure or complete success. Crucially, however, Thomas, in his praise of Gregory's literary qualities, does not insist so much on the saint's innovation in the particular style he employs in his writings. Rather, apart from offering general praise of the saint's endeavour to combine philosophy with rhetoric, Thomas praises Gregory for his orderly and successful way of introducing his arguments, even when they are somewhat unusual (ἄτοποι); the purity of his Attic vocabulary; the way he employs the various figures of speech (σχήματα), which includes his way of handling certain new inventions (καινοτομίαι); and the way the saint constructs his texts, combining beauty with loftiness. His conclusion is that each of the saint's writings constitutes a harmonious whole.[27]

One must not mistake Thomas's innovations (καινοτομίαι) with Metochites' καινόν. Metochites refers to Gregory's general tendency to innovate, while Thomas employs the term καινοτομίαι in a rather limited sense – handling the various figures of speech in an innovative manner. While Thomas does speak about certain inventions by Gregory, he is referring not to the saint's literary endeavours but to his scientific studies. Does he believe that contemporary authors should try to imitate Gregory? The evidence is rather ambiguous. Speaking about Gregory's poems, Thomas argues that all men are amazed when reading them; they resemble well-constructed bodies.[28] He underlines Gregory's inventiveness involving metre and rhythm. Everyone wants to imitate him, but no one is able to do so.[29] One wonders whether by saying this Thomas had in mind the controversy between Metochites, who praised Gregory of Nazianzus as an inventor of a new style of rhetoric, and Choumnos, who refrained from proposing Gregory as a model for his contemporaries. In any case, Thomas is not as optimistic as Metochites concerning the ability of his contemporaries to imitate Gregory's style. Thomas repeats his view later on, arguing that the writings of Gregory are beyond imitation.[30]

If trying to summarize Thomas's position towards Gregory, one might say that although he admires the saint's ability to write excellent speeches, he is reluctant to consider the imitation of Gregory's style advisable. In other words, Thomas would have shared Choumnos' reservations concerning the possibility of imitating Gregory in their day. Metochites' position is different. As noted, for him, Gregory is the writer par excellence. True, his style is difficult and incomprehensible to most of his contemporaries, but it is nevertheless worth trying to imitate the great church father. Metochites' maxim might be the following: only by trying to adapt one's style to the examples of Thucydides and Gregory of Nazianzus may one have any real claim to literary fame worthy of its name. While he does not discourage imitation of Aelius Aristeides, he also does not advise it without reservations and seems more enthusiastic when speaking about Thucydides and Gregory. These reservations he explained in the oration on Demosthenes and Aristeides, which he wrote near the end of his life.

Performance and literature

Stratis Papaioannou attempted to interpret the literary portrait of Gregory of Nazianzus that Michael Psellos created two and a half centuries before Metochites as an effort by Psellos to underline the literary aspect of Gregory's creation, neglecting his theological output somewhat, or at least relegating it to a position of secondary importance.[31] This view is noteworthy, although there are doubts concerning the innovative character of Psellos' views. For most Byzantine intellectuals, the literary qualities of language were always a major concern. It is a bit tenuous in the case of Psellos to speak of the creation of a new literature out of the old rhetoric. Papaioannou is correct, however, in stressing Psellos' interest in the literary qualities of Gregory's style.

At first glance, Metochites seems to share Psellos' predilection for Gregory's style. Metochites refers to the 'feast' (ἑορτή) of Gregory's language,[32] which was something ineffable and totally unexpected. He then emphasizes the 'variety' (ποικιλία) of his style,[33] the combination of the various 'colours of speech' (τῶν τῆς φωνῆς χρωμάτων),[34] and the employment of the different 'species of speech' (τῶν λόγων εἴδη).[35] Gregory is an inventor of a new variety of speech and is a benefactor of the human race.[36] What Metochites emphasizes, however, is his combination of lofty style and literary grace.[37] This combination is quite traditional, something most Byzantines admired not only in speech, but also in human conduct. The combination satisfied both the eager imitators of the loftiness of the classical Greek speech and the 'friends of feasts' (φιλέορτοι).[38] Were these φιλέορτοι men like Psellos, who shared the predilection of the orator of the eleventh century in Metochites' own times? It is possible.

Metochites characterizes the effects of Gregory's speech as a 'Dionysiac frenzy and possession' (βακχείᾳ τινὶ ... κατοχῇ).[39] One might be inclined to interpret this phrase as an expression of Metochites' admiration for the literary qualities of Gregory's style, which thrilled his audience, but one should not overlook the theological undertones of this expression. Metochites employs this phrase in other works when describing the spiritual elevation of men and their ardent wish to attain a stature beyond human capabilities, uniting with God.[40] Therefore, Metochites seems to return to the more traditional interpretation of Gregory of Nazianzus, as a great and innovative stylist indeed, who was first of all a great theologian, able to employ the graces of his style as a way of enhancing his theological message and making it more easily accessible to his various audiences. He also seems to be opposed to the trivialization of Gregory that adulterated the true qualities of his intellectual inheritance, as exemplified by Choumnos.

In Oration 14, Metochites includes a passage about a widespread practice of the Byzantine *theatra*, the gatherings where orators read their writings in front of small audiences, employing all manner of common performance tools. This is how Metochites ridicules the position of Choumnos, whose performances were presented as a caricature:

> If all piety and awe is due to Plato, and if anybody who dares to look in the face of his wisdom and expound a philosophic theory contrary to him is mad, how do you judge yourself? What will be your punishment? What will become of your admirable books, which you write as a philosopher against Plato, presenting them to all men without fear, as if benefiting and teaching them all? You convoke *theatra* (θέατρα) around yourself and you call all contemporary intellectuals to listen to your great wisdom and power and to hear your audacity against Plato and those famous men of antiquity. You sit in the midst of them while your writings are recited, and you behave as if taking part in an orgiastic feast and you express your approval with all manner of nasty movements: either you jump up from your chair or you fall and sit down and behave as a delirious madman making all sorts of gestures, shaking your head and your nape and contorting your body in all directions. Afterwards you offer many opportunities for discussion of your works to all those who see and hear you after they depart. They should have meditated on them and studied your wisdom and your noble arguments against the illiteracy of those men of the past falsely considered great with the utmost attention, gaining greater profits than any other men before them, but instead they turn the whole of their attention to your inspired talk, your licentious dance, and the manic frenzy which all accompany your talks, as they are able to see, and keeping them in their mind continuously, they always ridicule them, nasty men indeed. Woe to their nastiness, neglect and bad behaviour![41]

It is an important passage that helps us understand Metochites' attitude towards his contemporary authors and orators, who had high pretensions, entertaining even faint hopes of achieving the glory of ancient authors or at least of adequately imitating them. It is noteworthy that he employs several words often found in similar contexts: ἐπικροτεῖς, θέατρα, ἀναγινωσκομένων, ἀκροαταῖς, θεαταῖς.[42] Particularly striking is the inclusion of the words κόρδαξ and βακχεία. As seen above, the term βακχεία had a positive meaning in Oration 6, denoting the enthusiasm of the readers of the works of the great theologian Gregory. Here, however, the meaning is negative, denoting the excessive and lamentable enthusiasm of the audience for the false qualities of a bad speech. The verb βακχεύω is employed in a negative sense in Metochites' introduction to *Stoikheiosis Astronomike*.[43] One must not generalize: Metochites' criticism of Choumnos' literary practices does not signify a total rejection of the performative discourse of the Byzantine intellectuals, but he could not tolerate the excessive employment of certain performative tricks used to impress the audience. The combination of ἀκροαταί and θεαταί may offer a clue to the reasons for Metochites' criticism of

Choumnos' performance. Choumnos' way of reciting his speeches – himself or by way of a reader? – included visual effects that ran foul of Metochites' strict principles. One must keep in mind, after all, that Metochites advocated the combination of rhetorical grace with loftiness. His Oration 18, comparing Demosthenes and Aelius Aristeides, offers additional insight into his attitude towards the discursive culture of his time.

Back to the reality of beings: Oration 18, on Demosthenes and Aelius Aristeides, and rejection of traditional Byzantine rhetoric

Oration 18, on Demosthenes and Aelius Aristeides, is one of Metochites' late works, written at the instigation of his friends, despite his preoccupation with other matters at the time. Metochites had been reluctant to undertake such a difficult task because both men were so accomplished that any attempt at comparing them could prove to be ridiculous. Despite his reservations, Metochites ultimately yielded to the entreaties.[44]

Content of the oration

First, Metochites notes that both Demosthenes and Aristeides are products of their time. Demosthenes, living in a democracy, involved himself in public affairs to give free rein to his personal disposition. Being a difficult man prone to arguing, he constantly struggled with his opponents despite the hazards of such engagements. This proved to be an impediment for him. Demosthenes was always obliged to provide his audience with proof of his arguments.[45] By contrast, Aristeides, who lived under the safety of the Roman Empire and had no desire to become involved in politics, devoted himself to his literary preoccupations. Aristeides had nothing to fear from his audience. He was free to write whatever he wished. He usually composed speeches about events of the past that had long lost any relevance.[46] If Aristeides had lived during Demosthenes' time, he would have been obliged to adapt to the realities and requirements of that society or been accused of cheating his audience, like Antiphon of Rhamnus, the famous sophist of the late fifth century BCE who was forced to abandon the public assembly due to suspicions and concerns regarding the unrestrained use of his literary gifts.[47]

Demosthenes was always superb in his handling of the situation at hand. He grasped the essence of his subject and persuaded his audience of it. Even those who admired Aristeides' ability to treat his subject in a most convincing way were forced to admit that he was merely a perfect imitator of Demosthenes in that respect. This is the so-called loftiness ($δεινότης$) of Demosthenes' style. His art was his ability to project a disposition proximate to that of his city.[48]

Both orators were inventive, but they had to adapt their skills to the different circumstances of their life and times. This can be seen in the literary genres they employed. While Demosthenes mainly wrote deliberative orations, Aristeides, fond of the epideictic rhetoric befitting life under the emperors, composed declamations. Even his deliberative orations are fictitious, dealing with subjects of classical antiquity.[49] Demosthenes' primary aim was the facts themselves,[50] and even his enemies Philip of Macedonia and Parmenion recognized his positive qualities.[51]

Metochites considered Demosthenes fully equipped as an orator in all respects. His weapons were his sentences, constructed in such a way as to enhance their effectiveness. The periodic construction of his speeches was an important characteristic of his art, giving his thoughts a proper means of expression.[52] Men are generally unable to express their thoughts properly, but Demosthenes was most adept at formulating his thoughts and writing them down in a persuasive manner.[53]

Aristeides had greater opportunities to manipulate his subject matter, while Demosthenes was prohibited from doing so by the necessities of his political milieu. Aristeides was averse to using a simple style, even in those cases where the subject might have permitted some flexibility. His style exhibits a severity that surpasses even that of Demosthenes. It is old-fashioned, nowhere abandoning the road of the ancient writers he imitates.[54] By contrast, Demosthenes permits himself a certain dexterity.[55]

Generally speaking, Aristeides is an ardent imitator of Demosthenes. Even in his choice of vocabulary, Aristeides may be considered a new Demosthenes. In Metochites' time, however, Demosthenes was unsuitable as a stylistic role model for orators because the political and social realities of Byzantium differed radically from those of Demosthenes' day. Given that, the only proper example that could be followed by all Byzantine authors was that of Aristeides.[56]

The Metochites–Choumnos dispute revisited

Even a cursory reading of Oration 18 makes it evident how Metochites takes advantage of the opportunity to once more discuss facets of his dispute with Nikephoros Choumnos, though without reference to Thucydides. As noted previously, in Orations 13 and 14, Metochites praised Thucydides' oratorical style as the most perfect of all, and despite its notorious difficulty, recommended it as the model par excellence of good writing. No such musings are found in Oration 18, but the crux of the controversy with Choumnos is nonetheless addressed – that is, the necessity of using the so-called periodic style, or rather, the issue of the so-called δεινότης of style.

In Oration 13, Metochites had observed that his opponents were wrong to reject the periodic style, since their favourite author, Demosthenes, was himself a great admirer of it.[57] He implied that there was no real difference between Thucydides and Demosthenes, who was an ardent imitator of the great historian and had adopted the use of the periodic style under his influence. The latter becomes clearer in Oration 18.

In Oration 18, Metochites ventures beyond his treatises against Choumnos. Rather than Thucydides, he presents Demosthenes as the proper model of style, though, in fact, Demosthenes' style shares all the characteristics of Thucydides' as described in Oration 13: Demosthenes' style is lofty and majestic (δεινὸν) especially because of his fondness for complicated periods that most adequately express the meaning he wants to communicate. Metochites also stresses the compression (συστροφή) of Demosthenes' sentences, short and condensed yet meaningful at the same time.[58]

Enumerating the virtues of Demosthenes' style in Oration 18, Metochites reminds one of the way he summarized the main characteristics of Gregory of Nazianzus' style in Oration 6. Demosthenes combines beauty (ὥρα) and force or intensity (tonos). He is fond of the ancient way of expressing oneself and of the noble style of past times but does not neglect its elegance (καλλιέπεια).[59] In his speech for Gregory, Metochites praises him for combining the nobility and loftiness of style characteristic of old times and in addition for making his speeches elegant (καινῷ κάλλει). In this respect, Gregory was superior both to the modern orators, who cared only about the elegance of their style, and to the older ones, who mostly concerned themselves with its dignity.[60] Thus, Metochites finds yet another opportunity to recommend the δεινότης as the ideal of good writing. In Orations 13 and 14, the example of it is Thucydides, but in Oration 6, it is Gregory of Nazianzus, and in Oration 18, the utmost example is Demosthenes. This change in role models would appear to be significant, except that Metochites' views on the ideal style remain unchanged despite his recommending a different author as the personification of his literary ideal in each speech.

Metochites' perspective keeps a certain distance from Hermogenes' theories as expounded in *On Ideas*, where Thucydides' predilection for loftiness of style is sharply contrasted with Demosthenes' dexterity in combining different characters of speech whenever appropriate. Metochites does not deny this. What distinguishes Metochites' views from Hermogenes' is his tendency to mitigate or to even erase the differences between the two authors. In this regard, Metochites goes so far as to remind his readers that Demosthenes held Thucydides in great esteem and tried his best to imitate him.[61]

Metochites once again discusses the licentiousness of style (κόρδαξ and βακχεία) of modern orators in Oration 18. He states explicitly that Aristeides rejected this style altogether. The same terms are used in his speech on Gregory of Nazianzus. In Oration 6, Metochites had in mind the Asian style of late antiquity, pointing out that Gregory kept his distance from the Asian excesses, though not without succumbing at times to its graces, or at least this seems to be the meaning of the phrase: 'His style was superior to the old one because of its new grace, but it was also superior to the licentious modernity because of the dignity of its Greek loftiness.'[62] Gregory was able to combine both styles. His supposed originality consisted in this combination. According to Metochites, even Demosthenes was not averse to some licentiousness of style when the circumstances permitted it, in his private orations. Only Aristeides is adamant on this issue: any simplicity (ἀφέλεια) of style is to be avoided,[63] and Metochites seems to castigate Aristeides for it. It is noteworthy that Hermogenes also castigates Thucydides for it. Metochites, not mentioning Thucydides in Oration 18, seems to prefer to attribute the supposed deficiencies of his style as described by Hermogenes to Aristeides.

He admits that the solution of Demosthenes, who unhesitatingly employs a much simpler style in his private orations as Hermogenes points out, is much more consistent with the requirements of his profession; it would be improper for an orator to employ a pompous style when speaking about trivial private affairs.[64] This appears to be a veiled criticism of Aristeides. It is a typical case of the opposition between explicit words and implicit meaning, as Jakov Ljubarskij puts it.[65] Metochites implies that this inability constituted a serious deficit for an orator; according to the teachers of rhetoric, any orator should take into consideration the various circumstances surrounding his subject before composing his speech. That Aristeides refuses to do so or is unable to is not to his credit. On the other hand, one must also consider that Metochites is willing to admit that Aristeides is the most suitable author for the Byzantine orators to imitate. According to him, Aristeides has no true relation to circumstances (πράγματα).

Meaning of the oration

On the surface, Metochites seems to suggest that Demosthenes and Aristeides are equal,[66] even admitting that the imitation of Aristeides is the proper thing to do for his contemporary orators. Examining Oration 18 more carefully, however, reveals that his admiration for Aristeides is rather qualified.[67]

Aristeides developed his skills uninhibited by the political realities around him; he had the luxury of not needing to pay them any attention. On the other hand, Demosthenes had to cope incessantly with them, struggling to adapt himself to the ever-changing circumstances of Athenian democracy. Metochites clearly states that Aristeides is an accomplished and perfect orator – as far as he imitates Demosthenes. This is hardly unqualified praise of Aristeides.

It is interesting that Metochites constantly reminds his reader of the so-called πράγματα, the relationship between the art of rhetoric and the realities of life. The word πράγματα is constantly repeated throughout Metochites' speech: Demosthenes involved himself in all the affairs of his city, while Aristeides abstained from them, choosing instead to occupy himself with the wholly unrelated affairs of older times. Aristeides did not bother to be taught by those πράγματα.[68] On the other hand, Demosthenes obeyed those πράγματα, from which there was no escape, trying to adapt his habits and his thoughts to them.[69] Aristeides makes use of his natural skills in a way that surpasses the realities of life (πράγματα). This is demonstrated by the two orators' attitude towards the simple style: while Aristeides makes no concessions to it, avoiding it altogether,[70] Demosthenes, as Hermogenes points out, does not refrain from employing it in some of his private orations, where it seemed to be appropriate, dictated by the realities of life (πράγματα).[71] Coming to a conclusion, Metochites suggests that the imitation of Aristeides is appropriate for the times, and that anyway, no one could truly imitate Demosthenes, because the conditions of his life were entirely different from the current ones.

Thus, according to Metochites, the proper criterion for the evaluation of the art of rhetoric was its adaptation to the circumstances (πράγματα). This was hardly a ground-breaking idea. Most ancient teachers of rhetoric had clearly suggested such a relationship. Hermogenes remarks in his treatise *On Invention* that the diction of a text must be adapted to the circumstances and the persons involved in a certain situation; in short, the orator, like the poet, must reflect the circumstances addressed by his speech.[72] This is exactly what Metochites asserts in relation to Demosthenes, while implying something more: πράγματα are not only the affairs that each rhetorical speech had to deal with, but the social and political circumstances of the state the orator lived in as well. Demosthenes reflected the circumstances of his time, while Aristeides ignored the contemporary political and social milieu, choosing to concentrate on affairs from times different from his own,[73] composing speeches that were fictitious (πλαττόμενος).[74] In fact, by proposing Aristeides as an example for contemporary orators,[75] Metochites seems to be urging his fellow scholars to refrain from discussing the actual affairs of their society, not because it is wrong per se, but because they are not in a position to do so with any authority. This does not diminish his admiration for Demosthenes, who in his explicit view is the most important orator of all time. Leosthenes called the speech of Demosthenes 'beaten out by a hammer'. Apart from Demosthenes' style, he was referring to the orator's masterful handling of the circumstances addressed by his speeches.[76]

Metochites is not an isolated case. In the eleventh century, Michael Psellos was an ardent supporter of a turn towards the reality of human affairs.[77] Making such a change required practical and political wisdom and an awareness of the causes and consequences of events that transform human life. Psellos seems to be aware that the handling of harsh realities demanded certain qualities that many of his contemporaries lacked. This is a vindication of the political part of philosophy, which was neglected in Byzantium. In this respect at least, Metochites seems to agree with Psellos.

If this is the real meaning of Oration 18, one can interpret it as both a self-portrait of Metochites and a veiled criticism of the discursive culture of his own society despite Metochites himself providing numerous examples of a preoccupation with epideictic speeches. The speeches preserved in Vindobonensis phil. gr. 95 are specimens of almost all the subgenres of Byzantine epideictic rhetoric. Thus, by describing the literary activity of Aristeides, a practitioner of epideictic oratory,[78] Metochites also shines a light on his own activity in the process. The so-called *Presbeutikos*, Oration 8, a description of Metochites' mission to the court of Milutin, king of the Serbs, is the only one of his texts that touches on actual affairs of state. Metochites describes Aristeides as an 'emperor of himself' as far as his literary activities are concerned, and this applies to himself as well. The question is whether Metochites is, in general, satisfied with an activity so totally isolated from the society to which its author belongs. The answer is surely negative. The speech on Demosthenes and Aristeides may be read as a veiled but devastating criticism of the literati of his own time. By stressing the effectiveness of Demosthenes' speech, Metochites seems to castigate the total irrelevance of the speeches composed by his Byzantine contemporaries (and himself!) to the problems of their society. It was almost impossible for Metochites to express himself clearly in Oration 18, given that the regime of the state, the absolute monarchy, was the main reason for the bad situation. He hints at this in the beginning of his speech, when he states that the political environment of the Roman Empire protected Aristeides from attacks by his audience, but Athenian democracy did not protect Demosthenes from his.[79]

Metochites' Oration 11, *Byzantios*, on Constantinople, supports the assertion that the abandonment of affairs of life was far from an ideal for him. In this speech, Metochites' most extensive epideictic oration, the author compares life in Constantinople with life in other cities, drawing the conclusion that the citizens of Constantinople have more opportunities to enjoy life in its totality than citizens elsewhere. Near the end of the oration, Metochites points out that living in communion with as many people as possible and engaging in different affairs is much more valuable than living many years on earth without having the opportunity to obtain as many experiences as possible. Constantinople's value consists in offering its citizens such opportunities to a greater extent than any other city.[80] The word *pragmata* is prominent in this section of *Byzantios*, as it is in the speech on Demosthenes and Aristeides. It is evident that Metochites highly values involvement with the affairs of the world.

Metochites seems to conceal his true convictions under a somewhat qualified praise of Aristeides. At first glance, he presents Aristeides as a more convenient example than Demosthenes for the orators of his time, but it is clear that Demosthenes' rhetoric is closer to Metochites' heart. He feels nostalgic for past times, when orators could address real issues of their society and contribute to their solution. It is obvious that he wishes his contemporary orators were more pragmatic, admonishing and counselling their fellow citizens on the important issues of the day, but nonetheless refrains from suggesting such a radical break with the Byzantine rhetorical tradition of epideictic orations. He even advises them to continue imitating Aristeides instead of Demosthenes. At heart, however, Metochites seems to have been convinced of the perennial validity of the example of the politically engaged orator like Demosthenes. This is yet another sign of the elusiveness one encounters so often in Metochites' writings.

Emperor of himself: A self-portrait of Metochites?

At the beginning of Oration 18, Metochites laments that some of his friends had asked him to compare Demosthenes and Aristeides despite knowing that he no longer discussed literary matters, instead having become absorbed in astronomy, studying the dances of the stars and their majestic routes (πομπεία).[81] In the same treatise, he employs this very term to denote Aristeides' intention to exhibit his literary qualities to his audience and his ability to manipulate his speeches without taking into account the existing circumstances (καὶ πλὴν ἀτεχνῶς ἢ κατὰ τὰ πράγματα πομπεύων).[82] By employing this term at the beginning of his treatise, Metochites indicates that he has turned his back on his previous literary endeavours, focusing instead on his philosophical studies, under which astronomy was subsumed at the time. One may dismiss such a contention as a common Byzantine trope, in that most authors at the beginning of a text pretended to be unable to deal with the subject at hand for various reasons. In the case of Metochites, however, things were not so simple.

In Oration 18, Metochites calls Aelius Aristeides 'an emperor of himself and of the speeches'.[83] This stemmed from Aristeides being free to elaborate on subjects previously addressed by older orators without regard to the circumstances of his time. It is an observation that Metochites frequently makes about Aristeides, as shown above. Of note, Metochites employed the same term, αὐτοκράτωρ ἑαυτοῦ, in a rather positive sense in Poem 3, addressed to Gregory of Bulgaria. There, Metochites praises Gregory for being free to devote himself to the pursuit of virtue and knowledge without concern for anything else, since he had long abandoned worldly affairs. Such praise highlights once more the ambiguity of Metochites' self-representation. He extols Gregory's opportunity to devote his full energies and mental capabilities to his own affairs, but on the other hand he seems to sympathize with Demosthenes, obliged to consider current circumstances and to compose his speeches in accordance with them. Metochites refrains from castigating Aristeides for his total neglect of contemporary affairs and even admits that Aristeides is admirable for his rhetorical dexterity. What he adds afterwards is telling, however: he states that if Aristeides were living in another place and at another time, he would have been forced to take into consideration the circumstances of that time and place, adapting himself and his way of writing accordingly. He even admits that in another place, Aristeides might have been suspected by his audience of trying to deceive them and of behaving like a sophist, who would hold them in contempt, underestimating their capability to detect his deceit. In Metochites' view, Aristeides resembled Antiphon of Rhamnus, a famous sophist of the late fifth century BCE who was forced to refrain from all political activities because his fellow citizens had realized that his rhetorical dexterity was harmful and dangerous.[84] Further on, Metochites makes clear that Aristeides is inferior to Demosthenes, because even his admirers cannot but admit that his exceptional rhetorical qualities are due to his imitation of the latter.[85] He only recommends Aristeides as a useful model for his contemporary orators because epideictic rhetoric dominated in their time.[86]

Metochites presents Aristeides as a man who lived alone, dedicated to the graces of rhetoric and devoting his attention entirely to the audience in front of which he performed (ζῆν αἱρεῖσθαι ἑαυτῷ μόνῳ καὶ ταῖς τῆς ῥητορικῆς χάρισι καὶ θεάτροις ἐπιδείξεων).[87] Metochites had distanced himself from such absolute devotion to rhetoric at the beginning of the treatise, but one must keep in mind that the solitary life as realized by Aristeides was Metochites' ideal, or at least that is the impression one gets from Metochites' other works, including Oration 10, *Ethikos*, and Poem 3. In Oration 18, however, Metochites seems to subtly undermine the ideal of total devotion to one's literary studies; it might be a way to avoid the dangers of public life, but it is not an ideal with perpetual, absolute value. In another strange coincidence, Metochites quotes a passage from Demosthenes' third Olynthiac speech (ch. 32), where it states that man's thoughts are determined by the circumstances (πράγματα) surrounding him.[88] Metochites quotes this very passage in both Oration 5, in reference to Emperor Andronikos II Palaiologos,[89] and Oration 11, *Byzantios*, in reference to Emperor Constantine, founder of Constantinople.[90] Metochites quotes the Demosthenic passage in Oration 18 as proof of his view that he is able to adapt himself to circumstances and to subordinate himself to the necessities of life. Metochites stresses that adaption to the circumstances has nothing to do with deceptive inventions (ἀπατηλαῖς κομψείαις).[91] In all probability the term denotes the intricacies of epideictic orations like those by Aristeides. Metochites continues, saying that any orator who confronts the necessity of beings is forced to invent ways of coping with this necessity; by contrast, those who pretend to be affected by the circumstances of their speech have no share in any necessity and cannot be compared with orators like Demosthenes.[92] This is veiled criticism of Aristeides. Metochites implies that despite its merits, Aristeides' oratory had no relation to the circumstances (ἐνίσχετο τοῖς πράγμασιν).[93] The implication is that Aristeides cannot be considered inventive (εὑρετικώτατος) like Demosthenes.[94] This seems to be tantamount to a reluctant rejection of late Byzantine discursive modes, which were based on epideictic oratory and the *theatra*, and an awareness by Metochite of his own limitations as a writer who was a practitioner of the epideictic branch of rhetoric par excellence. Somehow Metochites considered the Byzantine *theatra* oppressive, curtailing the intellectual capabilities of his fellow authors and transforming them into mere puppets isolated from the real world.

Chapter 6

CODA – METOCHITES ON RHETORIC: VEILED CRITICISM OF LATE BYZANTIUM DISCURSIVE CULTURE

There is no doubt that Metochites was an accomplished orator in the way the Byzantines understood the undertaking. He does not insist, however, that he is both a philosopher and an orator, like Michael Psellos,[1] but appears instead to identify himself only as the former. Metochites describes his own course of studies,[2] that of Gregory of Nazianzus,[3] and that of his friend Joseph the Philosopher,[4] and he suggests a similar course for his student and collaborator Nikephoros Gregoras.[5] In each case, the study of rhetoric was at the time considered an indispensable part of the education of a Byzantine nobleman aspiring to be an accomplished and successful intellectual. Like Psellos, Metochites, after describing the branches of rhetoric, enumerates the branches of philosophy crucial for an accomplished scholar: logic, physics, mathematics, metaphysics and theology. The curriculum represents a gradual ascent towards the individual's knowledge of God. Metochites does not seem to consider rhetoric a fundamental branch of human knowledge, but certainly assigns it important propaedeutic value, contributing to the fashioning of language and giving man the ability to attack the enemies of the Christian faith by providing the necessary weapons. It is thus a required, albeit secondary, discipline. This should come as no surprise. Even Psellos, after being presented as the Byzantine orator par excellence,[6] creates his profile as an orator in a suggestive, subtle manner. Metochites' case, however, is different: no rhetoricizing of his persona, like that of Psellos, is to be observed;[7] he never presents himself as an orator. Metochites seems to imitate Gregory of Nazianzus, identifying himself as a philosopher.

Metochites goes a step further in trying to deconstruct the traditional rhetorical culture of Byzantium. According to recent research, the rhetoricians' self-consciousness had been growing from the eleventh century onwards.[8] It can be argued, however, that the self-consciousness of the Byzantine literati was high even before then, even if not explicitly stated by Psellos and his intellectual milieu. In any case, the intellectual climate of the early Palaiologan period was radically altered. The certainties of the early period had given way to doubts about the Byzantines' self-image as a result of the decline of the empire. The circumstances were ripe for reconsideration of traditional Byzantine values. Metochites' reassessment of the value of panegyric rhetoric is one element in his criticism of the Byzantine world view, but he did it through traditional means.

Almost all teachers of the art of speech known to the Byzantine scholars shared a certain admiration for Demosthenes and his political speeches, which they considered superior to the epideictic oratory of their contemporary orators. Discursive performance, which satisfied the need for entertainment, was viewed as inferior to practically oriented oratory. Political or civic speech, preoccupied with 'beings' (πράγματα), was thought a more trustworthy reflection of the truth than the panegyrical discourse, which involved fiction to a much greater degree.[9] Most Byzantine writers, however, neglected the political branch of rhetoric, limiting themselves to the composition of epideictic orations, which provided ample opportunities to exhibit their talents, unrestrained from the requisite political necessities. Like Psellos, Metochites appreciated the autonomous creativity of ancient writers,[10] among them Aristeides, and their authoritative power to fashion their speeches in the way they desired without bowing to social or political restraints as Demosthenes was obliged to do. He even goes so far as to nominate Aristeides to the canon for his contemporaries. He reserves his true admiration for Demosthenes, however. Despite the tradition of promoting Demosthenes, Metochites appears fed up with the practice of his fellows, who focused on the purely literary genre of epideictic oratory in contempt of political oratory in the broader sense.

The irony is that Metochites was one of the most accomplished orators of his time, but some of his speeches – like Oration 8, *Presbeutikos*; Oration 10, *Ethikos*; and Orations 13 and 14, against Nikephoros Choumnos – despite exhibiting elements of epideictic oratory, are more closely connected to the circumstances of late Byzantium, discussing real problems and even proposing solutions to them. Metochites addressed actual problems that occupied the minds of Byzantine intellectuals, although in a discreet and suggestive manner. The most important of these was the relation between the contemplative life and the active life: which one was more important? What was the true meaning of the active life?

Metochites' views on the models of good speech were not always the same, another indication of his repeated, characteristic elusiveness. In Orations 13 and 14, he evaluates Demosthenes positively but clearly considers him inferior to his preferred model, Thucydides. In Oration 18, Demosthenes is presented as superior to Aristeides. In Orations 13 and 14, Metochites seems to prefer the unadulterated δεινότης of Thucydides, which is castigated even by Hermogenes, while in Oration 18 Metochites appears more positive towards the mitigated δεινότης of Demosthenes. In the end, however, he advocates for Aristeides as the most appropriate model of style for his contemporaries, although in his heart Metochites was not convinced of Aristeides' superior value. One must not forget that in Oration 6, Metochites hails Gregory of Nazianzus as one of the greatest orators of all time. Is this another case of Metochites' elusiveness? The answer can only be affirmative.

Metochites attempts to conceal his disdain for the practice of his contemporary orators and in each instance adopts a different model of speech, which are in fact masks behind which Metochites hides himself. He never explicitly expresses his own views. Thucydides, Demosthenes and Gregory of Nazianzus appear to function as counterparts of Aristeides, the preferred model of his contemporaries. In each case, Metochites focuses on a quality of the first three orators in contrast to those of Aristeides. What is noteworthy is that Aristeides is also a mask of Metochites. Nobody was more familiar with the intricacies of epideictic oratory and the practice of the Byzantine *theatra* than Metochites. In mentioning Aristeides, he refers to the θέατρα ἐπιδείξεων, which that author so much appreciated. He was also aware that the audience largely defines the author, with community playing a greater function than the individual self;[11] this becomes evident in discussing the case of Demosthenes, who was forced to heed the political circumstances of his times (πράγματα) and the desires of his audience. Surprisingly, Metochites seems to appreciate the involvement of circumstances much more than the authorial licence of Aristeides to compose his speeches without taking the political circumstances into account. Without saying so explicitly, Metochites rejects such authorial license, which featured prominently for intellectuals from the middle Byzantine period onwards,[12] considering it a result of the circumstances prevailing in late Byzantium.

Even when discussing literature, Metochites remains an elusive intellectual. The contradictions one encounters reading his works are truly astonishing. Those and his elusiveness become more apparent in his writings on the relationship between the contemplative life and the active life. Despite his elusiveness, Metochites' self-image as an author and orator remains consistent on one point: he seems to have considered himself an author who defied the conventions of his time and tried to find new patterns of rhetorical discourse more appropriate for his talents and for the expression of his personal spiritual needs. In regard to the latter, Metochites expounded on the contemplation of beings in *Ethikos* and tried to construct a new image of himself – that of the pure intellectual devoted to studies of the ancient authors and to the contemplation of nature – which was radically different from the prevailing image of contemplation among his contemporaries – that of the monk devoted to the pondering the divine mysteries without caring so much about nature or ancient literature.

Part III

VITA CONTEMPLATIVA VERSUS VITA ACTIVA: THEIR AMBIGUOUS RELATIONSHIP AND THE AMBIGUITIES OF METOCHITES' SELF-IMAGE AS AN INTELLECTUAL

Chapter 7

'THE GREEKS SEEK WISDOM': POEM 6, FOR THE THREE GREAT PRELATES, AND POEM 5, FOR ST ATHANASIOS: THEOLOGY, GREEK LEARNING AND THE QUEST FOR A HUMANISTIC MONASTERY

Metochites' Poems 5 and 6 – praises of St Athanasios of Alexandria and of the three great prelates, respectively – are useful in understanding Oration 10 (*Ethikos*). Metochites dedicated Poem 6 to the three great prelates – Basil of Caesarea, Gregory of Nazianzus and John Chrysostom. The three came to be commemorated on 30 January after John Mauropous, the learned metropolitan of Euchaita, introduced their feast in the mid-eleventh century. At first glance, Metochites' poem looks like an encomium in verse, but there is more to it. Metochites does not restrict himself to the biographical details of the three prelates, but also provides a detailed account of their contributions to the enrichment and development of Christian doctrine stemming from their wisdom. At the end of the poem, he compares the literary style of the three prelates in a way that reminds one of Metochites' comparison of Demosthenes with Aelius Aristeides, in Oration 18. In essence, Poem 6 is a versified essay, like Oration 18, with some elements of rhetorical praise. Poem 5, for St Athanasios, is a more conventional piece of poetry, limited to a rather standard encomium combining praise and biography.

Metochites begins Poem 6 by stressing that it would be ridiculous for his readers to expect him to say anything worthy of the three prelates, whose virtues surpass any praise. Metochites glorifies the providence of Christ, who gave the men prominence at a time of severe crisis in his church. They managed to combat the enemies of Christ and guide the church to peace and tranquillity. Due to their virtue and wisdom, they are considered the most valuable examples of human nature and the utmost in human virtue; they proved that virtue is not unattainable, as had been argued in the past. Their wisdom was unsurpassable, combining superb knowledge of the Holy Scriptures and profound knowledge of secular wisdom, which they used as a powerful weapon against the enemies of the church. The language they employed in their writings was majestic. Their wisdom persuaded many to follow them; since these wisest of all men adopted the doctrines of simple fishermen, it was obvious to the people that the doctrines were true. Thus, something miraculous occurred: in the early days of Christianity, God strengthened the faith by employing the holy apostles, simple fishermen who lacked any formal wisdom, and who performed miracles, and then later, he brought forward and employed the three prelates, who persuaded learned people to Christian doctrine. Towards the end of the poem, Metochites examines the three prelates separately, highlighting their virtues.

It is almost certain that Metochites took advantage of the speech that John Mauropous delivered for the feast of the three prelates. One point made by Metochites that is not from Mauropous' text is, however, striking – that learned people were persuaded to adopt Christianity because the wisdom of the three hierarchs impressed them.[1] Here, Metochites seems to go beyond the permissible in Byzantium. If one accepts this assertion, then one could reasonably argue that the miracles of Christ had been insufficient to persuade people to adopt Christianity – that is, learned men needed something more: a rational argument, which the three wise prelates supposedly provided. Metochites does not dare utter such a view, which might have been considered no less than blasphemy in his time, but it is the logical conclusion of his statement.

Such a thought comes as no surprise. Metochites, more than once in his writings, attempts in a most sublime manner to undermine the traditional convictions of Byzantine society. This is abundantly clear in Oration 10, *Ethikos*, where the most important points he makes are that pleasure is not devoid of value for man and that one can connect with God and enjoy communion with him through the study of nature without knowledge of the divine revelation. He expresses similar views in Poem 10, on the harmonious laws governing the world that are, so to speak, a ladder leading to God. The poem for the three prelates offers Metochites another opportunity to issue veiled criticism on the absolute trust certain members of his society place in supernatural and irrational forces. Can Poem 6 be read as criticizing certain tendencies among the monks of his day? One must keep in mind that simple monks in Byzantium were generally reluctant to recognize the value of secular studies; they took care to subjugate philosophy to theology. Metochites appears to be trying to reinstate philosophy, Greek wisdom, to its once-revered position, and if not superior to the revelation of the holy apostles, at least equal to it. With the way paved for philosophy to be completely independent of theology, Metochites seems to set about creating a new self-image: that of the pure intellectual free of the traditional, prevailing conventions and doctrines of Byzantine society. There is a hint of this image in Oration 4, for St Demetrius, in the saint being willing to sacrifice the sacred and old religion of his forefathers for the sake of the true. The poem for the three prelates offers a preliminary outline of that picture, which is presented more fully in *Ethikos*.

As previously observed, Metochites devoted several of his writings to contemporary monks. In addition to Oration 17 for Joseph Rhakendytes and Poem 2 to the monks of Chora, he also wrote Poem 3 for his friend Gregory of Bulgaria, a retired bishop who lived as a monk in a suburb of Constantinople, Oration 16 for Loukas, abbot of the monastery of Chora, and Oration 19 for the ascetic saint John of Didymoteichon.

Gregory of Bulgaria was a prominent representative of the humanistic trend observable among certain monks of the Palaiologan period. As Metochites explicitly states in Poem 3,

> Your constant concern is twofold: to acquire more knowledge and to worship God. O blessed man in both respects, who loves those things and whose love is not unfulfilled, you manage to make progress in both respects: your virtue becomes even greater and you come thus nearer to God, but you also increase your learning, acquiring more knowledge, which is desirable, both ecclesiastical and profane; one can derive profit also from the secular knowledge, in order to walk easily along the path of the contemplative life, not encountering obstacles, not adulterating any of the doctrines of the pure faith of our Lord God.[2]

Service to God combined with striving for wisdom is Metochites' ideal in life and a theme in his work. In his day, the best place for realizing this ideal was a cloister like Gregory of Bulgaria's, the monastery of the archangel Michael. It is significant that in Poem 3 Metochites enumerates all those things that Gregory had abandoned.[3] In fact, the same things appear in the description of Metochites' own house in Poem 19, one of his poems to himself.[4] Thus, Poem 3 serves as subtle self-criticism.

Ultimately, the monastery of Chora seems to have been the realization of Metochites' ideal. There he gathered monks from throughout the state and provided them with the necessary means to pursue their purposes. In doing so, he also assembled a large collection of books, creating one of the most important libraries in the Byzantine capital. He points this out in poems,[5] as well as in Oration 16,[6] which is, essentially, a short history of Chora's restoration under the leadership of the abbot Loukas. Also, reminiscent of a Byzantine typicon, the oration contains instructions for the monks to follow. It is interesting that Metochites omits reference to the secular wisdom of Loukas, in all probability a rather simple man who lacked any sophistication of language and style, as Metochites asserts. After all, the setting at Chora was somewhat unusual: the most humanistic of all monasteries had an abbot who probably lacked any humanistic education. St John of Didymoteichon, addressed in Oration 18, is rather significant in this respect, having not been educated.

As previously noted, John was born the son of poor peasants during the reign of Emperor Basil II in the area of Didymoteichon. John soon abandoned his family, choosing the life of an ascetic in the mountainous areas of Thrace. He lived hidden in a ravine until an official who was hunting in the area discovered him, and after many failed attempts, finally persuaded him to establish a monastery. John gathered a group of monks in a simple building and acted as their abbot for a brief time, before retiring once more to the nearby desert, preferring to live in a ravine. He died not long afterwards and had almost been forgotten by his fellow citizens until Metochites, who had been exiled to the area, decided to write an encomium for him at the instigation of certain unidentified individuals, who honoured the memory of the saint.

John of Didymoteichon is the exact opposite of Metochites. A simple man, John, like most Byzantine ascetics, abandoned the secular world and founded a monastery at the instigation of a rich person, who, thanks to his connections, helped John create a monastic community. This is the commonality between John and Metochites; both men founded monasteries at the instigation of an important individual – Metochites by Emperor Andronikos II and John by an unidentified official of Didymoteichon province. The two monasteries differ from each other, with Chora being an important intellectual centre in the empire, while John's was a humble provincial monastery. Metochites seems to have abandoned the ideal of the humanistic monastery, to which he felt drawn in his earlier years, but this should not be interpreted as a wholesale abandonment of it. Rather, his fall from power made him more receptive to other forms of monasticism.

The Life of John of Didymoteichon ends with a section on the saint's miracles. Metochites does not seem to place much faith in the value of such supernatural phenomena. In Oration 18, on Demosthenes and Aelius Aristeides, he castigates Aristeides for visions he describes in *Sacred Orations*, which Metochites considers 'little stories proper for old women'.[7] In Oration 2, for St Marina, Metochites refers to the saint's two encounters with Satan himself, but describes the stories as fanciful.[8] These two instances strongly imply that Metochites had reservations about the stories. That Metochites takes on the traditional miracles of his church in his waning years is noteworthy as another sign of his habitual elusiveness. There is a suggestion in the text that Metochites is willing to adopt the mask of the retiring illiterate man he praises in Oration 19.

One may conclude that Metochites considered humanistic monasticism the solution to some of the problems of this life. The felicitous combination of calmness of mind, study of the ancient authors and contemplation of beings was the ideal of men like Joseph the Philosopher, Gregory of Bulgaria and Metochites himself. In *Miscellanea*, however, after describing the blessedness of those who live according to this ideal in terms reminiscent of *Ethikos* and Poem 3, Metochites adds a remark that clearly casts doubt about attaining such a dream:

> I know that even many such chosen men (in fact, life is too short to speak about all of them) neither stay completely untroubled in their thoughts, nor succeed perfectly and victoriously in this magnificent choice of life so as to live in serenity away from everything and pursue their calling undisturbed, but sometimes they have several dealings with those outside [the religious community] and concerning worldly affairs, both voluntarily, to some extent, and certainly involuntarily, and with one another.[9]

A small piece of land or a cottage may cause great anxiety to the philosopher who comes to possess it; therefore, one should take care to understand the real meaning behind such contradictory statements by Metochites and avoid superficial reconciliations. Metochites expounds unconventional views concerning the usefulness of secular knowledge and education in his usual elusive manner.

As noted, the wisdom of the three wise prelates is the main topic of Poem 6. After composing a long praise of their wisdom in general, Metochites describes in greater detail the literary merits of each prelate (beginning with v. 571). Unsurprisingly, of the three hierarchs, Gregory of Nazianzus is deemed the writer par excellence. Metochites insists on the novelty of Gregory's style,[10] as well as the beauty of his language (εὐστομίη).[11] Metochites believes that Basil of Caesarea and John Chrysostom are not to be commended for the beauty of their style, considered clearly deficient when compared with that of Gregory.[12] He concedes, however, that Chrysostom's language is 'well twisted' (*eustrophos*) and very efficient as a rhetorical weapon for persuading his audience and vanquishing his opponents. He also praises the fervour of his style, which resembles a fountain gushing out of the earth.[13] According to Metochites, although he was not particularly interested in the elaborateness of style of Basil of Caesarea,[14] the prelate employed a rather dignified diction,[15] which was quite effective and imposing; the brevity of his diction concealed great and ponderous thoughts.[16] Ultimately, what greatly impressed Metochites was the effectiveness of the three prelates' theological diction, with which they refuted and countered all arguments brought forward by their opponents. He leaves the impression that this effectiveness resulted from their Greek learning.

This is not the only time Metochites insists on the value of Greek learning as a weapon that can be employed in theological struggles for the sake of orthodoxy. In Oration 17, the funeral speech for his friend Joseph the Philosopher, Metochites describes the curriculum for Joseph's education, extolling in particular the value of his in-depth study of Aristotle's works on logic, an indispensable resource in the struggles.[17] In Poem 4, to Nikephoros Gregoras, Metochites advises his student to pay particular attention to the cultivation and embellishment of his literary style, arguing that style is the armour of one's thought.[18]

Metochites presents the case of Athanasios of Alexandria somewhat differently in Poem 5. He emphasizes Athanasios' effectiveness in his struggle against his adversaries; it is noteworthy that Metochites employs the same word, καίρια,[19] which he had used in the case of Basil in Poem 6 to denote this effectiveness.[20] There is, however, a crucial difference: although Athanasios was not unacquainted with Greek wisdom, having studied it for a long time, he did not pay particular attention to it, preferring to devote himself to study of the Holy Scripture.[21] Metochites points out that Athanasios, like the three prelates,[22] had been richly endowed by nature with special gifts that permitted him to accomplish his tasks in the most effective way.[23] Thus, in Poem 5, Metochites attributes Athanasios' effectiveness to the gifts of his nature, while in Poem 6 the accomplishments of the three prelates stem from a combination of the qualities of their nature and their Greek education. This difference may not be obvious from a cursory reading of the texts, but it is there, and it cries out for explanation.

The rhetorical culture of Byzantine intellectuals permitted them to present the same problem from two or even three different perspectives. One might assume here, as in other cases in this volume, that in Poems 5 and 6 Metochites availed himself of this technique from the *progymnasmata*. The issue he faced may be described as follows: is nature or education more important in life? Nature or nurture is a perennial issue, debated in Greek literature and philosophy since classical antiquity, that has been answered differently in various periods.

That said, such an explanation for the differences between Poems 5 and 6 appears rather trivial. Metochites was certainly interested in the possibilities of nature, which he regarded as a mighty and crucial force determining man's fate. In his orations, he frequently discussed the potential of human nature and the contribution of man's efforts to its development. In Oration 6, for Gregory of Nazianzus, he praises the quality of Gregory's natural gifts, considering him the supreme example of a man richly endowed by nature.[24] In *Ethikos*, Metochites deplores the tendency of most men to neglect the cultivation of the gifts with which nature has endowed them.[25] In Oration 5, the first *basilikos*, Metochites composes a long encomium on the natural attributes of Emperor Andronikos II Palaiologos.[26] He even goes so far as to point out that Andronikos' natural qualities more than compensated for his lack of formal education and the absence of time for proper study;[27] the emperor proved himself superior to the intellectuals of the imperial court.[28] The take on Andronikos somewhat resembles the attitude attributed to St Athanasios, who was confident in the gifts of his nature but did not bother to cultivate his speech. As pointed out elsewhere, Metochites seems to be fond of subtly and discreetly undermining in his later writings positions he had supported in previous writings, thus assigning his readers the task of pondering his positions, and whether he is hiding his true convictions, although he is careful to pay lip service to the traditional views of society. In Oration 14, his second invective against Nikephoros Choumnos, Metochites severely castigates his opponent for being overly confident in the potential of his nature while unaware of his deficient education.[29] In this case, Metochites appears to adopt the position opposite to the one he took in the case of Oration 5 and Poem 6.

One of the most sacred assumptions of Byzantine intellectuals was that secular education should be combined with the study of the sacred texts. Although Metochites seems to be a rather vocal exponent of this view in the late Byzantine era, presenting himself as the learned man par excellence of his time, the case of Poem 5 reiterates that one must be cautious in rushing to affirm that Metochites held one view or the other or that he preferred one image of himself to another; one should first study all his works carefully. In Poem 5, although not denying the value of secular education, Metochites is ready to admit that one may become a great theologian without paying much attention to grammar, syntax and rhetoric; this he applied to St Athanasios of Alexandria. Even when praising the secular learning of the three prelates, Metochites is careful not to state that devotion to secular learning is the only way of effectively and profitably studying the Holy Scripture and Christian theology in general. Metochites, the embodiment of so-called Byzantine humanism, is ready to praise Athanasios of Alexandria, whose literary style he deems deficient, side by side with the three prelates, famous exponents of the validity of Greek learning; he is also inclined to praise the illiterate St John of Didymoteichon side by side with the most learned and erudite Joseph the Philosopher. These ambiguities defy easy explanation, but they are an indication of the depth of Metochites' thought and his unwillingness to submit himself to the requirements of his intellectual environment. As a profound medieval thinker, Metochites is not averse to presenting his audience with various, often contradictory, images of himself, concealing his true views under a cloud of uncertainty. In other words, Metochites is a typical example of medieval esotericism.[30]

The theoretical foundations of Metochites' self-images need to be further clarified, including those centred around the notions of contemplation and the contemplative life in two of his most important works, *Ethikos* and *Byzantios*. Here as well, the nature of his thought was innovative, and again reveal the tendency to hide his true convictions behind conventional, seemingly trivial themes and commonplaces – in this case, on the contemplation of the world and nature. When examined more carefully, however, those convictions are revealed to be potentially detrimental to the established order and doctrines of the Byzantine church. At the same time, the self-image of the pure intellectual that Metochites has created displays certain inner ambiguities.

Oration 10, Ethikos: *The sage as contemplator of the world and denial of the monastic ideal*

Oration 10, *Ethikos*, is a peculiar work. Metochites explicitly affirms in Poem 12, to his friend and scholar Nikephoros Xanthopoulos, that in *Ethikos*, he presented views that people would not understand unless already knowledgeable of his thought.[31] There can be no doubt that the views Metochites was referring to were unconventional and likely not in accordance with those widely shared by his contemporary society. He had already hinted at the possibility of a man holding doctrines that did not conform to the common, old and venerable views respected by the members of his social circle in Oration 4, on St Demetrius. His covert message in *Ethikos* can be detected by closely examining Metochites' self-image as projected in this extensive work.

Ethikos is supposedly addressed to a young man who has been neglecting his studies. In it, Metochites attempts to persuade him to approach his studies with more vigour by explaining the advantages of a life devoted to the pursuit of knowledge. This allows Metochites to compose a praise of the *vita contemplativa* that is both convincing and captivating. He renews the ancient Greek protreptic speech to wisdom, which was quite common in the philosophical schools of late antiquity that had been somewhat neglected in his time. Metochites employs various literary techniques to persuade his addressee, or rather his audience, of the value of wisdom and literary studies and the importance of a life devoted to the cultivation of one's inner self. Of surprise is that except for some passing references to the value of the Christian faith, Metochites seems to neglect the religious dimension of the inner life of man. His main conclusion is that man, by closely examining the nature surrounding him, can come to realize that everything has been created by God; this focus on the study of nature is the contemplative life, the highest and most revered way of life. Man may happily adopt this way of existing and live happily, provided he severs all connections to the material world and withdraws to his study.

Any attempt to combine the contemplative life with an active life is hopeless: the man who tries to prove himself capable of combining these two different ways to conduct life will be condemned to bitter disappointment. Interestingly, Metochites offers his own case as an example of such a desperate, failed attempt. Thus, in *Ethikos*, Metochites creates another image of himself, but also touches on all the others from his writings as well – the young, successful bureaucrat, the saintly intellectual like the three great prelates, the intellectual absorbed by his studies like Joseph the Philosopher, and the author attached to the literary tradition of Byzantium. Discussion of two main themes in *Ethikos* – the contemplative life and Metochites' theory of pleasure – help in discerning the main characteristics of the image of the pure intellectual that Metochites creates of himself and in detecting inner ambiguities.

Content of the oration

Ethikos, preserved in Vindobonensis phil. gr. 95 with considerable losses of text, appears to be divided into the two traditional parts of an admonitory speech: in the first part, the author attempts to convince his reader of the value of the way of life he promotes, and in the second part, answers any objections raised by those who do not share his views and therefore reject or even denigrate the way of life he suggests to his audience.

Metochites begins his inquiry by noting that the negligence the young man exhibits towards his studies has made him overcome his own hesitations and proceed with the composition of this very speech to persuade him of the value of knowledge. He stresses that he has long since abandoned the contemplative life, so his praise of that particular way of life should not raise doubts about his sincerity; a man who praises a way of life he does not pursue himself is not to be considered credible, since it is evident that he does not look after his own best interest. Those scholars who praise the contemplative life fail to present an objective view of the whole matter. Rather, wishing to advertise their own lives, they praise all aspects of the contemplative life beyond any reasonable measure, thus undermining their credibility. This attitude is understandable – as all men have a natural tendency to praise their own lives – but their exaggeration seems to be the main reason that most reasonable men, who cannot believe such excessive praise, hold the contemplative life in contempt. That said, most men are deprived of reason; they live in darkness, unaware of the treasures hidden inside their soul. They live only according to their senses, which, although useful, are not the primary part of a man. Thus, they care little about the privileges that a proper education offers man. Metochites then proceeds to investigate the value of education (chs. 1–9).

The most important thing in a man's life is to have a correct view on God and his Son, who became man for our sake. He must also accept all the doctrinal positions of the Orthodox Church, avoiding dogmatic quarrels as far as possible. Any experiments in the realm of Orthodox doctrine are strictly prohibited for anyone who wishes to avoid the calumniations and accusations levelled by envious people trying to detect hidden heretics everywhere (chs. 10–16).

This situation had been exacerbated in Metochites' time, when men of dubious morality try to destroy a decent man different from them by exposing him as a heretic.

To live one's life according to the teachings of the church is of immutable value, while all other things are fluid and fleeting. But there is something else that is immutable and does not disappoint those who possess it: virtue. Virtue follows man even after his death, providing him with all manner of immutable, perpetual privileges. The spiritual delight of a virtuous man cannot be properly described. It is difficult, however, for a man to preserve his initial enthusiasm for a virtuous life undiminished; the temptations of social life are so strong that they may overwhelm even the most steadfast of men. This is why most virtuous men prefer a life of perpetual withdrawal from this world; these men hold those unlike them in contempt, not because they are misanthropic, but because they are well aware that this is the only way to preserve their spiritual serenity and enjoy the privileges of their life of choice (chs. 17–23).

All men long for wealth and glory, except for virtuous men, who, being aware of their transience, do not desire them. Virtuous men do, however, make an exception as far as education is concerned: education, like virtue, is something stable and trustworthy. No enemy can take them away from a learned man. All human privileges can be turned upside down except for a proper education. A learned and wise man does not care about the machinations of his enemies; even when enduring trials, he may turn to the treasures of wisdom and find consolation for his travails, while the uneducated man resembles a solitary traveller who falls prey to the hardships he encounters on his journey. The wise men who address us through their books are our best friends, advising, consoling and supporting us whenever we need them. That was the meaning of Plato's exhortation to young men to approach men of old age to obtain considerable profit. Plato could not have had in mind actual old men – who were most likely mentally incapable of helping young men in their endeavours – but writers and the sages of old, who speak to us through their writings (chs. 24–31).

Men tend to travel to faraway lands to learn about the habits of foreign people and investigate their history, enriching their knowledge and gaining invaluable new experiences. A learned man does not, however, need to undertake extended travels; he can learn whatever he wants while remaining at home and going through the writings of the past, where all human knowledge has been treasured. Socrates considered these writings real treasures. One may wonder what Socrates would have said in our day, when human knowledge has been considerably expanded and we are able to enjoy the fruits of the intellectual efforts of men of past times with hardly any effort. Men frequent public feasts where many good things are exhibited. Wisdom resembles such a festal assembly; all the results of the intellectual efforts of the past are exhibited through the writings of the sages (chs. 32–9).

The Greeks took advantage of the privilege of wisdom to advertise their own history. Thus, we know even the most minor details of Greek history, while knowing next to nothing about the history of other important peoples who did not take care to record their achievements by writing them down despite having all the institutions we so much admire in the case of the Greeks. The same applies to the Romans, whose glory became known to all peoples on earth. Learning their achievements by reading works of history is the greatest delight of all (chs. 40-5).

Plato has pointed out that delight is a force that creates an inner disposition linking us with the object of our desire. The delight we take in reading historical works is truly immense. Anyone who occupies himself with any writing of the past feels the same delight. Therefore, it is inherent in the pursuit of wisdom. The power of delight is considerable: it is to be observed in all human endeavours. Indeed, Epicurus and his followers believed that the pursuit of delight gives real meaning to human life. In any case the delight we feel through our effort to become wise and learned is the most sublime sensation, since it is linked directly with our soul. Even if the feeling of delight is to be rejected, we must keep in mind that it is unavoidable; therefore, we must accept it as a happy result of our endeavour to obtain knowledge, in the same way sailors accept good weather despite it not being their true goal. In any case, delight is not something altogether sinful. The delight we take in things material may be, but spiritual delight is certainly not. Even if perfection has nothing to do with delight, we may say that delight is the best thing we can obtain from our natural deficiency. It would be an exaggeration, however, to call delight a deficiency or an illness. Rather, it is something inherent in our nature: God gave it to us to keep our spirit strong. We should avoid all delight drawn from things material, but we should not be afraid of intellectual delight. We can make free use of it, provided we subject it to reason (chs. 46-53).

The delight that springs from our intellectual endeavours is immense. Nothing can be compared with our withdrawal from all public affairs and our concentration on our studies. As if viewing from a watchtower, a man frees his mind to travel the whole world, gathering all manner of experiences. After his travels are complete, his mind returns to itself and contemplates all those experiences it has gathered. Thus, it is able to discover the hidden reason of all things and to marvel at the workings of the divine providence (chs. 54-5).

At this point, Metochites introduces the second part of his speech, in which he refutes negative commentary against philosophy. Metochites states that his addressee may wonder why he has heaped so much praise on the contemplative life despite taking pains initially to affirm his objectivity. His response is that his objectivity does not mean that he will or should overlook the various advantages of the contemplative life. Metochites is aware that glory is not the privilege of wisdom, since even artisans may gain immortal glory through their achievements (chs. 56-7).

It is a pity that Plato did not understand this point and insisted that the philosopher is able to perform everything; however, this assertion was proved incorrect. On the basis of Plato's false assertions, men criticized philosophy as being a useless occupation, not realizing that they were thereby condemning the most important part of philosophy – that is, politics – which is the art of administering the affairs of this life in the best possible way, even if perfection is not always attainable (chs. 58-60).

Despite this, malicious men, taking advantage of certain inadequacies of men who clearly surpass their fellow men through their achievements, try to blemish the reputation of all virtuous men. Sadly, even learned men try to attack their fellow scholars, not realizing that in this way they are besmirching the reputation of their profession. The result of all these mutual accusations and calumniations is that nothing in this life may be considered fixed and settled; fellow turns against fellow, trying to blacken his reputation. One may wonder what great damage is done to wisdom by scholars' accusations against each other (chs. 61–7).

One may object that Metochites has no right to complain about the reputation of the scholars of his time, since he had abandoned the pursuit of knowledge of his own volition long before, to become involved in the affairs of the world. Metochites notes that he had once adopted the contemplative life but then decided to combine the contemplative life with the active life, not realizing the futility of such an endeavour (chs. 68–9).

Once a learned man becomes involved in the sordid affairs of this life, he becomes prisoner of his own occupations, unable to liberate himself and return to his previous way of life. He resembles those farmers who have abandoned their fields and decide to try to cultivate them once more after a long time, although the fields have been overgrown with weeds, which destroy the harvest (chs. 70–1).

The burdens of his family and the affairs of the state have persuaded Metochites that it is impossible for anyone who turns to the active life to cultivate his literary skills. He notes that some people argue, however, that the contemplative life is of no use, and the abandonment of it causes no damage to man (chs. 72–5).

At this point, missing folia considerably obscure the author's train of thought.

Some men are forced to lead a way of life they detest; some others adopt a way of life they consider unworthy of themselves, yielding to the opinions of other, more powerful men than themselves. Therefore, most men long after another way of life. All seek what is good for themselves, but they cannot agree about the real meaning of the word 'good'. Some identify this good with a life of pleasure, others consider the solitary life to be the best. Some others, because of their inability to act according to their ambitions, pretend to adopt a tranquil and unpretentious way of life, but as soon as the situation improves, they abandon it, revealing their heretofore hidden ambitions (chs. 76–81).

At this point, more folia are missing.

The situation is abhorrent: some men are utterly unhappy, while others are always successful. However, one who is in distress should realize that all men, bar none, are bound to suffer in this life and console himself that this is the common lot of all people, and he himself no exception; if he is unfortunate, he must expect that things may change for him, and fortune may bring him happiness (chs. 82–3).

At this point, more folia are missing.

We should try to liberate our fellow men from the tyranny of fortune. These men are in perpetual fear of death, whom they regard as a thief ready to attack. In any case we should remind them that bad fortune may change. A prudent man must change his inner disposition and confront the attacks of fortune with proper thoughts: even a tyrannical ruler may be discouraged by a man who is able to answer his questions with courage and self-confidence; a man who is persecuted by the tyrant must be aware that most men look at him with compassion and favour, while the tyrant is unable to control himself, since his soul is in constant turbulence (chs. 84–9).

Some people maintain that it is better for a man to live without making use of his mind, since it is the source of constant anxiety and embarrassment. The answer to this objection is that life resembles a military expedition; no soldier can take part in an expedition if he is unprepared and lacks the proper military training. The same applies to a musician who wishes to take part in a musical competition. Similarly, no man can live without the help of his mind and reason, which guides him on the difficult path of this life (chs. 90–1).

Metochites states his preference for suffering instead of being deprived of the privileges of the life according to the mind (chs. 92–5).

The mind is one of the gifts given to man that distinguishes him from all other animals. If we accept the arguments of our opponents, we may say that pigs are happier than men. But this is insanity. If the life of the mind is pleasant, too, we may thank God for his dispensation. But if the life of the mind happens to be accompanied by certain minor distresses and temptations, they are far too trivial to lead us to reject the most noble gifts of our nature. Reason governs the ship of both our life and our world, administering it in a just and proper manner. Nothing belonging to the realm of the mind is unstable and dubious. As Plato writes, science holds all our thoughts fast, protecting them. It is a great pity to reject our intellectual property for the sake of carnal delights. Men who are deprived of their mind and reason are deprived even of material benefits (chs. 95–100).

In short, any man who has the gift of word and reason is able to contact God and pray to him in a most persuasive manner, as Metochites did when he was in need (ch. 101).

Theoria: *A mask most beloved, but a mask nevertheless*

In *Ethikos*, Metochites discusses at length his decision to abandon the contemplative life and to embrace the active life. He states that he deplores that decision and considers that turn in his life a hard strike of bad luck. It is not surprising that most earlier Byzantinists took at face value the section comprising chapters 68–72 of *Ethikos*,[32] believing that Metochites strongly regretted his decision to abandon the contemplative life. Those views are of no real value, however, if one takes into consideration the way Metochites employs certain masks in his works, which, far from conveying his own views, function as mechanisms for concealing them. Metochites when deploring his abandonment of the contemplative life is simply putting on the mask of an ancient sage troubled by his life in the world, ardently desiring to free himself from its constraints. In *Ethikos* and in *Byzantios*, he subtly undermines the mask of the intellectual yearning for the life of the mind, simple and pure.

Even after a cursory reading of *Ethikos*, one gets the impression that Metochites' purpose was to extol the life of the mind, as described by Plato, Aristotle and other philosophers of antiquity, under the mask of a teacher advising a young man who has neglected his studies. The young man's identity is never revealed, and he likely never existed. The invention of an imaginary addressee was a device of the protreptical orations of late antiquity that Metochites adopted for *Ethikos*. He introduces the device in chapter 1 to warn his audience against taking everything said by him at face value. Adopting the role of a teacher, Metochites distances himself from his true self. It is a way of alerting his audience that he has put on a mask.

In any case, *Ethikos* deals with the problems of the contemplative life, to which the concept of *theoria* (θεωρία) – broadly speaking, 'contemplation' – is crucial. In antiquity, apart from referring to sending state ambassadors, known as θεωροί, to the Oracles, the word *theoria* also meant 'viewing or beholding something', and from there it developed the additional meaning of 'considering or contemplating a certain object'. This, in turn, gave rise to yet another meaning, 'philosophical speculation' or 'theory' (as opposed to practice).[33] The word soon came to refer to 'spiritual contemplation', which was not always clearly distinguished from philosophical contemplation. The word can also refer to 'knowledge of God', which is identical in meaning to theology (θεολογία). In the Christian era, *theoria* may also refer to the mystical contemplation of the divine realities, which lie beyond the grasp of human mind, a state attained by certain ascetics after long and painful preparation.

Monastic *theoria* had no value for Metochites, or at least that is what he conveys in *Ethikos*. Metochites is not interested in a supernatural paradise. Rather, paradise is the life of the mind, which can be realized on this earth. The beatitude of life no longer consists of devotion to God and his church, but in an intellectual effort by man to obtain knowledge through his own efforts. The contented man is no longer the monk, but the intellectual. It is, so to speak, a Byzantine version of 'die Wiederkehr gelehrter Anachorese' (the return of learned reclusiveness), as Ernst Kantorowicz described the movement that originated in the West in the twelfth century. As observed in Metochites' Poem 6 for the three great prelates, the abandonment of this world and its problems was no longer a monastic ideal, but an intellectual principle.[34]

In chapter 54 of *Ethikos*, Metochites speaks in rather metaphorical language about the incessant theory of beings, the privilege of a man who has abandoned all worldly cares to concentrate on intellectual investigations. This concentration presupposes the proper preparation of one's mind through education and virtue. The individual is then able to let his mind wander all about the world and its essence, which is immense, and to examine everything as if his mind had been placed atop a watchtower. Such an investigation, similar to initiation to a mystery, resembles a spiritual journey. The essence of the world is like a vast, calm sea, on which man travels with the ship of his intellect, inspecting the various, ineffable beauty of beings. The human mind returns afterwards to itself and enjoys the fruits of the journey; it examines the inner meaning, the essence, of everything, arriving at its inner core and thus realizing that everything is the product of a wise Creator:

> The same is the case, I think, with the function and preparation of our rational faculty, the good management and progress of our intellect that comes from the influence of education, especially when our mind, as regularly happens, after it

engages with virtue, renders all other human concerns of secondary importance, and lives for itself alone, and its activity becomes the contemplation of existing matters. There could thus be nothing more pleasant among human beings than the moment when a person turns entirely to himself and to the acceptance of, pleasure in, and discourse with books and wisdom, and focuses his mind, as far as possible, away from all other preoccupations onto a stable, utterly independent, unswerving and undivided permanence that is also free and undisturbed. Afterwards, as in a solo pipe performance, he allows his mind to be completely unfettered, and as if from a high vantage point becomes a careful overseer who observes the entire world and its boundless essence. When he opens his eyes, he can see everything in a sequence, easily and with no effort. He can see the countless harmonies of everything that exists, with which he engages; he comes into contact with something that is truly blessed and profoundly divine, with no fear or slackening, I think, without feeling fatigue or hesitation once he embarks upon this endless course. Every time he sets forth, it is as if this were an untroubled celebratory procession of the Muses, and a journey; never ending but not tiring; without a destination but quite pleasant, free of external distractions. This person has relieved the vessel of his mind from everything else and unfurled the sails of contemplation, and he throws it into the matter of the entire universe, as if onto a calm, serene sea. He sails all over, he visits and enjoys many places that he fancies and considers the best, and he embraces the countless beauties of what exists. Then, because he grows extremely beautiful himself, due to his association with what is most beautiful, as they say, he returns home as he chooses, and begins pondering and examining what he has seen, and seeks refuge in the meeting place and council chamber of his thought in order to seek out and discover the truth in what he has seen. When he retrieves the meaning and reason mingled together in every single thing and finishes his examination, he is astonished and admires the inventor and craftsman, who is God, with a truly ineffable sentiment that suddenly makes him feel ineffable pleasure.[35]

The object of Metochites' *theoria* is the world and its beauties. He regards such a preoccupation as a feast in some of his works.[36] Metochites is not interested in certain intellectual essences that lie beyond the grasp of his mind, despite employing the terminology of the ancient mysteries in the passage above.[37] He is satisfied with contemplation of the world, which is realized after the soul, detaching itself from the body, occupies a vantage point from which everything can be seen.[38] The contemplative life is identified with examination of the inner meaning of visible things, which reveal their structure to man. All structured things do not, or could not, result from accident, but instead have been created by a wise Maker. It is in this way that Metochites attains an understanding of God.

Such a conception of the contemplative life is characteristic of an intellectual trend in antiquity, especially in Hellenistic times. This trend has its origins in the late Platonic dialogues (*Timaeus, Laws, Epinomis*) and in some lost dialogues of Aristotle. Plato associated stars with certain divinities and considered the whole world an entity possessing a soul. Therefore, by examining the world and the sky, the philosopher came upon a divine reality. The Stoics adopted certain elements of the Platonic theory, adapting them to the needs of their own philosophy. They claimed that the divine Logos permeated the entire world, giving life to it and contributing to its order and maintenance. Even the early Christians adopted elements of this theory, considering it a useful argument for proving the existence of God and the divine Providence. Later, with the emergence of Neoplatonism, the search for a cosmic god gave way to the more sublime pursuit of a god beyond the capacities of the human mind.[39]

Metochites does not seem to be interested in a mystical knowledge of God, such a thought itself being the result of the enlightening of the human mind by God, who is willing to reveal some of his hidden characteristics to the philosopher or the ascetic. There is no place for a god who cares for men in this trend of Hellenistic mysticism under discussion,[40] nor is Metochites satisfied with the Christian revelation, which supposedly answers all questions concerning God and the creation of the world. Instead, he wants to find for himself answers to the questions concerning the world and its creator, and this is to be achieved through intensive study of the creatures inhabiting it.

One must keep in mind that Metochites presented himself as the resurrector of the scientific study of astronomy in late Byzantium. He wrote an eloquent expression of the inner necessity that pushed him to occupy himself with astronomy – that is, study of the world surrounding man. It reveals the intellectual foundation of Metochites and his students, like Nikephoros Gregoras, who imitated his teacher and built upon his astronomical studies – and their belief that the scientific study of nature could lead man to God. This was not an entirely heterodox position even among the conservative Byzantine circles of Metochites' time. The ascetic writers had absorbed ancient teachings on the study of nature as a journey to God. Many Byzantine theologians were eager to argue that the study of nature, so-called natural contemplation, was the second stage of man's journey towards God, the first stage being man's effort to cleanse himself of his passions, and the third being mystical contemplation of God. There are many variations on the theme of the three-part journey of the soul of the ascetic who wishes to approach God, but the stage of contemplation of nature appears to be a fixture in all of them.[41] When a Byzantine reader came across the word *theoria*, however, he expected to find something more than a mere description of man's effort to understand the mysteries of nature through the scientific study of natural phenomena, in which Metochites seems to be interested to the point of excluding any expectation of something more. The reader expected revelation of the divine realities. There can be no doubt that a passage by Metochites in *Ethikos* was inspired by Philo Judaeus' introduction to the third book of his treatise *De specialibus legibus*. Philo wrote as follows:

> Once upon a time I was occupied with the study of philosophy and with the contemplation of the world and of everything in it, and was obtaining a blessed fruit out of it, coming always into contact with divine words and doctrines, out of which I was obtaining a great delight, although I could not satiate my desire

for them; I did not entertain any mundane and petty thoughts. I was not crawling like a worm among the carnal pleasures, and the desire for glory or wealth, but I looked like a man who was travelling through the air, high up, because of the enthusiasm of my soul, and I had the impression that I was going round together with the sun, the moon and the whole sky and the world. At that time, I was stooping and creeping as if from the top of a hill and I was looking down from the air, stretching the eye of my intellect and examining the ineffable spectacles of the earth. I considered myself very happy because I had completely avoided the damages suffered from mortal men.[42]

The view from above, as Pierre Hadot puts it, is one of the 'spiritual exercises' in the philosophy schools of Greco-Roman antiquity at which students learned how to hold in contempt the pleasures of this life, longing for the delights of the intellect.[43] The philosopher should learn how to observe the earth from above, as such a view gives him the opportunity to realize that the earth is just a tiny part of the universe, devoid of any real value. The true philosopher must, therefore, learn to regard everything from a cosmic perspective, gradually transforming himself into an integral and valuable part of the greater universe and living in harmony with the eternal and unchangeable laws governing it. The view from above leads man to live in accordance with his true nature, which is in fact a part of the universe. Philo deplored his decision to become involved with the administration of public affairs, which contaminated the purity of his intellectual life.

The second part of Metochites' passage is drawn from another treatise of Philo, the well-known *De vita contemplativa*, a description of the life of a group of Jewish ascetics, the so-called Therapeutai, who lived in the desert near Alexandria. Philo wrote as follows:

They used to pray twice every day, at dawn and at sunset. When the sun rose, they asked for happiness, for true happiness, that consisted in the divine light enlightening their own intellect. At sunset they asked that their soul, relieved from the burden of the senses and all sensible things, might enter its own study and chamber and dig up the truth.[44]

The real meaning of the contemplative life according to Philo consists in the contemplation of the world and its beauties, which leads to knowledge of God.[45]

The scientific examination of the world as the real meaning of the contemplative life is encountered once more near the end of *Ethikos*. After rejecting the 'unfair' accusations of those who deny the value of the contemplative life, Metochites draws yet another picture of the sage who contemplates the world. This time, however, he employs another Platonic image, that of the governor of the ship who maintains a steady helm:

The genuine grace of rationality, however, is human beings' only exceptional advantage and the best there is. It is the supervisor and teacher of true bliss and proper behaviour throughout the world and indeed in every human being individually, foreseeing and regulating every situation; as Aeschylus aptly says, it is seated alone on the stern of the city and directs all things, governing them all efficiently, so that they are made serviceable. By 'city' one could refer to anything one likes, be it the eternity of life and the world as a whole taken as a true unity, or each person individually, in whom rationality and the mind preside authoritatively as noble guardians and kings of nature, anticipating and foretelling what is best for him, considering matters thoroughly and establishing appropriate laws for every deed and action, until they establish a perfect legal order, equality, justice, and in the separate sections of each person a balanced constitution, where no one can step over the threshold, as the proverb says, nor shoot wide of the mark.[46]

Metochites takes the city Aeschylus refers to at the beginning of *Septem contra Thebas* (v. 2) and compares it with the whole world and with the soul of the individual sage, who takes care to live under the precepts of reason. The theory that the whole world constitutes a city governed by the laws of God is primarily Stoic,[47] and was widespread in Hellenistic and Roman times; some Greek and Latin fathers of the church later adopted it.[48] The same comparison appears in the first part of Philo's *De somniis*, where the Judaean philosopher, discussing the meaning of Psalm 45.5, interprets the term 'city' allegorically:

> The psalmist calls the world 'a city of God'; the world drunk the whole cup of the divine drink, and becoming happy, takes a delight which cannot be taken from him and is inextinguishable and perpetual. On the other hand, he may refer to the soul of the sage, inside which God is said to walk as if in a city.[49]

The passage of Philo employed by Metochites highlights his main perspective: the world is closely related to the soul of the sage; the contemplation of the world may transform the soul into a small world, in imitation of the wider universe; and the order and eternal laws of the universe govern the soul as well. This is the real meaning of the contemplative life.[50] Man can imitate the universe, imposing its laws on himself and becoming a useful part of it. This idea originated in the Platonic Republic and was widespread among philosophers in late antiquity, especially the Stoics.[51] By adopting this theory, Metochites tries to lay the foundations of a new morality. Virtue is no longer the result of the conscious application of the precepts of the Christian religion in one's own life but is instead the corollary of man's contemplation of the universe and its eternal laws. Although not clearly expressed, this was the underlying idea of the author, who may not have had any problem with a simple fellow following the laws of his church blindly but was probably unwilling to let his fellow scholars adopt such a simplistic attitude towards morality. By reviving the ancient understanding of *theoria* as contemplation of the world, Metochites was clearly trying to undermine then-popular monastic *theoria*, the constant struggle of the monk to liberate himself from the tyranny of his passion and realize a vision of God even in this life.

Metochites was fond of the works by Philo Judaeus, whom he considered a kindred spirit, a scholar who had suffered considerably after abandoning the delights of the pure contemplative life. Among the numerous passages in Metochites' works influenced by Philo, two further instances in *Ethikos* where the contemplative life is described in accordance with Philo's precepts require acknowledging. They concern the origins of the concept of abandonment of the world, a theme often encountered in Metochites' works. The sage's desire to abandon this world and its pleasures so he could concentrate on his own studies as Metochites described it actually had few similarities with monastic withdrawal from the world and the seclusion of the ascetic as practised by the Byzantines.[52] Even in speaking about the sage's desire to abandon the world for a virtuous life, Metochites draws his images from Philo in *Ethikos*:

> As a consequence, most of them actually flee from us and reject our choices with full consciousness and strength, not because they hate mankind – how could this be possible? They are lovers and followers of our one, common benevolent God, the master of us all – but on the contrary, they wisely seek absolute tranquillity for themselves and also manage to repel anything that might forcibly lead them away from there to disruption and distraction. They wish to fulfil their aim with as much calm and peace from perpetual change as possible. They flee association and co-existence with the many in the cities, as if these were destructive plagues on good reasoning, and they run from every plot that matter contrives, preferring instead isolation from all things as a companion for their desires and expectations, thus strengthening their initial way of life. Just as the winds blow on the mountains bestowing bliss, so, too, the breezes sent by the merciful divinity relieve their labours and the flames of their temptations, and the rising of certain stars produces an ineffable pleasure, a rising that only these people really know, which by means of a betrothal guarantees their coming prosperity and keeps their thoughts in a unified and permanent movement unaltered by any influence.[53]

Metochites employs terms that would have been familiar to his Christian audience: the abandonment of worldly things reminds of monastic withdrawal from the affairs of this world as practised by Byzantine monks. Equally widespread was the image of the human mind travelling in a sea at the time of spiritual contemplation.[54] It is indicative of Metochites' mindset, however, that he does not turn to a traditional ascetic authority to describe the sage's abandonment of this world, instead preferring Philo once again. The passage from Philo's treatise *De vita contemplativa* is as follows: '[T]hey live outside the city walls in gardens or solitary fields because they look after a total isolation, not because they are misanthropic, but because they know that any contacts with men of a different character are of no use and may bring damage to them.'[55] There are many similar passages in the works of Philo,[56] who stresses the sage's philanthropy in spite of his desire to live by himself.

Philo's works were well known in Byzantium. Authors constantly quoted him, and he is well represented in Byzantine theological florilegia. Metochites' use of his works is not strange or unexpected. What makes it noteworthy is Metochites' tendency to avoid using any other author who discusses the spiritual itinerary of the man who wants to devote himself to his studies and to approach God. The ascetic works of Byzantium are full of such descriptions. Metochites prefers to present this itinerary from a clearly Platonic perspective. The use of Philo, or rather the mask of Philo, who was heavily influenced by the Platonic journey of the soul as described in the *Timaeus* and the *Phaedrus*, may be easily explained as the result of Metochites' tendency to suppress the Christian elements in the description of the soul's quest for knowledge, substituting them with Platonic versions, which were far more original. This can clearly be seen in Metochites' Poem 4, a piece addressed to Nikephoros Gregoras, where he describes the original human quest for knowledge:

> Philosophy is the most important part of <human> education: it undertook a noble, glorious, and most exalted task, i.e. to explore each one of the plans of God, who created the universe, <understanding how each creature was created>; man tried to comprehend the mind of his creator, the almighty Lord of everything; his ambition was to prove that everything had been created according to a plan, and not by chance, as a result of the creative movement of a wise leader, who had brought into being everything in a rational manner from the beginning, and had continued to guide everything after its own interest always, according to specific preordained laws. Such a desire caused philosophy to be born among men: some mortal men who looked at what took place in our world did not proceed any further, but lived like prisoners of their senses, resembling the souls of the other animals that have neither reason nor mind. But some others, observing things diligently, investigated them, spending great effort; it was necessary not only to look at them but to examine what they saw, i.e. their condition, their nature, the way they were created, why they remained stable, how things that were identical remained always the same, while things that differed from each remained always different; they needed to look closely at the way differences remained there always: some are blended, some unmixed, some are disunited and some united. They took great pains to explain all these things, and they wanted to prove them stable, self-sufficient and wisely made, since it was impossible that such beautiful things would be created most stable and remain stable forever by mere chance. Accordingly, philosophy became a champion of the excellent works of God. Man is proud because he has managed to investigate the wise plans of God and to understand the functioning of each creature and the wise purpose of God.[57]

This passage may be considered a commentary on that of chapter 54 in *Ethikos*. The examination of the natural phenomena by mortal men was the main reason for the development of philosophy.[58] Men attempted to explain the world around them, they admired it, and the explanation they found was that everything depended on God, who created everything. Therefore, philosophy is the result of the scientific investigations of men. The target of science is knowledge of God.

There are many philosophical passages describing man's journey towards philosophy.[59] All depend on Plato's *Timaeus* 47a, here as a free translation:

> According to my view, sight was a great benefit for us: no doctrine of those we now teach about the universe would have been expounded, if we had not seen the stars, the sun or the sky. But now we have seen day and night; months and years, equinoxes and tropics helped us to form a sense of number and year and to make investigations about the nature of the universe. From those investigations we invented the genre of philosophy.

Philo Judaeus used this passage extensively in his writings.[60] In all probability, Metochites may have taken the idea from Philo and utilized it in *Ethikos*, Poem 4, and in several chapters of the *Miscellanea*.

The question remains: did Metochites' real thoughts correspond to the image of a late antique sage like Philo that he was fond of projecting? There is no definitive answer. The details of that image require additional study to discover certain other aspects that have not yet been revealed.

Journey of the mind

Metochites was fond of the Platonic image of the journey of the mind. In the *Miscellanea*, he presents vivid elaborations on this theme, which he also discussed in chapter 54 of *Ethikos*. In his essay on the meaning of the myth of Epimenides and of Aristeas of Proconessus, who had slept for many years before being resuscitated by miraculous intervention, he offers an allegorical explanation of these stories. He states the following in the *Miscellanea*:

> The myth implies, as I said, that men are dreaming and are not really alive in this illusory life. But if they abandon the material world, waking themselves up, they enjoy another contact and communion with the real being. Because of this withdrawal from that life and avoidance of any contact with matter, they are able to bring to their fellow men messages concerning the real, intelligible life and the substantification, which are most beneficial for our life.[61]

Speaking about Aristeas of Proconessus, Metochites notes, 'His soul left his body dead very often and after retiring from it for a certain number of days, it came back, entered that lifeless corpse and Aristeas was shown alive once more.'[62]

Metochites' source is an essay by the second-century CE orator Maximus of Tyre: 'I think that Epimenides implied that the life of men on this earth resembled a long dream, lasting for many years ... Life here is really a dream; the soul, which is buried inside the body, is barely able to have just a dream of real things because of its satiety and insolence.'[63]

Metochites seems to have been fond of Maximus of Tyre. In all likelihood, he imitated the style of Maximus' short essays when composing his *Miscellanea*. Metochites' use of Aristeas and Epimenides to describe the contemplative life would have come as a surprise to his contemporaries. Mythical figures who were known as pagan magicians would have hardly been considered an appropriate example of the life of the mind, even for the more open-minded among Metochites' contemporaries. Metochites hastens to deny that their stories are real and interprets them allegorically, like Maximus of Tyre; the Stoic theory that in sleep the human soul is free from the constraints of the body underlies the passage from Maximus.[64] Metochites' interest in these figures of the distant Greek past is, however, idiosyncratic, if not heterodox.

Metochites struggled all his life with the issue of reality. Which beings are real? As shown above, in Oration 18, on Demosthenes and Aelius Aristeides, he describes rhetoric as the art of dealing with real things. Endeavouring to understand the meaning of the contemplative life, he defines it as the effort of man to liberate himself from the tyranny of his flesh and to fly towards the intelligible reality. Even in the idiosyncratic description of the active life as defined in Oration 11, *Byzantios*, Metochites tries to work out the reality of beings hidden behind the facade of everyday life and the occupations of residents of the imperial city. The true sense of his preoccupation with the problem of the contemplative life comes to the fore in *Byzantios*: it is his struggle to understand reality, to uncover the hidden meaning of the visible things, to enter their core and detect their real sense. It is no accident that in *Ethikos*, Metochites refers to the 'meaning and reason mingled together in every single thing', which fills his heart with an ineffable joy.[65] This way of viewing reality is inspired by Plato's quest for the understanding of the real essence of things, which he identified with their 'idea'. In this respect, Metochites' Poem 10 is of interest.

Poem 10, the harmony of beings

Poem 10, Metochites' most extensive poem, deals with the science of harmonics. In fact, it is a praise of music. Metochites is not interested in the science of music per se, but regards it as a means of proceeding towards an understanding of the world, which he considers a harmonious whole, governed by God through the eternal laws of music. Poem 10 is therefore the counterpart of *Ethikos*. In *Ethikos*, Metochites attempted to discern the inner reason of beings; in Poem 10 he tries to do the same in regard to their inner harmony, which is the same thing. Both texts have a cosmological perspective, and in this respect Poem 10 also deals with the problem of the contemplative life: the only minor difference is that the sage is presented not as a philosopher who has withdrawn to his study, but as a skilful musician, who through the study of the laws of harmony, discovers the creative power of God inside all things of this world. In the concluding verses of Poem 10, Metochites displays a true enthusiasm for the way God works through his creatures based on universal laws of music:

> I love the science of harmonics very much. A great love, distinguished above others, takes possession of my heart, as I take delight in it, admiring the fact that

it is a habit inherent in all the good things of this life, giving them their essence and beauty, safeguarding their proper conduct and pouring out a glorious grace that reaches the eyes of both body and mind in a most evident manner. I try to put myself in its footprints as best as I can: I see some of its marvels and my heart takes pleasure in them; some others are invisible, so I try to see them with my imagination, imprinting their design on its tablets; so I have a sweet hope, so I acquire a shadow outline of the perfect order. With great joy I admire all these myself and I meditate upon the great, ineffable and incomprehensible power and creative wisdom of my Lord. O blessed, invisible, most wise and powerful king of everything, the sky, the earth and what lies between, Lord of all beings visible and invisible, that is, the angels, the intelligible servants of your glory, I feel a great pleasure mixed with fear: how did you manage to bring into light all these through the most effective power of your mind and your ineffable wisdom? How impudent it is for someone to wish to reach the depths of all things! He tries in vain! Who is able to count the grains of the sand of the sea, who is able to find out the traces of the course of a ship in the barren sea, or the traces of the flying of a glorious eagle, which is the fastest of all birds, in the sky? It is equally impossible for us to determine the course of your thought, and to understand how you manage to create everything most easily, and how you manage to preserve them stable, binding them with the laws of the science of harmonics; you do not leave anything to chance, you do not allow anything that is ugly to be created; nothing unreasonable can be seen, resembling an ill-fitting cloth, the inferior product of the inexperienced mind of a bad tailor. O most powerful Lord, whatever you create with your wisdom is adorned in a most reasonable way, being most prominent for all those who observe; its construction is regular, based on the laws of harmonics, being the product of the combination of λόγοι, each one of which is perfect; their combination with one another is perfect, too.[66]

This text is a hymn of the world similar to the optimistic hymns of the world composed by Stoics and some early church fathers.[67]

In *Ethikos*, Metochites had remarked that the purpose of man's observing the marvellous works of God is to discern their rationale (λόγοι),[68] their inherent inner reason. The sage who tries to identify these λόγοι is filled with an ineffable joy that takes possession of his whole being. The motif of the sweetness of the heart, the spiritual pleasure in *Ethikos*, is also encountered in Poem 10. The science of harmonics is called an ἕξις σύμφυτος here, which recalls the σύγκρατος λόγος of *Ethikos*. Metochites stresses that he uses both his corporeal and his mental eyes to understand the workings of the laws of music. This assertion stems from a previous discussion in Poem 10, where Metochites investigates the true nature of the mathematical entities. According to him, the entities have a separate existence (contra Aristotle), but men are obliged to start with investigations of their visible, material representations before being able to proceed to a more holistic approach at a later stage, after gradually being liberated from the influence of the material world. There is no such clear distinction in chapter 54 of *Ethikos*, where Metochites speaks about the contemplation of nature in general terms, insisting on the intellectual aspect of it, though its more material aspects are not neglected. His perspective, however, is clear: study of the mathematical sciences – arithmetic, geometry, astronomy and music – starts with the observations a sage makes based on his study of the material world, but it must proceed further into the true essence of things, discovering their hidden purpose. This is 'contact' (*epaphe*) with God himself.[69]

The word ἐπαφή (touch), which Metochites uses in *Ethikos*, denotes an apprehension of something tangible and familiar to the one who touches it. Both pagan and Christian authors used it in reference to direct contact with God. Metochites, uninterested in the mystical speculation of the monastic circles of Byzantium, considers the scientific study of beings an adequate means of approaching God, as true contact with him. Metochites appears to appropriate the term ἐπαφή from the mystical Byzantine theologians, remove it from its original context, and apply it to the scientific study of the world that may lead to direct contact with God. This was not a totally arbitrary procedure. In fact, Metochites reintroduces into Byzantine thought the older perspective of the cosmic religion as he had found it in the works of Philo. As he puts it in Poem 10 (vv. 510–12), by the observation of the laws of music, 'the functioning of the mind, which directs and sets in motion everything from the beginning is revealed'.[70] Here he is referring to the divine mind. The same quest to understand the workings of divine providence through science can be found in another important author of late Byzantium, Emperor Theodore II Laskaris, who in his two extensive works – *Manifestation of the world* (Κοσμικὴ Δήλωσις) and *On natural communion* (Περὶ φυσικῆς κοινωνίας) – expressed views similar to those of Metochites.[71] It is this direct contact with God which creates a sense of ineffable delight in his soul. Metochites makes frequent reference to 'spiritual delight' in his works and in *Ethikos* provides a rather long explanation of the term.

Spiritual delight: Criticizing Byzantine monasticism and discovering a new dimension of the contemplative life

Pleasure or delight (ἡδονή) usually had a negative denotation in Byzantine texts, most often referring to carnal desires, which resulted in the fall of man from Paradise and his subsequent condemnation by God. The doctrinal intricacies of the Christian religion were not, however, solely responsible for Byzantines' negative attitude towards all forms of delight. A long tradition of philosophical discussion had pondered the meaning of pleasure, culminating in the refutation of Epicurus' view that pleasure was the real purpose of human life. Although even Plato, and to a greater extent Aristotle, recognized a certain necessity of pleasure in human life, the late Platonists were almost unanimous in rejecting it, consigning it to a subordinate position, if any. Thus, the Christians inherited a tradition of rejecting pleasure that they then strengthened through their own inherent abhorrence of everything carnal or bodily.

Metochites discusses the problem of pleasure at length in *Ethikos*.[72] Employing an old Platonic metaphor, he readily admits that pleasure resembles a nail, which attaches the soul of a man to the object of his desire (ch. 46). What interests him is not the concept of pure pleasure, but spiritual pleasure – the delights that come to man as a result of his literary activities, or in other words, the pleasure of the contemplative life. He insists that there cannot be anything wrong with this; it should be readily accepted by man as a necessary corollary of his literary endeavours. Fulfilling his duty as an Orthodox Christian, however, Metochites does not forget to condemn the carnal pleasures. He also references Epicurus and his followers as examples of the false notion of pleasure and its meaning, but he also states the following:

> I think that the pleasure that comes to educated men and to those who have devoted themselves exclusively to this attitude and activity in their lives and have preferred this to anything else, the pleasure that arises from engagement with and about education, is truly and in all respects graceful, appropriate and fitting for human beings, as well as highly beneficial. For this pleasure is superior in comparison to all other pleasures, and everyone who had experienced it and profited from it even moderately will agree. But we should certainly not offer it to the unhallowed – let those who are unmoved by these better things, the utterly deaf and insensate, who restrict pleasure to the body alone, as animals do, close their ears! As I just noted, in this case the pleasure is great, extremely beautiful, and pure, partaking exclusively of divinity, pertaining to the very soul more than anything else, and uncontaminated by excessive burdens and stains. It brings the soul into incomparable indulgence and relaxation, and in a quite beautiful way it makes the soul more pliant and overflowing with mildness, while at the same time it equips it greatly, stimulates it, and prepares it to undertake the tasks that pertain to it, namely the intellect and knowledge, as we said previously. In this way, both the mind and the pleasure are in the best possible condition, the mind by being active but also charming, the pleasure by being both vehement and chaste, as is the case with the spectacle of the sky, which we sometimes see assuming an overwhelmingly beautiful combination of colours when at noon on a sizzling summer day it suddenly pours rain, so that the moisture becomes interwoven and intertwined with the rays of sunlight above and diffracts the rays of fire and embellishes them until it creates a beautiful combination that is unexpected and extremely pleasant.[73]

He then repeats the same idea:

> The Academic doctrine says, 'Pray that we not be ill, but if we be ill, pray that sensation be left to us.' 'Very well, we shall feel no pleasure, and this would be better' says this very treatise – 'for this is truly a sickness and not an entirely healthy state' – but for those unable to escape the feeling of pleasure by natural necessity, there ought to be some calculation of the benefit and realization of their situation. In this case, there is much benefit indeed – that is, the intellectual

progression of those who choose the pleasure linked to education and the crafting of rhetorical speeches. Indeed, in his treatment of tyrannical power, the tragic poet Euripides says, 'If injustice is necessary, it is best to act unjustly, putting forth a statement both completely irrational and inappropriate for a free spirit.' For injustice is never acceptable, not even for the reason Euripides puts forward.[74]

Metochites states that his wish would be to be free from all passions, but since it is impossible for any human being to be free from the influence of the lesser parts of his soul, he is inclined to accept spiritual pleasure as the lesser evil, so to speak. Therefore, spiritual pleasure is something inevitable and totally permissible for an intellectual like himself.[75]

Metochites, though distancing himself from those who reject pleasure altogether, still agrees with them that carnal pleasure is to be rejected but also criticizes those who identify carnal pleasure as the whole of pleasure. He does not suggest that these men are slaves to their pleasure, but simply adversaries of any and all pleasure. Metochites strongly disagrees with them, castigating them for their complete lack of good taste: indeed, there is a pleasure that may be accepted by all men, and this is the spiritual one. The delight experienced by all those intellectuals of Metochites' circle involved in various literary and scientific activities seems to have been the target of those who denied the value of pleasure altogether. To identify the opponents of Metochites as a particular group, which may have been the target of *Ethikos*, requires investigating the sources of this passage. Metochites likely drew inspiration from Synesius of Cyrene, the Neoplatonic philosopher of late antiquity who in the treatise *Dion* discusses the problem of pleasure at length. One particularly telling passage is as follows:

> I wished that our nature was always inclined towards contemplation. But this has been evidently proved to be impossible. Therefore, my wish would be to cling closely to what is best in a partial way, but to have also the possibility to make certain concessions to my own nature and to experience a certain pleasure, giving to my life a delightful taste. I am well aware that I am a man; I am neither a god, so as to be able to offer resistance to all the temptations of pleasure, nor a wild animal, so as to experience only the carnal pleasures. What is left is to find a middle road. But what other may this be than the occupation with books and education in general? Is any other pleasure cleaner than this one? Is any other pleasure more devoid from any passion? Which pleasure is less involved with matter? Which is less polluted than this one?[76]

In the same text, Synesius quotes the passage from Plato's *Phaedo* about pleasure as a nail in a way that resembles the quotation of Metochites.

Synesius criticized the illiterate monks of the fourth century who were unable to appreciate the value of Greek learning and literature, arguing that the only safe way towards God was through the teachings of Christ. Synesius castigated the monks' ignorance and inability to combine the old, Greek *paideia* with the new,

Christian religion. His views were incompatible with a trend in Christian ideology that although not always dominant was encountered quite often among monks throughout the history of early and medieval Christianity; the view that secular knowledge was to be rejected altogether became widespread among monks and other zealots, who were eager to argue that the Christian religion was not only superior to all earlier forms of human knowledge, but had successfully superseded all other previous forms of religion. Christianity was a revelation God accorded to all men to lead them to salvation. Synesius felt the need to admit that in certain exceptional cases, secular education might be irrelevant to salvation. This is the case of Anthony of Egypt, the founder of monasticism, who enjoyed a special relationship with God and whose divine gifts were so exceptional that they rendered any other knowledge totally useless. Ordinary men, who cannot attain the spirituality of an Anthony or a Hermes Trismegistus, are not to be discouraged from further pursuing their literary studies and enjoying the fruits of the experience of men from centuries past treasured in their books.

This trend in Christianity lost some of its vitality and influence after the combination of Greek learning and Christian teaching effected by the great church fathers of the fourth century, who, far from adopting the Neoplatonic, heterodox positions of Synesius, were able to preserve the purity of their religion while at the same time taking advantage of Greek learning, which they presented as a useful weapon for Christians in combatting heretics and other opponents of their faith. Greek education was never abandoned in Byzantium, but the opposite trend never completely disappeared; ultra-orthodox monks were always to be found in Byzantine monasteries. In the lives of the saints, a popular genre of Byzantine literature, one frequently encounters the motif of the man who abandons his studies – an unnecessary embarrassment – to concentrate on the performance of his ascetic duties, the only true guarantee for his salvation. These monks were clearly expressing their mistrust of their fellow humans who remained devoted to Greek learning; some monks considered too much confidence in one's knowledge a satanic temptation, which would certainly lead a man astray. John Mauropous, Eustratius of Nicaea and Eustathios of Thessalonike were prominent representatives of the so-called Christian humanism in Byzantium, but they co-existed with many other religious people unwilling to share their enthusiasm for the combination of Christian virtue with Greek learning that these prominent prelates of the Byzantine church were so eager to promote. Gerhard Podskalsky has collected numerous passages from Byzantine texts that attest to the survival of this tendency among certain circles in both middle and late Byzantine society.[77]

Throughout *Ethikos*, Metochites insists on the combination of Christian virtue and Greek *paideia*, as one might expect from a prominent representative of the tendency to be friendly and open to Greek learning and reading literature despite it possibly being a dangerous undertaking in medieval times.[78] Maximus Planoudes represented this tendency in the late thirteenth century.[79] Metochites' decision to adopt Synesius' theory on pleasure can hardly be considered accidental. Like Synesius, Metochites had in mind the conservative circles of the Byzantine church, which were always reluctant to adopt a more positive position towards Greek education. The early part of Emperor Andronikos II Palaiologos' reign coincides with the two patriarchates of Athanasios of Ganos, an austere and uncompromising monk who wanted to renew Byzantine society through the strict and severe application of Christ's laws. There was no room in Athanasios' vision of a renovated Christian society for Greek learning. Certain Constantinopolitan intellectuals hated Athanasios, who despite this enjoyed the lukewarm support of Andronikos II. The historian George Pachymeres, a contemporary of Metochites, offers a starkly negative picture of the patriarch in his *History*. It is not known whether Metochites had in mind Athanasios and his followers as those unable to raise themselves up to the high standards of Greek learning as he himself understood them. He probably did not, but he was hardly unaware of the anti-intellectual tendencies in Byzantine society, which gained renewed impetus in the mid-fourteenth century due to the Palamite controversy.

Metochites was a typical product of late Byzantine humanism. Although well versed in the theology and doctrines of his own church, he remained aware of the value of Greek literature and was more than willing to share the fruits of his intellectual curiosity and the delight he took from it with the members of his circle. One can now better understand his assertion in Poem 12, to Nikephoros Xanthopoulos, that *Ethikos* is the treasury of his inner thoughts, ideas inaccessible to those uninitiated in his way of thinking. Metochites could not openly express his thoughts about the contemplative life and its delights, because they diverged from the dominant position – that of the Orthodox Church – on these matters. According to the church, *theoria* was the contemplation of things divine only, and the only pleasure permitted was that which springs from man's devotion to God and mystical contemplation of him.

It is hardly a coincidence that Synesius' *Dio* is extensively quoted by the anonymous author of the dialogue *Hermippos*, who may be identified with Ioannes Zacharias Aktouarios, a contemporary of Metochites.[80] Ioannes Zacharias was a fervent admirer of Greek learning and a friend of Joseph Rhakendytes, who was close to Metochites. Thus, it appears, Metochites was the mouthpiece of the intellectual circle that formed at Chora around Maximus Planoudes in the late thirteenth century. Members of the circle emerged as the primary exponents of the so-called Palaiologan Renaissance, which was characterized by a renewed interest in the treasures of Greek literature and philosophy and an insistence on formulating new answers to old problems through intensive study of the works of the Greek philosophers regardless of whether the answers might differ from the prevailing views of most members of society.[81]

Scholars like Planoudes and Metochites cannot be considered revolutionary. In fact, they were typical products of a culture built on two pillars – Christianity and Greek *paideia*. Periods of neglecting Greek literature alternated with periods when the study of Greek literature enjoyed renewed interest, but a disconnect between the two constituent parts of Byzantine civilization can be observed throughout the empire's history: a religion based on direct revelation of God cannot be easily reconciled with a philosophy based on human reason. That the two elements were not only divergent but irreconcilable became evident at certain times due to dramatic events, such as the trial of John Italos, the condemnation of Eustratius of Nicaea, and the Palamite controversy.[82] Gregory Palamas explicitly condemned travels of the mind as a satanic aberration among intellectuals of the day and took great pains to restrict *theoria* to its traditional sense of the contemplation of God, excluding any alien, pagan influences that might distort its true meaning by his definition. Metochites' message is an interesting testimony to the vigour of the intellectual circles of late Byzantium, in that they continued to enjoy their reading of Greek literature and were unashamedly inspired by it without any sense of remorse for turning their backs on their traditional religion. Most Byzantine intellectuals from the eleventh century onwards valued science.[83] Those from earlier years could not have imagined that by the middle of the fourteenth century the value of secular education would be called into question and that the Byzantine church had fallen under the control of intransigent monks, represented by Palamas. Of course, the Palamites failed to extinguish the intellectual trend represented by Metochites. In the mid-fourteenth century, Nikolaos Kabasilas, a friend of Nikephoros Gregoras, would repeat Metochites' thinking in a new guise: virtue is to be combined with learning; a saint who is illiterate is inferior to a saint who is learned.

There is another aspect of Metochites' vindication of pleasure that should not be overlooked – an affirmation of the value of human life uninhibited by doctrinal reservations. Like Psellos in the eleventh century, Metochites sought to rehabilitate the human body in the broader sense,[84] rejecting the Christian interpretation of the Platonic doctrine of the soul, which had dominated Byzantine thought since the early period. Metochites denies the absolute value of monastic *apatheia* (lack of any passions), thus denying the total renunciation of the body as advocated by the Byzantine church. This comes close to the vindication of the political man, who moderates the divergent demands of both body and soul.[85]

As Metochites shows through his works, intellectual delight was obviously an integral part of the mask of the intellectual that he projected as himself, but how astonishing for readers familiar with that Metochites to then be confronted by another mask of Metochites – that of the pious Orthodox taking delight in the monastic life. In Oration 16, addressed to the monks of Chora on the death of their abbot Loukas, Metochites describes his delight at taking part in the official singing of hymns in the monastery's church.[86]

In assuming the mask of a man actively participating in the political life of his state, Metochites seems to abandon the mask of the ancient sages – Philo, Gregory of Nazianzus or Synesius – but once again he speaks of pure delight, which seems fitting for the intellectual part of his soul. He describes taking the same delight at the marvels of monastic life in Poem 2.[87] The same interpretation would clearly not apply to Poem 2, written in all probability before Metochites fell from power, if one followed the path of scholars using the biographic-historical approach and interpreted Oration 16 as an expression of the disappointment of an old man who had lost everything and had taken refuge in the monastic ideal. One must admit that Metochites' self-image as a sage like Philo or Synesios in *Ethikos* is just a mask, which will give way to another as soon as Metochites addresses another audience, like the monks of Chora, who would expect a different posture from the founder of their monastic community. Even in the text of *Ethikos*, however, Metochites

Politics and their value

Reading *Ethikos* provides an opportunity to view Metochites as a learned man completely persuaded of the value of the contemplative life and purely intellectual pursuits but who was forced by adverse circumstances to instead concern himself with affairs of state. He was more than willing to don that mask, but it is not a completely accurate picture. Although Metochites' praise of the contemplative life seems to be rather unqualified (esp. chs. 54–5, where his extolling of the advantages of the life of the mind peaks), in other passages he keeps his distance from limitless praise of such a life.[88] Even at the beginning of the treatise (chs. 4–6), he states that he is not prepared to extol his subject beyond certain limits. The same is repeated later: it is erroneous to maintain that only an author's memory remains immortal, since this privilege belongs to other men as well – e.g. artists, painters, sculptors, etc.[89] This view on the immortality of writers was discussed by Plato in *Symposium* (209d), and repeated by others. In Metochites' times, this view was contested with some vigour by Thomas Magistros in the treatise *On kingship*. It is possible that Metochites was involved in a discussion with Thomas – a younger contemporary, friend and correspondent of his – wishing to correct his views, which Metochites likely thought stemmed from a superficial awareness of the importance of education. Metochites emphasizes the inner life of the intellectual, rather than the external advantages, such as the post-mortem fame he will enjoy; the real fruits that wisdom offers its servants are the virtues that help them to live a decent life on earth and to be rewarded by God in the future.

In another moment, Metochites maintains his distance from unqualified praise of wisdom. He points out that Plato was initially confident that any philosopher was adequately qualified to perform any form of service to the state, even correcting the evils of human society, but Plato's own multiple failures forced him to admit that most men were not prepared to accept rule by philosophers.[90] Instead of reconsidering his views, however, Plato came close to condemning politics altogether and avoiding all involvement in public life. Metochites castigates such an attitude, arguing that politics is the best part of philosophy. A politician is not someone who performs all his duties perfectly, but someone who has an acute awareness of his own limitations and manages through perseverance to govern the state even in the most adverse of circumstances, adapting himself to the requirements of the particular situation.[91]

Crucially though, Joseph Rhakendytes, the philosopher and close friend of Metochites, had a view of politics identical to the one Metochites refutes in *Ethikos*. In the introduction to his extensive *Encyclopaedia*, Joseph states the following:

> I considered the contemplative life the most desirable of all, because it is devoid of any passions and it is much more suitable for a man to adopt, than the active

life, which deals with politics and depends on the moderation of human passions. The philosopher from Stageira makes our life dependent upon these two ways of life. The reason for this is our judgement about these two lives: the contemplative life is exclusively devoted to the logoi ... while the political one, which moderates our passions, deals with the inferior part of our soul, not being able to reach the level of pure reason; it is administered by the inferior part of our soul. The political life listens to the admonitions of reason but disobeys them like those servants who are hasty and rush before listening to the instructions attentively. Listening to reason and its admonitions, the political man attempts to adapt himself to those instructions and is ready to proceed to what is good, but he desists through impatience to act so for the reason we mentioned. He has many achievements, but many failures as well. He champs at the bit of reason and rushes leaderless. He, too, is to be praised for these achievements, although he does not achieve good in any perfect manner.[92]

Joseph Rhakendytes' perspective is clear: the contemplative life is unequivocally superior to the active one.[93] Joseph recognizes the relative value of the active life, but he would never consider politics to be the best part of philosophy. The contrast between a life without passions and a life with measured passions is prominent in the passage quoted above. Joseph recommends a life deprived of passions, while Metochites' view seems to be more moderate. One must not forget Metochites' proclivity to defend the active life in a disguised manner. By defending politics, he defends himself. One must read between the lines of *Ethikos* and not take at face value Metochites' assertions about his disappointment in failing to combine the two ways of life. As observed previously, Metochites is an artful writer, able to undermine the views he appears to adopt. *Byzantios* is eloquent testimony to Metochites' tendency to defend his choices surreptitiously.

In Metochites' day, Joseph Rhakendytes was but one scholar who defended the contemplative life in an uncompromising manner.[94] The anonymous author of the dialogue *Mousokles*, who in all probability belonged to the circle of Joseph Rhakendytes, views those involved in political life with contempt: 'What sort of reputation will all those whom you admire so much for founding certain cities, for making their laws and constitutions, for building houses, cultivating the earth and travelling the sea, really gain? None of these occupations reveal any good thoughts behind them, they are simply an annoyance and a vanity.'[95] Thus, the author of *Mousokles* denies the value of the active life altogether, adopting a position far more radical than that of Joseph Rhakendytes. On the other hand, John Kantakouzenos in his *History* doubts the capability of the moral orations (οἱ μὲν ἠθικοὶ τῶν λόγων) to improve the life of man, preferring those authors who deal only with the actions of men.[96] Was Kantakouzenos targeting Metochites' *Ethikos*, among other works?

Metochites' views were certainly influenced by the discussions among the Constantinopolitan intellectuals of his time, even if he did not have the texts quoted above in mind while composing *Ethikos*. Therefore, one must be cautious with the evaluation of the contemplative life in *Ethikos*. Metochites was certainly sometimes willing to wear the mask of the pure intellectual, but even in these cases his usual elusiveness is evident: he does not reject politics altogether. He seems to have doubts about the absolute value of the contemplative life as expounded by his friend Joseph. Metochites' Oration 18, the comparison between Demosthenes and Aelius Aristeides, is another case of the perpetual conflict between the contemplative life, personified by Aristeides, and the active one, represented by Demosthenes. Metochites proceeds to issue qualified praise of Aristeides, but does not refrain from expressing his admiration for Demosthenes, the man of action. The same occurs in *Ethikos*: Metochites presents himself as a disappointed intellectual who abandoned the life of the mind, but at the same time he undermines that image. In Oration 17, the funerary speech for Joseph Rhakendytes, Metochites praises his already deceased friend without qualification. Joseph, in the introduction to his *Encyclopedia*, speaks in a manner reminiscent of Metochites:

> The contemplative man is absolutely devoted to reason. If somebody is deemed by God worthy of leading such a life, he approaches that quiet mountain of Zion, and spreads his own wings for flight, travelling through the air: then he has the opportunity to observe with the unobscured eye of his mind the miserable life of mortal men and to realize how turbulent and vile it is; he will see how the immaculate souls, after being bound to the body which resembles a shell, are carried off violently from their repose ... Seeing those disturbances of his fellow men and the disturbance created by those numerous strange things which are able to destroy a soul, and of which our present life is filled, he blesses himself for being able to avoid such adverse circumstances, and feels pity for those who go up and down, being unable to come up out of their difficulties, and to strive for real goodness, but being used to their miserable fate they prefer their own doom, running far away from that blessed conduct, because they consider the things escaping them permanent and those that are fluid eternal.[97]

Metochites appears to be using Joseph's introduction to his *Encyclopedia* in the funeral oration, written near the end of his literary career. One may explain that as the compulsory, so to speak, exaggeration of an orator wishing to praise his friend at all costs, or it could be Metochites once more wearing the mask of the pure intellectual towards the conclusion of his life.

In any case, Metochites seems to be in a discussion with his friend while composing *Ethikos*. The discussion itself is a valuable testimony to the intellectual debates of the late Byzantine era and helps in understanding certain nuances and tendencies in the empire's intellectual circles, which, though differing on the issues, were not irreconcilable. Those engaged in the discussions conducted them in a rather amicable and confidential manner until the outbreak of the Palamite controversy around the mid-fourteenth century. The intellectual debates then took a turn for the worse, with the controversy contributing to a hardening of the front line separating the humanist intellectuals of Metochites' type from the more conservative circles of the Orthodox Church. Even in the earliest stages of the controversy, there was something of a line dividing conservatives like Choumnos and the more open-minded thinkers like Metochites. A short passage from Choumnos' second treatise against Metochites is particularly telling:

> You believe that you walk on ether and fly over the clouds, being over the whole earth and the seas, and living together with the stars. You would like to wear wings made of wax like Daedalus and fly to the sky in order to meet the sun, which comes out of darkness and shadows, burning to ashes whatever runs across him.[98]

This brings to mind the expression 'to walk on ether', employed by Metochites in *Ethikos* (ch. 55), immediately after the description of the journey of the soul (ch. 54). We are left with the impression that Choumnos is ridiculing Metochites for it. One cannot say with certainty whether Choumnos was a precursor of the conservative tendencies and trends of the mid-fourteenth century, but Metochites would certainly have been targeted by the Palamites if he had lived a few years longer.

Self-destruction of the intellectuals and Nikephoros Choumnos' response

There is still another aspect of Metochites' self-image as an intellectual: he is a pessimist as concerns the reputation of the scholars of his time. He complains time and again about the apparent neglect of wisdom shown by them, even among intellectuals. Metochites warns of a looming danger for all those involved with the *logoi*: they are being led astray by their excessive zeal to praise the object of their love, inventing all sorts of false advantages of learning that are devoid of substance. The result is that even men of some standing cannot bear to listen to their false praises and come to hold education in contempt, mistrusting those devoted to it.[99] The motif is later repeated (chs. 57–60). Plato is presented as a prominent example of this false attitude towards learning. He was eager at one time to prove the superiority of philosophy in all respects, but as he went from one disaster to another in his political activities, he realized that men were not willing to accept his supposedly salvific teachings. As a result, he withdrew from political life, and in doing so, cast doubt on philosophy's ability to govern his fellow men. As noted previously, according to Metochites this was tantamount to the rejection of the best part of philosophy – politics. Metochites insisted that in spite of Plato's contentions, politics stood as a legitimate endeavour for all those willing to accept that perfection was unattainable and therefore adapted themselves to the circumstances to govern the state as best they could.[100]

It is clear that Metochites' assertions here diverge somewhat from his previous unqualified admiration of the contemplative life. It is as if he sought to defend his own decision to combine the contemplative and the active life: a politician must not strive for perfection, but govern the state, taking into account the political and social situation. Most men, however, being unaware of the limitations imposed on the politician or indeed on any other man struggling in this life, were unwilling to judge a politician's achievements objectively, instead castigating his failures, believing him totally worthless and incapable of achieving anything. This stems from envy. Those judging persuade other men that since they are in a position to detect the failures of the politician, they are the only ones who can manage the affairs of this life successfully.[101] This is also the case with the evaluation of wisdom. Most scholars are unable to recognize the achievements of their peers, so they try to denigrate them to the best of their ability instead.[102] As a result, striving for wisdom is considered an unworthy occupation for any prudent man, and the contemplative life as a whole becomes identified with the ridiculous quarrels of ambitious scholars, who do not realize that through their vainglory and their ardent wish to destroy their opponents they cause great damage to wisdom itself.[103]

Among the writings of Nikephoros Choumnos there is a short treatise addressing '[c]ertain fellows that should not feel annoyance if those who maltreat the *logoi* enjoy a good reputation among those who are ignorant, although they are stupid and awkward'. It is almost certain that in writing this treatise, Choumnos was responding to Metochites' complaints in *Ethikos* about the reputation of scholars.[104] Here is a relevant passage from Choumnos' treatise:

> Some people are greatly annoyed by the fact that ignorant men behave impudently towards those best men – i.e. those who have important literary successes to their credit, and try to slander them, employing as judges those who have nothing more to do with education than handicraftsmen. They are eager to do whatever they can against them, in a way I do not approve of. But even those true sages who are supposedly unfairly dealt with would not approve of this attitude. Anyhow, they consider this attitude horrible and are eager to attack them, because they believe that they treat those learned men unfairly. But I offer the only advice I have to those who are rightfully indignant against those envious men but in a way which is not to be commended. My advice is this: let those crazy people enjoy the fruits of their madness without any impediment but refrain from being angry and accusing them. It is impossible for men of such baseness (you see their character!) to harm whatsoever those good men, whose wealth may neither be stolen by anyone nor be confiscated.[105]

It should be clear to anyone who compares Choumnos' short treatise to *Ethikos* that Choumnos had in mind Metochites' objections to the attitude of his contemporary scholars towards certain learned men. It is rather strange, however, that Metochites refrains from identifying those men of such good reputation for whom he seems concerned. From what he says in *Ethikos*, one may get the impression that the author speaks in general terms about wise men of both past and contemporary times, while Choumnos seems to refer mainly to the past.

In any case, one has the feeling that Metochites was not particularly happy with his self-projected image as a pure intellectual forced to abandon his most beloved studies. Even the life of the intellectual absorbed in his studies is not free from problems created by peers unable to abstain from malicious criticism. This was a problem innate to the *theatra*, which, Metochites believed, contributed to the destruction of the intellectual elite of Byzantium. This is something also encountered in Oration 18, on Demosthenes and Aelius Aristeides, and again the controversy between Metochites and Choumnos: is the portrait of the pure intellectual that Metochites fervently praises really so admirable? Is not Metochites a critic of the discursive culture of his own society?

Oration 17, for Joseph Rhakendytes: A new type of saint?

Metochites' Oration 17, the funeral speech for Joseph Rhakendytes exhibits several traits of a hagiographic work. He titled it 'To a friend on the occasion of the death of the great philosopher and new Joseph'.[106] His use of the adjective 'new' suggests that Metochites considered Joseph a new kind of saint, like Michael the New Martyr of Egypt, in whose honour he had written Oration 12. The two behaved differently in notable ways from the saints who came before them.

Renuntiatio is a motif of many hagiographic texts, which stress the willingness of the saint to put his love for Christ above all else, forsaking his or her family, wealth and secular dignities.[107] In this regard, Joseph abandons his native island and his parents for the sake of Christ, leaving Ithaca for Thessalonike and later travelling to other places.[108] In his story, the motif of renunciation is combined with another common theme, peregrination, but with a distinct difference. In most lives, the saints rush to join a monastic community after renouncing family and country,[109] but unlike them, Joseph takes his time, first moving to Thessalonike, where he devotes himself to his studies and the pursuit of virtue,[110] in all probability, remaining a layman there. Joseph pretends to be illiterate because of his deep humility, performing the most humbling manual work. When his true identity becomes known, he prefers to move on out of humility.[111] The Life of St Athanasios the Athonite, the founder of cenobitic monasticism on Athos, relates the same story, and it is quite likely that Metochites was aware of it.[112]

Joseph is finally tonsured when he joins a monastic community on Mount Athos.[113] Metochites' description of Joseph's ascetic endeavours there is replete with the usual motifs of Byzantine asceticism: fasting, constant praying and the like.[114] The section contains an interesting story: Joseph, travelling from Thessalonike back to Athos on foot, falls ill with fever and is forced to take shelter in a small church near the road; there some barbarian robbers enter, meet Joseph, and want to rob him; however, after realizing that Joseph had no possessions, they decide to carry him to a nearby village and leave him there, so that he may take care of himself in an appropriate manner.[115] A similar story appears in the Life of St George of Choziva (seventh century), who is protected by some robbers because of their respect for his exceptional moral qualities.[116]

Metochites then speaks about Joseph's journey to Constantinople, motivated by God, because he did not want Joseph's talents to remain hidden and also because Joseph wished to obtain more knowledge.[117] The latter is another difference from the traditional hagiographic literature, in which the saint typically abandons his studies to become a monk. In Constantinople, Joseph assumes the care of a certain monk, Makarios, who was ill.[118] This resembles a similar story in *Lausaikon*.[119] What is interesting is that Joseph, against the expectations of the reader of the funeral oration, distances himself from Makarios, without completely abandoning him, following the advice of his friends – one of whom may have been Metochites himself! – who were distressed by the hardship Joseph had to suffer because of Makarios.[120] Is Metochites thus indicating his disapproval of such a motif?

Joseph denies the patriarchal dignity offered to him four times.[121] This is a rather common theme in Byzantine hagiographic texts.[122] What Metochites' text lacks is any mention of miracles performed by Joseph, either during his life or posthumously. Is this absence an indication that it is wrong to interpret Metochites' text as a piece of Byzantine hagiographic literature? No. The absence of miracles is intentional: Metochites wanted to present Joseph as a new type of saint, one who was more secularized and more in line with the sensibilities of the intellectuals of his time. Indicative of Metochites' mood is that the adoption of monastic qualities is called the 'pursuit of virtue',[123] not 'union with God' or something more traditional. In this, Metochites tries to reintroduce the moral virtues of antiquity into the Byzantine social code under the cover of Byzantine monastic qualities. More significantly, he combines the pursuit of virtue with the pursuit of knowledge in a hagiographic text. In this way, Metochites subtly undermines the traditional image of the saint despite seemingly crafting such an image himself in some of his hagiographic works – Oration 2, for St Marina, Oration 19, St John of Didymoteichon. His oration for Joseph is a case of Metochites wearing the mask of the ancient sage once more.

Ethikos reveals Metochites once again exhibiting inner ambiguity. He seems to extol the contemplative life, praising the inner tranquillity of the sage and his detachment from wordly affairs, considering such a life the road towards true and constant happiness. Metochites does not try to leave the reader with the impression of at least superficially conforming to the requirements of Byzantine orthodoxy. The contemplative life is the ideal of Greek philosophy, and Metochites presents himself wearing the mask of a Greek sage of ancient times. No other way of life can safeguard man's serenity and calmness of mind.

The active life is a source of constant worries and troubles, as Metochites himself came to realize during his long public career. At the same time, however, Metochites undermines his own position, subtly defending those who embark upon a public career, even if they are unable to attain perfection in carrying out their duties. He goes so far as to dispute the views of Joseph Rhakendytes, a man he greatly respects and appreciates.

Did Metochites ever try to reconcile his opposing masks, creating another mask comparatively free from inner tensions and contradictions? The answer can be found in *Byzantios*, in which Metochites tries to present a picture of himself free of ambiguity.

Chapter 8

ORATION 11, *BYZANTIOS*: THE SECULAR BODY OF THE CITY AND A SECULAR WORLD CONTEMPLATED

Byzantios is one of the most complex and perplexing works by Metochites. On the surface, it reads like a typical praise of a city, a literary genre from late antiquity that the Byzantines neglected somewhat but made use of as a subgenre incorporated into encomia. Metochites' choice of the genre for expressing his inner thoughts is indicative of his penchant for literary experimentation in the style and the content of his speeches. Of note, *Byzantios* is one of his longest orations and was not intended for public presentation. *Byzantios* is considered an adaptation of earlier models; the author probably refers to the late antique encomia of cities, like the *Panathenaikos* of Aelius Aristeides or the *Antiochikos* of Libanius, which he took into account while composing his own praise of Constantinople. The importance of *Byzantios*, however, lies in his adaptation and treatment of the contemplation of nature, a motif also encountered in *Ethikos*. Although such contemplation takes place in a very different setting from that of *Ethikos*, Metochites insists that every citizen of the imperial city partakes in a special privilege – to examine nature through its 'exact copy', the city itself. What is the meaning of this assertion, this concept? Is *Byzantios* the counterpart of *Ethikos* and in what respect? Does it help Metochites put on another mask and create a self-portrait more coherent and convincing than the others seen so far?

Content of the Oration

Metochites begins *Byzantios* in typical Byzantine manner, by pointing out that it is his duty to praise Constantinople because it is his home town, and by stressing that the city is full of marvels that capture the attention of any man who is able to appreciate its beauties. (chs. 1–2) He mentions the emperor Constantine the Great, who founded the city (ch. 3), and also makes a passing reference to the Palaiologoi dynasty, the successors of Constantine and the lawful rulers of the city (ch. 4). As is typical with speeches of this sort, Metochites enumerates the difficulties one encounters dealing with such an immense subject: even if an accomplished orator were to treat just one of the marvels of the city enumerated, he could not do so in a satisfactory manner, because no man's abilities are sufficient for such a difficult task. As for Metochites, he has long since abandoned literary activities, so his difficulty is thus greater still (ch. 5). Regardless, he will attempt to accomplish this rigorous task, driven by his great love for the city. No one would berate somebody who tries to fulfil a challenging pursuit if he ultimately fails (chs. 6–7).

Metochites wonders how he will proceed with his speech, unable to find a proper beginning for it. He ultimately chooses to speak about geography first (ch. 8), stressing that Constantinople enjoys a certain privilege compared to all other cities on earth: it is built on a peninsula and thus able to enjoy all good things offered by the sea while at the same time avoiding all the dangers that come by it (chs. 9–10).

This observation would have been evident to all those attending his speech – residents of Constantinople – therefore it is difficult for the author to praise this aspect of the city (ch. 11).

The position of Constantinople on the threshold of two continents permits it to function as a bridge linking them (chs. 12–13). At the same time, all products of the two continents come to the city, enriching it immensely (chs. 14–15). The position of Constantinople has been praised by many authors, but none so aptly as Herodotus, who castigates the citizens of Chalcedon for choosing to build their city where they did instead of the promontory opposite them that was not yet inhabited at the time (chs. 16–18).

Constantinople is constantly bathed in sunshine, being immersed in all the beauties of its natural environment (chs. 19–21). The dry land of Attica and the rocky landscape of Delphi cannot be compared with Constantinople, which is fortunate in its ports, being placed at the crossroads of all the commercial routes of the Mediterranean and Black Seas (ch. 22). It is admirable to observe how the Black Sea, which is so rough and frightful, is tamed by the Bosporus Straits and approaches Constantinople like a lover who comes to his beloved gently and quietly (ch. 23). Then the Black Sea empties itself into Propontis, which resembles a vast, calm lake (ch. 24). It is a marvel for an acute observer to see the reflections of the stars upon the surface of Propontis at night; one has the impression that the sea imitates the sky (chs. 25–7). At the same time if somebody goes beyond the city limits of the Bosporus straits, he is amazed by the ferocity of the elements of nature, which are in constant turmoil outside the city (ch. 28). Therefore, Constantinople combines all the adversities of nature, taming and exploiting them in a most effective way (ch. 29).

After a short praise of the landscape of Thrace, Metochites concludes his section on the land of Constantinople, pointing out that the city is the heart of the world, generously sharing its treasures with all men of all countries (chs. 30–3). There is a minor gap in the manuscript at this point, after chapter 33, but it is clear that Metochites has moved on to the next, and most extensive, section of his speech, on the relationship that existed between Constantinople and the Roman Empire (ch. 34). The section begins with praise of the city's founder, Constantine the Great, who is compared to Alexander the Great, founder of another famous city, Alexandria. Constantine's main concern was to build an imperial city that would serve as a firm and fixed centre for his empire. In reality, Constantine brought a plan of God to fruition. This explains Constantine's spectacular success. The city serves as a monument to his great ability and statesmanship (chs. 35–6).

Constantinople is the capital befitting such a huge and strong empire in its extent and magnitude. No one may deny that Constantine chose the most appropriate place on earth to build his new capital. The ancient cities had countryside, called *chora*, surrounding them, and the Roman Empire seems something like that, an 'area' (χώρα) around Constantinople, such is the suitability of the city to the whole empire (chs. 37–40). Constantine considered many cities as potential capitals of the restored empire, but none of them was as suitable for this purpose as Byzantium (chs. 41–6).

The city came to prominence slowly and gradually attained perfection, like all living organisms (ch. 47). It already boasted a glorious history. It was inhabited by Dorians, the most martial of the Greeks (ch. 48), and became a target for conquerors because of its prominence; whoever controlled Byzantium controlled all of Greece (chs. 49–50). Constantine built a new city there to reign over his empire (ch. 51). The expectations of the city's founder came to pass, as demonstrated by Christianity becoming the established religion of the Roman Empire as soon as the city was founded (ch. 52). Constantinople experienced no decline at all, unlike other imperial cities in the past. All miracles took place after Constantinople's foundation, clear proof of the providence of God. The city served continuously as the capital of the empire (chs. 53–7). Constantinople stands as a creation of the two most important nations on earth, the Greeks and the Romans – the Greeks functioned as the material basis of the city, while the Romans gave it its shape and form (ch. 58). Things of beauty from throughout the world were gathered in Constantinople, adorning it and making it most beautiful (ch. 59). Everyone who has eyes may see those things for himself (ch. 60). Even time, which destroys all good things with its passing remains idle in the city (chs. 61–2). Instead of destroying the beauties of the city, time makes it even more beautiful (ch. 63). This applies both to the walls of the city as well as to all the buildings inside it. The city resembles an evergreen plant, and even its ruins contribute to its glory, appearing so strong that one wonders how it became possible for them to be ruined at all. They also affirm the city's glorious and illustrious past. In any case, the citizens of Constantinople do not need the confirmation offered by the things of the past, since the city is constantly refurbished and is perpetually glorious (chs. 64–6).

It is impossible for a single man to praise all the marvels of the city. The churches are scattered all over it, functioning both as treasuries of all things necessary for the preservation of human life and as havens in which anyone may take refuge (ch. 67). Who can describe the porticos, the other buildings, the statues and the other works of art that adorn the city? (chs. 67–70) All the countries on earth have contributed to the embellishment of Constantinople (chs. 71–2). Like the gardens of the countryside provide each city with all necessary things, in the same way, all the cities on earth send Constantinople whatever it needs. The city is the common hearth of earth. One wonders how it became possible for so many things to be gathered in just one place; such a thing has never happened in the past (chs. 73–4). Many cities would have been content, even quite proud, to possess just one of the numerous marvels of the city, but the city does not seem to be satisfied with them, instead always adding something new to its previous treasures, resembling the ever-inventive and creative power of nature (ch. 75).

Even in front of the city, there are certain suburbs that resemble a constellation surrounding Constantinople, but the city offers many gifts to other cities as well (chs. 76–9). It resembles the nature of the universe: nature draws waters from the earth and returns them to it through the clouds. The city obtains all the beautiful things from the earth and returns them through its generosity (ch. 80).

The city is an offering to God. This is proven by the multitude of churches scattered throughout it. The great protector of the city is the Virgin Mary, who governs it and saves it from misfortune. The numerous churches of the Virgin Mary built in Constantinople are proof that the city is devoted to her (chs. 81–6). It is impossible for anyone to describe the greatest marvel of all – the church of Hagia Sophia. If the city is the soul of the whole world, then Hagia Sophia may be considered the soul of the city, being the soul's soul of the world (chs. 87–92). Plato writes that heaven is the teacher of wisdom. The same applies to Constantinople (chs. 93–4). It is not only the teacher of human wisdom, but it is also a guide, initiating us into the mysteries of life and essence. The city is the link uniting the whole world to each of its organic parts, the common fatherland of all men on earth, being their common state. It is much better for one to live for a few years in Constantinople than to enjoy a long life in a place where he will not have the opportunity to have so many memorable experiences, where there will be a total 'absence of life'. A desert where life is absent has no value. By contrast, the citizens of Constantinople, even if they live a short life, get to observe many things and to interact with all manner of different people who come to the city, so may be considered truly blessed. The founders of the city regarded their creation as a universal theatre, where all good things that exist on earth are exhibited (chs. 95–104).

Metochites moves on to a description of the special relationship between the city and God. Constantinople is the source of the Orthodox faith, irrigating the entire earth with it (chs. 105–6). The city has never abandoned the Christian faith, since its founding by Constantine, the only emperor to become a saint. The see of Constantinople is the only one of the five ancient patriarchates that kept its faith intact (ch. 107). Here three of the seven ecumenical councils took place. Its prelates have taught the whole world through their admirable writings (chs. 108–17).

After offering a short summary of the contents of his speech (chs. 118–22), Metochites proceeds to the final part of his praise of Constantinople, comparing it with other famous cities (Babylon, Antioch, Alexandria and Rome, chs. 123–37). This was the standard conclusion of Byzantine encomia, whether of persons or inanimate things.

The advantages of the other cities are known only through writings referring to them, as they themselves have since been irretrievably lost. Constantinople's marvels, however, are still visible to everyone. Babylon had a great wall surrounding it, but it was nevertheless a barbarian city that could not be compared with the Greek city of Constantinople and the civility and freedom it enjoys. Moreover, Babylon was deprived of any havens, having no sea near it. As far as the two Macedonian cities of

Alexandria and Antioch are concerned, nobody may deny that they were once powerful, but have now lost everything, even their Christian faith, having fallen under the yoke of the barbarians. Moreover, while Alexandria's and Antioch's power did not extend beyond the limits of Africa or Asia, respectively, Constantinople controlled three continents simultaneously. Not even Rome can be compared to Constantinople, because being deprived of noteworthy havens, it cannot function as a commonwealth of all men from every corner of the earth like Constantinople.

Constantinople as nature

Readers of the short summary of *Byzantios* above can readily discern that Metochites insists on the comparison of Constantinople with nature. After describing the taming of the waters of the Black Sea in front of the city, he concludes that its blending of opposite things into a harmonious whole makes Constantinople a true copy of the world, which consists of different elements combined into a whole.[1] Then he goes a step further. Constantinople is not just a copy of the world (οἰκουμένη), it is the heart of the whole universe and the source of its life.[2] This statement is somewhat mitigated when Metochites specifies that Constantinople is the heart of the Roman state, which he considers a living organism; the city safeguards the ongoing existence of the state.[3] He further employs the metaphor of nature in comparing Byzantium – initially rather small before its transformation into a glorious city – to living organisms that start from simple beginnings, developing other natural properties over time.[4] He then explains his thought process: like all beings, Constantinople consists of form and matter, the material basis of it is in the form of the Greek people, while Romans shaped the amorphous material into a harmonious and well-constituted whole.[5]

The metaphor of nature occurs once more: Constantinople is a unique creature of God, like the sun or heaven. It resembles the evergreen plants, adorning itself with all sorts of marvellous things that are impervious to the ravages of time.[6] In one of the most striking images of the city, its functions resemble the administration of the earth's waters by the all-powerful nature of the universe. Metochites stresses that he is employing the metaphor of nature once more.[7] This image is later enhanced: the protector of the city is the Virgin Mary, who also protects nature itself.[8] Employing the previous image of the city as the world's heart, Metochites wrote that, indeed, the city resembles a heart; through its perfect functioning, life is distributed to the different parts of the world.[9] There is also another aspect to the city: it has its own soul in the form of the church of Hagia Sophia, which is the soul's soul (the ψυχῆς ψυχὴ), so to speak.[10] The image of nature thus assumes a religious dimension that until that point has been hardly discernible.

The concept: Sources and background

The metaphor of nature that Metochites employs has distinct layers. First, there is the city akin to a human body: the city has a heart and soul and is the source of life, which is diffused to all parts of the empire. Such portrayals of cities became widespread in Greek antiquity, especially among the Stoics.[11] Second, the city resembles a plant: the city gradually develops and grows bigger and bigger like a plant. It also resembles evergreens. Third, the city takes on a larger scale, resembling the entirety of nature, which appears to be synonymous with the whole world. This is the actual meaning behind Metochites' contention that the city is an 'exact copy' of the sky above, displaying on its surface all manner of marvellous spectacles. This leads the author to an interesting conclusion: contemplation of the city resembles contemplation of the world. In fact, he seems to identify the city with the entire world.

There can be no doubt that Metochites had certain sources that he drew on either consciously or unconsciously. On the unconscious level, Metochites seems to have been inspired by terminology commonly invoked in the church in Byzantium. Body and plant imagery was widespread among Byzantine theologians, who drew inspiration from the texts of the New Testament, some of which were indebted to Stoicism.[12] Paul the Apostle referred to the church as the body of Christ (Eph. 1.23), while John the Evangelist compared the community of Christ and his disciples to a vine (John 15.4).

On the conscious level, Metochites seems to draw inspiration from two sources. He uses the phrase ψυχὴ ψυχῆς, which is found in *Quis rerum divinarum heres sit*, the well-known treatise by Philo Judaeus, Metochites' favourite author.[13] There are also parallels with the works of Plotinus, who employs a similar expression, ψυχὴ αὐτοψυχῆς.[14] The universal soul of Plotinus is the source of life diffused through the 'body' of the world. One might dismiss this connection as far-fetched, but Metochites employs another phrase in the same context – that of the 'absence of life'.[15] The phrase seems to have been taken verbatim from Plotinus' writings. In accepting this connection, one must acknowledge that Metochites places Constantinople into a larger cosmological context, which is ultimately inspired by the cosmological picture of the Platonic *Timaeus* as interpreted by the Neoplatonists. The life given by Constantinople to its organic parts is identical to the Neoplatonic concept of life, which is a product of the world's soul, itself diffused throughout the world.

The image of the administration of the waters of the earth by nature has certain affinities with Aristotle's *Meteorologica*, as interpreted by Metochites' friend Nikephoros Choumnos. There is not enough substance, however, to warrant its investigation as a source of Metochites' application of the image of the world or nature to the city, which consists of multiple layers defying superficial examination.

Contemplation of the city as counterpart to the contemplation of nature

In chapter 93 of *Byzantios*, Metochites adduces the view of Plato, who argued that heaven is a teacher of men, exhibiting a variety of spectacles and harmonious combinations; Metochites asserts that the same applies to Constantinople, which is a heaven on earth and a cosmic theatre of wisdom. All lessons and all sciences are taught in the city. Constantinople is the heir of the glorious cities of the past, the fame of which has long since been extinguished, but it is also much more than that: the city offers to all men opportunities for experiences that they could not enjoy if they had remained idle in their own countries.[16] Metochites clearly states that Constantinople resembles a command post, a peak, from which a man can examine all things on earth.[17] He employs the same image in *Ethikos*: the man devoted to his studies resembles a man sitting atop a watchtower, from which all things on earth can be examined one by one in a most satisfying and appropriate way.[18] As previously noted, Metochites draws this comparison from Philo Judaeus. The perspective of the passage from *Byzantios* is the same. The citizen of Constantinople is almost identical to the wise man of *Ethikos*. Metochites employs similar terminology in both texts. The watchtower and the *epopteia* of the things of nature are common to both, albeit with a crucial difference. In *Ethikos*, Metochites considers the contemplation of nature the activity of a solitary man who abandons everything and cuts ties to society to devote himself to his studies. In *Byzantios*, the man who examines things of the earth is not a solitary sage, but a citizen of a great city. What is the real meaning of this change in perspective?

In *Ethikos*, Metochites deplores the fate of the scholar who became involved in the affairs of this world against his wishes. Although he remembers his previous literary activities and longs for a carefree life devoted to knowledge, he is unable to break the bonds that shackle him to this world. Metochites presents himself as the victim of just such a situation: he becomes involved in the affairs of the Roman state, unaware of the dangers menacing any man with literary ambitions. Thus, he is a man shattered by the burden of administering the state, a responsibility that fell upon his shoulders and robbed him of all hope of restarting his literary activities. This is hardly a credible representation, since Metochites never abandoned his studies and continued to be a prolific author long after he became a close collaborator of Emperor Andronikos II Palaiologos. Such expressions of self-pity do not seem particularly sincere. In fact, Metochites was flattered to be assured of his ability to successfully combine his literary studies with his obligations as a public servant. In a letter to Metochites, Thomas Magistros extols this particular virtue of Andronikos' powerful minister.[19] Metochites' assertion that it was difficult to be both a successful author and a servant of the Roman state are plausible, but his claims of utter disappointment with his literary activities cannot be taken at face value.

Byzantios is the counterpart of *Ethikos*. On the one hand, *Ethikos* is a rhetorical description of the contemplative life and a lyrical praise of the merits of such a life; the narrative of this life being irretrievably lost for Metochites is simply a rhetorical device he employs to enhance the persuasiveness of his assertions on the absolute value of the contemplative life. On the other hand, *Byzantios* is a description of the *vita activa* as exemplified by the life inside the most important, most illustrious city in the world, Constantinople. There is, however, a paradox. The contemplation (ἐποπτεία) of nature, that most distinctive privilege of those who lead a contemplative life, is accorded to all citizens of Constantinople provided they have the ability to realize that their city is an exact copy of the world, governed by the same eternal laws that govern the universe. It is important to always bear in mind that Constantinople is the seat of the imperial government. Metochites is one of the most prominent members of said government, so he has ample opportunity to observe the laws of nature, as he administers the Roman state, the heart of which is Constantinople. It is evident that Metochites somewhat exaggerated the complaints raised in *Ethikos* about his inability to enjoy the fruits of a true contemplative life, since as a politician he had ample occasion and capacity to contemplate the nature of the world through the administration of the state and its capital.

These considerations may lead one to the conclusion that *Byzantios* is an apologia of the active life so denounced by Metochites in *Ethikos*. In writing the praise of a city, Metochites is answering his own objections to the active life of a politician as set out in *Ethikos*. The main argument of this apology is that the politician can enjoy exactly the same sort of spiritual fruits enjoyed by the scholar devoted to his studies. This is possible because an inner relationship links life in a city with life in a hermitage: both lives can lead man to the contemplation of nature, provided he is willing to be initiated into her mysteries, as she unveils herself to both the sage and the wise administrator of a state.

At the heart of Metochites' contentions obviously lies the ancient Platonic and Stoic concept of the totality of the world, which is governed by the eternal and unchangeable laws of nature like a city encompassing the whole universe.[20] What truly bears emphasizing, however, is that through these contentions, Metochites confers a spiritual content on the active life that was far from inherent to it. With this, these two ways of life, which philosophers before Metochites viewed as opposites, become identical for him. This reconciliation, so to speak, of two opposites, ultimately results in the total subordination of the active life to the contemplative life. This is, therefore, neither a combination nor a reconciliation of two concepts on equal terms: rather, the contemplative life absorbs the active life. Metochites ignores that governing a state, or its imperial city, was, indeed, the diametrical opposite to living the solitary life of an ancient sage. His picture of late Byzantine Constantinople as a small world governed by the same laws that govern nature, though rather impressive as a literary creation, is merely a creation of his imagination, deprived of any real value either for understanding the mechanisms of a medieval state or for properly evaluating the contemplative life of a Byzantine scholar. One may object on the grounds that this was not the purpose of Metochites' praise of Constantinople, where exaggeration was, to a certain degree, unavoidable. The way Metochites tries to defend himself and his involvement in the affairs of the state, however, is indicative of a certain, self-serving posturing. By subordinating the administration of the state, at the time in great peril, to his fantasies about a universal state centred round Constantinople, Metochites was hardly rendering a useful service to that state. Aelius Aristeides was permitted to present Rome as a universal city, because he was living in the second century CE. In the troubled years of the early fourteenth century such an image was not only misleading, but dangerous. Metochites failed to restrain his own imagination, instead letting it lead him astray. However, in his depiction of Constantinople as a universal city, as a city almost identical with the whole world, there are some truly innovative and rather fascinating traits. In some respects, Metochites was quite prescient.

The body of the state and its theological implications

Metochites' conception of the state as a huge body was not ground-breaking. As already observed, under the influence of Platonism and Stoicism, the idea of a great world city governed by universal laws became quite widespread in the political literature of both the Hellenistic and imperial eras. It formed the foundation for the concept of the church of Christ as a body, developed mainly under the influence of St Paul, who contributed greatly to the dissemination of the idea among Christians.[21] Although the concept of the state as a body was not alien to Byzantine authors, Metochites' insistence on it held particular significance in the ideological context of the early fourteenth century. His vision of it stems from the concept of the church as the body of Christ. While the soul of that body is Constantinople, the soul of Constantinople itself is the church of Hagia Sophia. The religious dimension of this imagery is evident: the church is the source of life, and via the city, rivers of real life are distributed to all the limbs of the larger body of the Roman state. Some ecclesiastical authors – anxious to persuade their audience of the church as the only source of real life – often stressed the life-giving power of Christ, the head of the church. Metochites saw things somewhat differently: although his vision contains a religious dimension, he tended, to an extent, to secularize the image of the church as the body of Christ. Admittedly Metochites takes care to place Hagia Sophia[22] – a church of Christ, the Wisdom of His Father – at the heart of the city, but this perfect life permeating Constantinople and invigorating the limbs of the Roman state resembles the life given by the world's soul to all living beings as described by Plotinus. Furthermore, it seems to display few similarities with Christian life treasured inside the church and provided through the Mysteries to all Christians, who constitute the body of Christ. At the same time, Metochites seems to revive the ancient image of the state as a body, which despite being the source of the image of the body of the Christian church, had been somewhat neglected in Byzantium.

What is the real meaning of the attempt to revive the ancient image of the body of the state invigorated by its capital? This same tendency to secularize the image of the body of the church and transfer it to the state appears in several Western European texts.[23] Metochites could hardly have been insensitive to the somewhat heterodox implications of that image. The world's soul was a Platonic and Stoic concept conceiving the world as a living organism,[24] a view that could hardly be reconciled with the basic tenets of Christian cosmology,[25] as Metochites' contemporary, Nikephoros Choumnos, was quick to point out in *Adversus Plotinum de anima*, his long refutation of Plotinus' doctrines.[26] This is probably the reason Metochites concealed the origins of the imagery by presenting the church of Hagia Sophia, or even the Virgin Mary herself,[27] as the state's ultimate source of life. This, however, is hardly sufficient to prove that theological discussions on the life of the church by Christian authors inspired Metochites' image. Constantinople seems to have usurped the place of the Christian church, heretofore the sole distributor of the grace of God. In other words, in Metochites' imagination, the traditional place of Christ as the heart of the body consisting of all Christians seems to have been usurped by Constantinople, the distributor of life to the citizens of the Roman Empire. In this construct, there no longer seems to be a place for abstract theological speculation concerning the centrality of God in the body of the faithful who collectively constitute the church. In Metochites' imagery, the imperial city effectively usurps the place of the church as the centre or heart of the body of the Roman state. This transposition might have been facilitated by Byzantine imperial ideology shared by all Byzantines: they viewed their state as a replica of the heavenly state, and God himself served as the prototype for their emperor. In Metochites' thinking, the body of the whole world replaces the heavenly kingdom. Of additional interest, Metochites remains silent on the place of the emperor in *Byzantios*.

A similar image appears in Oration 4, for St Demetrius, considered the soul of Thessalonike, his native city: '[T]hat brave martyr of Christ takes the place of the soul of the city; he is much more than any natural bond, any governing mind and reason; he is the completion and cohesion of the city's being and its form. He also becomes the leader, superintendent and protector of every action.'[28] The passage is full of philosophical terms and certainly reminds one of the passages from *Byzantios*, but in this case, Metochites emphasizes theological undertones, probably because his aim was to praise a saint, not a city.

In trying to explain Metochites' attempt to secularize the notion of the body of the church, one must remember that in all those cases where he employs the image of the world or its body, his main concern is to prove that the human mind is capable of comprehending the world and its creator independently of official religious institutions. This is evident in his representation of the sage who contemplates the world in *Ethikos*, where only a cursory mention of Christian revelation is made, at the beginning of the treatise. The same applies to the image of the contemplation of the world through the scientific study of its harmonious laws, as described in Poem 10, on the science of harmonics. Metochites, following ancient philosophical tradition, considers the world a trustworthy guide towards wisdom; by examining the various limbs of the world, man comes to an understanding of its basic functions and realizes that this harmonious whole must have been created by a supreme being. Therefore, the rejection of religious or apocalyptic elements is inherent to the image of the body of the world (or of the world's city) as employed by Metochites.

In writing *Byzantios*, Metochites did not merely wish to present the public with a pamphlet of political theory. He also wanted to explain his views on politics in a way that would provide justification for his decision to combine the life of a scholar with that of a politician. The absence of religious undertones in the image of Constantinople would have been quite natural in the work of a scholar like Metochites. His entire thought process stood far removed from the official religious discussions of the church fathers and theologians, who tried to define the nature of the church as Christ's body. Metochites would have been opposed to any attempt to interpret *Byzantios* as a document refuting the main doctrines of the church to which he himself belonged even though its content is obviously far removed from the religious sensibilities of the guardians of orthodoxy. It appears, moreover, that some intellectuals of Metochites' time were rather irreligious, making him a mere representative of the zeitgeist. His vision of a secular social body like that centred around Constantinople represents the dream of a group of scholars dissatisfied with the images used and projected by the official church and longing for something else. This is the reason for the secular image of Constantinople as a body that lives by the life of the world's soul. It is the reason for his utilization of Plotinus' thought.

Metochites' secularization of the state is a result of his secularization of the classical Christian *theoria*, which he did in *Ethikos*. The world contemplated by the sage in *Ethikos*, though created by God, had an autonomous life devoid of influence by any external, metaphysical entities. It was inevitable that Metochites would represent the body of the state, an exact copy of the larger world surrounding it, as an autonomous entity functioning with its own laws, independent of the will of God. Metochites secularized both the contemplative and the active life in a way that surely estranged some of his contemporaries to a certain extent.

The state without an emperor

In *Byzantios*, Metochites refers in brief to the ruling Palaiologan dynasty, according to him the legitimate successors of Constantine the Great, founder of Constantinople. Metochites points out that the ruling emperors, Andronikos II Palaiologos and his co-emperor son, Michael IX (and possibly also his wife Eirene), contribute to the importance of the imperial city, ruling it wisely and adorning it with their virtues.[29] Metochites makes no other mention of the Palaiologoi in *Byzantios*. Keeping in mind that most Byzantine orators wasted no opportunity to mention the emperor in a work, and given that Metochites was no exception to this rule, his restraint concerning his emperor and protector in *Byzantios* seems surprising. As previously noted, the city is presented as the soul of a worldwide empire, but the empire appears to lack an emperor. What lay behind this ominous omission? This question leads to another one: what is the relationship between *Byzantios* and the Byzantine reality of the early fourteenth century? Did Metochites believe that the majestic image he paints of Constantinople, the centre of a worldwide empire, corresponded to reality? This last question is clearly rhetorical. Metochites was acutely aware of the empire's severe decline when composing his works, as the *Miscellanea* clearly demonstrate. In *Byzantios*, Metochites underlines that fortune and nature act in concert in the case of Constantinople,[30] but had earlier asserted in *Ethikos* that these two concepts are contradictory.[31] Constantinople is not a real city but a symbol of the active life, as demonstrated above. That the ruling Palaiologoi are mentioned only in passing is indicative of Metochites' intentions. It serves as a signal to the reader not to take his account of the origins and the development of Constantinople at face value.

The omission of the emperor from the picture becomes stranger when one considers that Metochites had in the past written praises of two cities, in which he took the opportunity to praise the emperor as profusely as possible. In Oration 1, *Nikaeus*, to Nicaea, Metochites presents Andronikos II as the symbol of the glory of the reconstituted Roman Empire after the disaster of 1204.[32] The same idea is further developed in Oration 7, the second *basilikos*, in which Metochites includes a colourful portrait of the 'body' of the Roman state. The emperor has revived the ancient province of Asia Minor, transforming it into a well-functioning entity with inner cohesion. The body of the whole structure is well built, and the entire province is protected by a series of castles that together resemble a chorus. This imagery, probably inspired by Aelius Aristeides, was re-utilized in *Byzantios*, where Metochites used it in describing the islands near Constantinople. Metochites even uses the Stoic term *sympathein* to explain the interaction of the various parts of the province with the rest of the world.[33] What clearly distinguishes this picture from the one of Constantinople in *Byzantios*, however, is the distinct connection of the body of the province of Asia Minor with the emperor Andronikos II: in the second *basilikos*, the body of the city belongs to the great emperor.[34] It is also noteworthy that in discussing the advantages of monarchy over republic in the *Miscellanea*, Metochites compares the city with a body and the monarch with the mind or soul of the body, implying that the emperor and the mind of the state are identical.[35]

One could object to the assertion that the omission of the emperor in *Byzantios* is significant when compared with the second *basilikos* by arguing that in the latter, a speech written specifically for Andronikos II, the connection of the body of the city with the emperor was unavoidable. One must keep in mind, however, that such an objection could apply to *Byzantios* as well. That Constantinople is represented as an exact copy of the cosmos could have led Metochites to a reference to the emperor, since according to official Byzantine ideology the emperor, the leader of the cosmic body, also had an archetype, which was none other than the Heavenly Father himself. That both God and his replica on earth, the Byzantine emperor, are absent from the pages of *Byzantios* seems to be deliberate.

One might argue that Metochites, like some of his Western contemporaries,[36] believed that the empire existed independently of its emperor, but such a contention is far from certain. A tentative explanation for this seeming anomaly may be sought in Metochites' intention to secularize the image of the body of the state. If he had mentioned the emperor, he would have also felt the need to mention God. A reference to the emperor unaccompanied by a reference to his divine model might have seemed rather strange to Metochites' audience, if not outright blasphemous, when one considers the implications of the picture of the city as painted by Metochites. He may not have wanted to further complicate the image of the city as a copy of nature. Therefore, he purposely kept the emperor out of the picture. The image of Constantinople he depicts corresponded to his inner thoughts and dreams. As discussed, in writing *Byzantios*, Metochites sought to present an account of his personal choices and preferences: he considered himself an ancient sage who was adept both in the active and in the contemplative life. Constantinople was a symbol of the active life. Metochites did not deny the existence and providence of God but had no use for the mystical sensitivities of some of his contemporaries, nor was he satisfied with the basic contention of his church, which considered itself the true distributor of the mystical life of Christ. Therefore, the omission of the emperor from the image was to be expected.

Another issue is whether the absence of the emperor may have had any political undertones. One might argue that his absence was the author's reaction to an emperor responsible for the empire's decline. That Metochites was more than willing to praise Andronikos II in other cases should not be held as an objection to disqualify such an interpretation. As observed previously, Metochites had a tendency to distance himself from his own positions whenever necessary, but it is hardly convincing for another reason. Metochites had realized that the causes of the empire's decline lay in the distant past: the men governing the state during his time were unfortunate heirs of the bankruptcy that had occurred before them; their only duty was to administer that failing state in an attempt to preserve some remnants of its previous glory. Many passages of the *Miscellanea* can be read as a direct refutation of certain chapters of *Byzantios*.[37] One must avoid trying to explain the omission of the emperor in *Byzantios* as an expression of Metochites' disappointment with the contemporary state of public affairs. Instead, one should look to Metochites' choice to spiritualize the reality of his Constantinople by transforming it from a real city into a symbol of the active life. In an almost doomed state, the only thing left for an intellectual was contemplation of the city as a symbol of the interaction of the world and the once-glorious Roman Empire. Such a symbol could serve to enrich his own spiritual life while remaining completely disconnected from the reality surrounding him. The emperor had no place in such an idealized picture of Constantinople.

Niels Gaul has argued that the decline of imperial power in the Palaiologan period led to increased self-confidence for orators like Thomas Magistros, who, imitating the orators of the Second Sophistic movement of late antiquity, projected an image of themselves as defenders of the independence of the empire's cities and as protectors of the dignity and rights of their citizens.[38] This may be another plausible explanation for Metochites' depiction of the capital of the empire as an entity lacking a sovereign emperor.

Back to reality, but what kind?

Metochites insists that anyone who enjoys the privilege of contemplating the imperial city experiences the opportunity to reflect on a tangible reality. In *Byzantios*, the author notes that a citizen of or visitor to Constantinople finds themself in communion with as many people and things as possible.[39] The city is also described as a market full of men and various things, which provides those who visit it with περιουσία.[40] The term περιουσία, which follows the word εὐζωΐα (good life), here denotes something more than mere 'property'. Rather it signifies the possibility of the citizen of Constantinople to have an inner connection with the things he possesses and that gives real meaning to his life and to his whole existence. Metochites uses the term οὐσία (essence) in connection with the term 'life' (ch. 94). Περιουσία and οὐσία are almost identical in meaning.

This brings to mind what Metochites said in Oration 18, on Demosthenes and Aelius Aristeides, regarding the bearing circumstances (πράγματα) had on

Demosthenes and this distinction from Aristeides, who had neither the desire nor the possibility to take into account the social and political conditions of his time. When Metochites uses the term πράγματα in *Byzantios*, however, he appears to mean something more than the material conditions of contemporary life or even its political and social dimensions. Instead, πρᾶγμα refers to a concrete reality. In this case, it is likely a reality more coloured by the Platonic theory of ideas as the ultimate rationale, the true essence of all things, rather than by the real condition of Byzantium in Metochites' time. It is no accident that Metochites is reminded of Herodicus of Selymbria, whom Plato presents in the *Republic* as an example of a long but futile life deprived of any inner meaning.[41] Once more, Metochites discusses the value of a περιουσία of all good things safeguarded by a real life,[42] even if that life is rather short. Metochites speaks about the glorious life afforded by those πράγματα,[43] giving the impression that he has in mind only the external circumstances of life, employing the metaphor of life as a theatre: the citizens of Constantinople live in the middle of the theatre of the world and thus can draw the attention of all other people towards themselves. That life in Constantinople is described as a life full of light, while life without the privileges afforded its inhabitants is described as the life of men imprisoned inside the earth, deprived of any light, who resemble the blind,[44] once more recalls Plato, who used the famous allegory of the cave to describe the life of men who lacked the privileges of real knowledge.[45]

It is partially correct to argue that Metochites did not employ these images consciously. Metochites did not write *Byzantios* as a systematic philosophical or theological treatise. He merely composed the speech as an expression of his inner thoughts, to be understood only by those initiated into his way of thinking. No systematic exposition of a philosophical system is to be found in *Byzantios*, but Metochites' readings and his philosophical inclinations are evident in every passage of the speech. This can be demonstrated by even a cursory comparison of *Byzantios* with *Ethikos*, which is a more systematic exposition of its author's teachings on human life. Several images of *Byzantios* – for example, the contemplation (ἐποπτεία) of nature, the contemplative life, the theatre of life, even the image of the market – are drawn from *Ethikos* and reworked somewhat to fit the differing context. The result is that the characteristics referring to the contemplative life are transferred to the active life of the citizens of Constantinople. Thus, Metochites spiritualizes the involvement of a citizen with the πράγματα, the affairs of his city, the main component of an active life, to such an extent that the active life is transformed into a peculiar form of the contemplative life. The crux of *Byzantios* is that the abandonment of the contemplative life, so much deplored by Metochites in *Ethikos*, was more than rewarded by his involvement in the reality of his native city; the change in course gave him the opportunity to contemplate the affairs of the city as he would have contemplated the eternal truths, the πράγματα, the laws of nature, had he remained a philosopher detached from the real things. In this way, consciously or unconsciously, Metochites transforms the active life into its opposite, into a peculiar form of the contemplative life.

It seems that Metochites took the Platonic ideal of the philosopher-king quite seriously. *Byzantios* may be considered the theoretical documentation, though in a rather oblique form, of that ideal. It is evident that Metochites wanted to present himself as the ideal man of action, one sensitive to the needs of the human intellect and who managed to combine the requirements of his profession with the philosophical investigation of the mysteries of the world. That was one of the numerous masks Metochites wore during his career, but also the mask that successfully combined and represented the various other masks he donned at various times. It is a mask that reveals no internal contradictions and is coherent, combining the mask of the intellectual and of the man of action in a dialectic manner. It creates a self-image that appears to take into account the various traits of Metochites' 'personality' detectable in his writings and reconciles them to a certain extent, smoothing the dichotomy between the contemplative and active life so pointed in *Ethikos*. The self-image presented in *Byzantios* may be regarded as another mask alongside the others employed by Metochites, but without doubt, it was closer to his heart than all the images of himself he had previously sketched.

Chapter 9

CODA – NATURE AND BEING: ELUSIVE CONCEPTS

'Nature' and 'being' are two important terms and concepts in Metochites' works. Like other elements of his writing – such as his ambivalence in evaluations of the contemplative life versus the active life – their use is illustrative of his elusiveness. In some cases, he appears to state a preference for the life of the mind, but in others he seeks to justify the life of the politician in his city; ultimately, however, he seems to prefer a combination of the two ways of life. The same tack is to be observed in his evaluations of nature and being. Metochites seems to give different answers to the question of whether nature or being should be viewed positively.

Nature versus law

It might seem preposterous to try to determine what the term *physis* meant to a Byzantine writer of this later period and even more preposterous to suggest that said author attempted to express his innovative views by manipulating the various meanings attributable to the term. It is, however, worth attempting with Metochites, a writer not averse to innovation in his works.

Following the philosophical tradition of his time, Metochites employs *physis* in an ambiguous manner. It generally denotes nature in its entirety – that is, the created world – and in this context, it carries positive connotations. Metochites only rarely employs the term in this manner and actually seems to avoid using it in the sense of the entirety of creation, of both heaven and earth. One of the rare exceptions to this is found in Poem 10, on the science of harmonics, where the author uses it to assert that a 'harmonic disposition' exists in all natural things as well as those things invented by wise men through art.[1] There is another interesting passage in the *Miscellanea* where Metochites, discussing the advantages of contemplation of the world, argues that the wise man participates in the 'feast of the created nature and its miracle-workings'.[2] This passage is rather similar to one in *Ethikos* (ch. 54), where Metochites praises the contemplative life, identifying it with the contemplation of 'beings'. This is hardly unusual: Christian writers, though denying that nature was an independent entity, accepted it as a positive force guided by the Creator. In the mid-thirteenth century, Emperor Theodore II

Laskaris saw nature as a unifying force safeguarding the functioning and cohesion of the universe.[3] Metochites is an heir to a long-established theological tradition,[4] but at the same time being quite innovative. Like certain Western writers of the twelfth century, Metochites perceives the universe as an entity composed of diverse elements and governed by an all-encompassing divine power.[5] This is not a mere triviality or literary topos. Metochites was an ardent student of the mathematical sciences of the quadrivium as well as an pioneer in astronomy, so in his case, adoration of nature is combined in one person with a scientific curiosity, something heretofore unseen in Byzantium. In *Byzantios*, Metochites discreetly refers to the 'world-soul', an idea closely connected to nature by authors during the Western renaissance of the twelfth century.[6] In *Ethikos*, Metochites presents man as a microcosm, an idea capable of giving birth to both contemplation and science.[7]

In most cases, however, when Metochites employs the term 'nature' (φύσις) in a cosmological sense, it denotes earthly phenomena, as opposed to celestial phenomena, and has certain negative connotations. Following philosophical tradition,[8] Metochites believes that while the unchangeable and eternally functioning laws of mathematics govern celestial phenomena, earthly phenomena – or more properly, phenomena of the sub-lunar world – are determined by the laws of physics, which in lacking the consistency of the laws of mathematics are unpredictable and changeable. This opposition between the laws governing the celestial sphere versus the laws governing earthly phenomena led Metochites to view mathematics as superior to physics, contrary to his opponent Nikephoros Choumnos.[9]

The same dichotomy appears when the term *physis* denotes human nature in general. In most cases, true to Christian, and especially the ascetic, tradition, Metochites presents human nature as something negative,[10] something that needs to cast off by the virtuous man who strives to reach God and attain the blessedness he has promised all true believers. This meaning appears primarily in Metochites' hagiographical works. Such a position is hardly surprising. The saints fought against the limitations of human nature, and by overcoming human passions, left behind their sinful self and attained sanctity. Human nature as an adversarial force that requires constant struggle to overcome is not, however, the only connotation of the *physis* when denoting human nature in general.

In Metochites works, *physis* also has an overtly positive meaning: it is something given by God to man that distinguishes humans from other animals, or in other words, a special gift to the species; it is thus closely connected to the rational part of the human soul.[11] This meaning is especially prominent in *Ethikos*, one of Metochites' most secular works. There he solemnly declares that even if in some cases the life of the mind is accompanied by misfortunes and accidents that destroy man's happiness, he prefers the nobility of nature – that is, the gift of reason.[12] He even urges the young man to whom *Ethikos* is supposedly addressed to also prefer this life, instead of one deprived of prudence, care and acumen, resulting in living like the irrational beasts, without sorrows, neither thinking of nor understanding anything of human affairs that occur in 'nature'.[13] It is evident that Metochites identifies reason with the noblest part of human nature. He goes so far as to call both reason (λόγος) and mind (νοῦς) the 'king of nature', who imposes the best regime inside the soul of man.[14] The Platonic undertones of this passage are evident.

At the beginning of *Ethikos*, Metochites clarifies that the most important part of human nature is man's ability to attain knowledge through the proper use of reason. Therefore, those unable to employ the rational part of their nature are to be condemned.[15] Also warranting condemnation, however, are all those who deny the value of pleasure, an integral part of human nature.[16] Metochites does not deny that human nature has certain inherent 'mutinous impulses', but reason keeps these in check.[17] Nature is something unpredictable, connected to matter.[18] He even asserts to his readers that 'nature is something anomalous, the body filling her with innumerable changes'.[19] He praises men able to vanquish their nature, almost certainly having in mind men like Joseph the Philosopher, Gregory of Bulgaria and St Demetrius: 'Full of pride, they rise very high and triumph over nature, to which they did not yield at all or succumb or flee or shame. I would say instead that these people are the fairest prizes of nature or its admired statues, who resemble the firstborn of a more complete, flourishing and solid expression.'[20] Metochites was quick to 'correct' his previous statement: nature was not truly an adversary of those men; indeed, their exemplary personalities are to be considered nature's most important products.

The same ambivalence appears in the evaluation of 'life according to nature', a philosophical term previously employed by the Stoics. In *Gnomikai Semeioseis*, Metochites applies the expression to the simple and unpretentious life led by the Scythian nomads, who are assessed as men living outside society and therefore not forced to conform to the evils of civilization:

> From the beginning Scythians have been used to a light, easy and painless way of life, which is devoid of any troubles; that life has no point of contact with the life of other men; therefore, leading this simple life according to nature, they have denounced all sorts of complicated thoughts, intrigues, judicial procedures, arguments and counter-arguments, plots, defences and calumniations, and all human fascinations.[21]

Here Metochites greatly appreciates that no judges, orators, lawyers or attorneys are to be found in Scythian society,[22] but this is not the case in Oration 7, the second *basilikos*, where instead he castigates the nomadic way of life in harsh terms: '[T]hey do not know justice, they have no idea of any proper state, they do not know any laws, any conventional way of life's organization, any elementary harmony and setting-up of a proper society, they are unaware of the laws of nature, they know nothing good.'[23] The contrast is striking. Here Metochites, referring to the Ottoman Turks, busy pillaging the eastern provinces of the empire in the late thirteenth century, stresses that the nomads lack any sense of the elementary laws of nature. While in the private *Semeioseis Gnomikai* Metochites gave free rein to his thoughts concerning the 'noble savage', who lives according to the laws of nature,[24] in the more solemn second *basilikos* he condemns him for the same exact reason: not living according to the laws of nature. This dichotomy also appears in

Oration 8, *Presbeutikos*, Metochites' account of his diplomatic mission to Serbia on behalf of Emperor Andronikos II. In this work, an amalgam of two literary genres – a *presbeutikos logos* and a *Hodoiporikon* – Metochites, adapting himself to the requirements of both genres, speaks in the first person.[25] Reporting the accusations of the Serbs against the Byzantines in direct speech, Metochites wrote as follows:

> [T]he solemn oaths to which we had faith disappear as if they have been never exchanged at all or as if they were exchanged long ago; and the excuse might appear rather plausible, and the pretence might be rather serious and noble, but the oaths will be violated and completely broken, after they have cheated us for a short while like in the theatre or in dreams; our opponents are very clever and quibblers.[26]

Metochites' response to the Serbs' accusations is significant: '[N]othing is sacred to them, no bad thought, speech or act is abhorrent to them; they pay no attention either to the divine laws, or to the providence of God, or to human justice; they do not believe in it.'[27] Metochites' criticism in *Presbeutikos* resembles his objections to the nomadic way of life in the second *basilikos*. Without saying so explicitly, Metochites considers the Serbs to be barbarians like the Turks, who do not share the values of Byzantine civilization. On the other hand, the Serbs' objections to the Byzantines' attitude is based on the conception of the 'noble savage': civilized but mischievous men cheat and destroy the innocent children of nature, who are unable to understand the intricacies of civilization and fall to the traps of their enemies. If unaware of Metochites' praise of the simple and noble life in *Semeioseis Gnomikai*, one might consider his criticism of the 'natural' ways of Turks and Serbs unequivocal, but this is not the whole truth. Metochites seems to have been aware of the advantages of the simple but noble life of the 'uncivilized' peoples, and he was willing to view his own way of life in a critical manner. His whole mission to Serbia is interpreted based on this perspective: the Byzantines represent the civilized and articulate society, while the stubborn and reckless Serbs represent the noble savages' primitive but robust society, the advantages of which Metochites is somehow ready to accept.[28]

Discussing the idea of nature during the twelfth-century renaissance, M.-D. Chenu pointed out that according to certain representatives of this current of Western thought, man can break free of the material universe through the metaphysical part of his nature, but at the same time remain a part of the latter.[29] *Mutatis mutandis*, the same may be affirmed of Metochites. His thinking is not a total break from the bonds of medieval speculation about nature and the universe. Man's bond with God was not fully severed. Metochites stood as testimony to this tension as experienced in fourteenth-century Byzantium. A similar line of argumentation can be found in the works of Michael Psellos in the eleventh century.[30] On the one hand, there is no doubt that the positive evaluation of nature, for both Psellos and Metochites, is one of criticism (veiled to a greater or lesser extent) of established Byzantine church doctrines. On the other hand, the negative evaluation of nature by Metochites might in some cases explain his tendency to be elusive in his evaluations of the world outside himself and in the way he represents himself in his writings. This can be seen more clearly by examining Metochites' evaluation of being.

The value of being: Metochites' ambivalent answer to a perennial problem

Essay 58 of Metochites' *Miscellanea* deals, unusually for a Byzantine text, with a perennial philosophical issue: 'Whether it is better for man to be born or not born.' In the old-school fashion of the *progymnasmata*, Metochites quotes the arguments of those who deny the value of human life and then attempts to refute them.

Metochites starts with the famous quote from Ecclesiastes 4.3 – 'better than both is he who has not yet been, who has not seen the evil that is done under the sun'[31] – and a dictum of Pseudo-Plato from *Epinomis* (974a3–7) affirming that no man would have wished to live once more, fearing to once again experience the troubles of life.[32] He also adduces an argument from Homer: '[F]or every good thing there are two sorrows.'[33] He admits that human life is full of innumerable grave sorrows, some caused by nature, others brought about through deliberate action; regardless of one's choices in life, it is his due to suffer. Metochites then denies the validity of these arguments; movement and progression of being are preferable to absence of being and motion. The attribute of God most applicable to him is 'essence'. All human beings long for life; they cling to it with all their might. A long and happy life is generally regarded as the most valued thing a man can have. Through the continuation of human life, divine providence has arranged for man to share in the eternity of being. It is God's natural goodness that endows man with the gift of life, his divine energy working within man. It is evident to all that the greatest gift in life is essence combined with contemplation, allowing humans to admire the marvels of creation, which resembles a great theatre. In short, only through existence can man enjoy the gifts of God and perceive of him and his nature.

Metochites concludes his essay by asserting not only that human life is just a dream and a theatrical performance, but that it is most profitable for man to abandon this performance as soon as possible and be transferred to paradise, where the enjoyment of eternal bliss awaits. Here, once more, is the ambiguity so prominent in Metochites' writings. While he seems to defend human existence and life on earth, in the end, Metochites changes tack, defending the eternal existence of human life in paradise. In doing so, he even rejects the value of human life, declaring: '[S]urely this is the best fortune for us, to be born into this world and after a short while be transferred from here in a noble manner, whenever it befalls us, and after we have passed our lives here behaving well, and thenceforth to take possession of that other, unchanging world.'[34] This, however, contradicts his initial statement that a good and long life is preferable to a short one. Metochites made a similar statement to the foregoing in *Byzantios*.[35]

The issue Metochites addresses recalls the famous line from *Hamlet*: 'To be or not to be, that is the question.' Hubert Dreyfus and Sean Dorrance Kelly, commenting on this verse, rightly observe: '[T]he very idea that he [Shakespeare] understands this as a choice open to him indicates that his culture no longer takes it for granted that God determines these fundamental facts of our existence.'[36] The idea is that human life is something miserable, defying rational explanation, and that it would be better not to be born at all rather than suffer life's innumerable calamities. Sophocles also railed against being born and recommended dying as soon as possible once born.[37] Sophocles was in all probability influenced by verses of Theognis.[38] Euripides, one of the most pessimistic classical authors, describes the miseries of human life in the lost tragedy *Cresphontes*, considering those alive to be unlucky and the dead to be lucky.[39] It is possible that Euripides was influenced by Herodotus' description of the customs of certain barbaric tribes that organized feasts upon the death of their members and mourned whenever a baby was born.[40] Pseudo-Plato quoted the passage from Euripides in the dialogue *Axiochus* (368a), which contains similar passages from other Greek poets deploring human life and praising death as the only solution to human problems. Many Greek authors of late antiquity shared this pessimistic approach to life, the most prominent among them being Dio Chrysostom, a favourite of Metochites. Dio Chrysostom touched on the subject in Oration 23, in which he examines the question of whether the happy man may exist. The passage from Ecclesiastes that Metochites quoted on the matter is just another example of this *contemptus mundi*.

The only positive value that Metochites attributes to life on earth is the possibility of contemplating the marvels of the universe, seeming to adopt Aristotle's view that a life of contemplation is the best possible life.[41] This admission does not, however, disparage or dismiss the impression a typical Byzantine might have been left with after reading an essay denying the value of life. In pointing out that human life is a stage towards salvation, Metochites took care not to offend the theological sensibilities of those readers who might have objected to a low estimation of earthly life. By subtly undermining the necessity of this stage and by denying the value of longevity, however, Metochites turned one of the most important Byzantine convictions on its head. Metochites' devaluation of two key concepts – that of nature and of being, though relative – aids in understanding his elusiveness: Metochites was unable to find his place in the world, the value of which he entertained serious doubts. With that, it became inevitable that the images he created of himself at various stages in his career would lack inner coherence and appear contradictory. By adopting the various masks in his writings, Metochites imitates life itself, for if being is a grand performance, the life of the individual is a performance as well.

CONCLUSION: METOCHITES, A PHILOSOPHER OF HIS TIME

Elusiveness was a distinct characteristic of the true philosopher in the medieval and early modern eras. Leo Strauss called it 'an intelligible necessity for all times'.[1] Philosophers, to shield themselves from personal danger, concealed their true views. Metochites was no exception. The way he chose to present himself in his works highlights this elusiveness and resulted in some startling contradictions, through which he projected certain images of himself, or masks, concealing certain aspects of his personality and thinking.

In addition to employing masks to allow elusiveness, Metochites also used his own theory of life as a theatrical performance. Pointing to others' elusiveness, he painted the contradictions of ancient authors as deliberate attempts to conceal their true views, and in his own work, adopted devices to create images of himself and other people to meet the expectations or the limitations of his audience. Preoccupied with having rejected the contemplative life for an active life, serving the emperor, Metochites examines both himself and other people – among them Joseph Rhakendytes, in Oration 17, and Gregory of Bulgaria, in Poem 3 – from this perspective. As a pattern, it helped him mould the images he projected in a most effective way. Sometimes, however, he issued praise for a life of action. In Oration 4, he presents St Demetrius as a successful young statesman, while in the autobiographical Poem 1 he expresses his gratitude both to God and to Emperor Andronikos II for promoting his career tending to affairs of state.

Metochites also attempted to propose a new model for the art of discourse. This constitutes another piece in his pattern of crafting self-images and others, this one evident by examining Orations 6, the funeral speech for Gregory of Nazianuzus, Orations 13 and 14, inveighing against Nikephoros Choumnos, and Oration 18, comparing Demosthenes and Aelius Aristeides. Metochites bristled at blindly following the precepts of his contemporaries, who advised their fellow orators to avoid potential stylistic, logical and grammatical traps of their art by using as their models those ancient authors who employed an easier, more accessible style. Instead, he preferred Thucydides to those authors whose style was smoother and easier, and he made no secret of his admiration for Gregory of Nazianzus. He acknowledged that Aelius Aristeides' writings were proper models for his contemporaries, but an attentive reader of Metochites would understand that he believed Demosthenes to be far superior to Aristeides. Metochites' view on the superior quality of Thucydides' writing explains his preference for a style that was difficult even for his contemporaries.

At the same time, Metochites' adversary Nikephoros Choumnos argued that no room was left for any contemporary author to create anything new; the great orators of the past had already accomplished everything.[2] Metochites' view was largely similar; he admitted in the prologue to the *Miscellanea* that it was impossible to use speech in any new way whatsoever, since everything possible had already been anticipated by others.[3] Despite this, Metochites was more audacious than Choumnos. His 'innovation' in the art of discourse, however, was imitating the most difficult authors of antiquity. Did Metochites not realize that this represented a more conservative approach than that of his opponents? In any case, in Orations 6 and 18, referring to authors of antiquity – that is, to Gregory of Nazianzus and to Demosthenes and Aristeides – he projected an image of himself as an audacious writer not hesitant to break with the literary conventions of his time, all the while donning the mask of a traditionalist here and there by offering lip-service to the Byzantine tradition of rhetorical discourse.

Metochites' work exposes that his innermost desire was to justify his 'abandonment' of his literary studies and to find a way to project an image of himself that combined his intellectual pursuits and his political profession. This is best illustrated by Oration 10, *Ethikos*, and Oration 11, *Byzantios*. Metochites, an admirer and apologist of the contemplative life, did not share the prevailing conception of it – that is, monasticism – in his day. He revealed no particular fondness of traditional monastic contemplation and may have even found the lack of education characteristic of most Byzantine monks repugnant. His excessive commendation of the value of secular learning was probably rooted in doubts regarding contemporary monasticism. He most certainly preferred the ancient Greeks' *vita contemplativa,* studying the world and its eternal laws. That aside, Metochites freely admitted that his political preoccupations had prohibited him from devoting himself to his studies to the degree he wished. Quite often he projected the image of a man sorry about this outcome, but at the same time, he did not agree with those who rejected the active life altogether. Despite Metochites' solemn statements on the impossibility of combining a life of contemplation with politics, at heart he was not averse to such an idea.

Metochites subtly explored a combination of the contemplative life and the active life in *Byzantios*. There he presented living in Constantinople and actively participating in the city's social and political life – Metochites being the citizen of Constantinople par excellence – as the ideal means for contemplating the mysteries of the world, because Constantinople represented a mirror of the world (like many cities before it).[4] In short, his involvement in the active life of the citizens of Constantinople, as described in *Byzantios*, more than compensates for his 'abandonment' of the contemplative life, as he admits to having done in *Ethikos*. In this way, Metochites reconciles the contradictions between the images of himself that he projects in *Ethikos* and his other works. Being in theory an ardent defender of the contemplative life, he transformed the life of a politician in the late Byzantine Empire into a form of the contemplative life, because such a politician supposedly had the opportunity to explore the mysteries of the whole world from the vantage point of the empire's command post – the capital of Constantinople. After all, Metochites seems to have been convinced, to a certain degree, of the value of the combination of the two ways of life despite his professed doubts, relativism and elusiveness. It is the only image he projects of himself that presents as cohesive, well balanced and reasonable, reconciling to a certain extent the various other images of himself encountered in his writings. That combining of the two lives and, more significantly, the way he does it was certainly an innovation in his day. The image drawn in *Ethikos* of the intellectual deploring the abandonment of his literary studies is faint by comparison, a mask Metochites may have used simply as a trick. It is devoid of any autobiographical value.

With the mask employed in *Byzantios*, Metochites, despite his notorious elusiveness, reveals a basic aspect of his ideology, or maybe of his theology in a broad sense: he viewed the smallest details of everyday life through the prism of the eternal truths of the world and nature. *Byzantios* is an impressive treatise indeed, but despite its author's inventiveness, it is a thoroughly medieval piece of work. The typological interpretation of Constantinople – as a mirror of the world and governed by the eternal laws of nature – is the most eloquent testimony to Metochites' commitment to the Platonic understanding of reality, which remained dominant in the Middle Ages. Far from offering a realistic picture of Constantinople, Metochites creates a conceit (or mask) out of the real city that corresponds to his inner needs and dreams. Metochites likely considered his conception of the life of a politician as another form of the contemplative life to be innovative. He must have been quite proud of the concept, but with it he remained a prisoner of the preconceptions of his time. Therefore, one must be careful not to confuse Metochites' self as presented in his works, autobiographical or not, with the modern concept of man's own self.

Far from providing an opportunity to discover the development of Metochites' own personality and conscience as a process of overcoming the traumatic experiences of childhood or as a harmonization of different experiences that take place in one's deeper consciousness, Metochites presents his own self as an idealistic reflection of certain eternal truths, or rather, as the realization of some of the eternal possibilities granted by God to human nature. His ceaseless attempts to interpret his own life as a constant wavering between the contemplative and the practical life makes that clear. The Platonic understanding of reality prevented Metochites and others in the medieval era from presenting true portraits of themselves free of religious undertones. In Metochites' works, one cannot discern the nuances of feeling and the power of self-examination found in modern autobiography. Metochites considered his life a realization of an eternal exemplum that went beyond himself. He endeavoured to manipulate the facts of his own life to adapt them to that exemplum, which helps explain the heavy rhetorizing in his works.

Like all medieval authors who spoke about themselves, Metochites idealized the events of his life to present them as further proof of the validity of the eternal truths that he believed determined everything in this world. He accomplished this using the tools provided by his rhetorical education, but this should not discourage examination of these rhetorical pictures to try to discover or grasp his true disposition and persuasions, although it is not always possible to fully do so.

Metochites had a generally pessimistic view of the affairs of this world. The way he discusses the issue of being versus not being clearly indicates this. Metochites, unconvinced of the value of living on this earth, tries to avoid the trap posed by this question, which required a positive answer from a Christian, by insisting on the value of eternal life, with which virtuous men are rewarded after death. This allows him to withhold a positive evaluation of life on this earth. In this instance, his conviction led him to a certain relativism, which makes it difficult to identify his true self under the multiple masks he employed during his long literary career. It is a relativism that somewhat undermines his Platonic convictions as well as the picture of the 'contemplative' politician he draws in *Byzantios*. A man entertaining doubts about the true value of being is prone to constantly reversing previously held views and changing masks.

Metochites was not a systematic philosopher in the modern sense of the term. He had no interest in comprehensively discussing certain philosophical questions, adducing all the arguments pertaining to them in a systematic manner. In some cases, he preferred to provide answers that may not have corresponded to his true convictions, restrained by a theocratic society and its servants, who kept a vigilant watch on intellectuals fond of philosophical innovations and thought experiments. In such instances, he wears the mask most appropriate to the circumstances. In certain cases, however, he subtly subverts those very masks by consciously contradicting himself. In this way, he challenges the attentive reader to discern his real views by patiently comparing the various and even contradictory answers he has given to questions in differing circumstances and in trying to discover his true self under the masks. This is how Metochites' works should be interpreted – that is, as his attempts to create certain masks for himself. One must take those contradictions as intentional and serious.

Metochites did not consider himself a modern lobbyist or an aesthete, but a serious philosopher and a politician who managed to remain a philosopher amid turbulent times. He lived in a world whose values had been severely undermined. His relativism and the high degree of elusiveness in his self-representation were by-products of this reality. He intensely sought to find a solution to the perennial problem of the intellectual's place in the fluid and often quite inimical world surrounding him. His way was to take part in the social life of his times without losing the perspective of a philosopher. This is what he describes in *Byzantios*, but was there such a possibility in the declining Byzantium of the early fourteenth century? Metochites seems to have thought so. He might have been wrong, but at least he tried to offer something new to his contemporaries. That may be considered as his most important legacy.

Ihor Ševčenko long ago casually noticed Metochites' employment of certain masks.[5] This eminent Byzantinist was the first to draw the scholarly community's attention to the importance of Metochites' writings and initiate proper philological study of them. It was inevitable that some of Metochites' internal contradictions would not escape Ševčenko's notice, but he did not proceed any further, sometimes falling victim to the biographical approach to Metochites' work and taking at face value his statements about his misfortune of abandoning the contemplative life. This book shows how masks were an integral part of Metochites' projected self-image. To a certain extent, this stemmed from the rhetorical education that Metochites received. Convention required all Byzantine authors to display this rhetorical 'ethos', which enhanced adaptability to various circumstances, but Metochites took it a step further. He wore masks not only when discharging his public duties, but also when engaged in discussions with public audiences or his close friends about the perennial problems occupying Byzantine minds, such as the problem of the contemplative life, the value of being, the value of politics and so on. This is a sign of someone seeking a proper identity, of a self constantly constructed and reconstructed, compelled to reconcile his inner compulsions and the necessities of society, negotiating, so to speak, between himself, his rhetorical education and his social environment. Despite sometimes exhibiting a grandiose sense of self in aggressively trying to prove superiority, Metochites may have recognized his ongoing changing of masks as a never-to-succeed yearning to project an image of his self as a unified whole.

Metochites' quest should be interpreted as a social phenomenon. The once-powerful Byzantine state had disintegrated during his lifetime and with it also fell an old but powerful ideology that provided the Byzantines with a deeply held sense of identity in its social and cultural stereotypes. Metochites, a sensitive and clever observer of reality, could never find a mask that allowed him to consistently communicate with his audience and readers. The mask of the traditional contemplative man of his society, the monk, did not fit him; he was too educated and clever to adopt such an obsolete instrument in the long term. The mask of the successful politician failed to fit as well; Metochites was painfully aware that the state was no longer governable. Even the age-old mask of the sage contemplating the marvels of the world in a state of perpetual serenity proved to be inadequate; Metochites the active politician knew such a mask to be unrealistic.

In a sense, Metochites had lost his orientation. At odds with his social and cultural environment, he found himself without a proper role to play on the stage of this life. Putting on the mask of the active politician contemplating the world through governing the affairs of Constantinople might have appeared to him as his last refuge.

APPENDIX: WORKS BY THEODORE METOCHITES

Below is a brief overview of each group of Metochites' works.

Orations

The orations of Metochites are preserved in Vindobonensis phil. gr 95, which was likely copied under the supervision of the author himself. This collection probably represents the entirety of Metochites' rhetorical production from his youth until the end of his career. It is unknown whether all his rhetorical works were included in it, though the answer is most likely negative.

The main issue involving the manuscript is whether the orations appear in chronological order. Ihor Ševčenko studied the matter thoroughly and concluded that the works were, indeed, copied chronologically. No one has yet been able to credibly refute Ševčenko's arguments, which are well founded and convincing.

Oration 1	*Nikaeus*, encomium of the city of Nicaea
Oration 2	For St Marina
Oration 3	For the archangel Michael and the angels
Oration 4	For St Demetrius
Oration 5	First *basilikos*, praise of Emperor Andronikos II Palaiologos
Oration 6	For St Gregory of Nazianzus
Oration 7	Second *basilikos*, praise of Emperor Andronikos II Palaiologos
Oration 8	*Presbeutikos*, account of Metochites' diplomatic mission to Serbia
Oration 9	Funeral speech for Empress Theodora Palaiologina
Oration 10	*Ethikos*, protreptic speech on education
Oration 11	*Byzantios*, for Constantinople
Oration 12	For Michael the New Martyr of Egypt
Oration 13	First speech against Nikephoros Choumnos
Oration 14	Second speech against Nikephoros Choumnos
Oration 15	Prologue to an imperial chrysoboullon
Oration 16	Funeral speech for Loukas, abbot of the monastery of Chora
Oration 17	Funeral speech for Joseph Rhakendytes (Joseph the Philosopher)
Oration 18	Comparison of Demosthenes and Aelius Aristeides
Oration 19	For St John of Didymoteichon

Readers are referred to *Theodorus Metochites: Orationes* (2019), edited by Ioannis Polemis and Eleni Kaltsogianni.[1]

The orations may be divided into the following groups:

1. For members of the imperial family: Orations 5, 7 and 9
2. For funerals of his friends: Orations 16 and 17
3. For cities: Orations 1 and 11
4. For saints: Orations 2, 3, 4, 6, 12 and 19
5. Occasional: Orations 8 and 15
6. Antirrhetical: Orations 13 and 14
7. Non-rhetorical: Orations 10 and 18

At first glance, Metochites' rhetorical works are conventional examples of the main literary genres of Byzantine rhetoric. Metochites took great care to collect all his speeches to save them for posterity, as did most scholars of his time – such as Gregory of Cyprus, Nikephoros Choumnos and Thomas Magistros – and some of the past – for example, Nikephoros Basilakes and Michael Choniates. His orations are what one would expect a high-ranking Byzantine official to write in an effort to bolster his reputation and strengthen his ties to the imperial family. Time and again, Metochites praises Andronikos II for his generosity to his people and his care of the state. Half of his orations refer in one way or another to Andronikos II and his entourage. The majority of those collected in Vindobonensis phil. gr 95 were probably delivered to an audience. One may imagine Metochites presenting his Orations 5 and 7 before the entire imperial court. The same applies to Oration 1, *Nikaeus*, an encomium for the city of Nicaea, and Oration 9, the funeral praise of Empress Theodora, delivered during the service.

Metochites may have presented some of his orations on their feast day, although this is not indicated in any of the texts. The lavish praise of Andronikos II in Oration 12 suggests that it was delivered in front of the emperor himself. The same is likely for Oration 2, for St Marina, but less so for Oration 3, for archangel Michael and the angels, Oration 4, for St Demetrius, and Oration 19, for St John of Didymoteichon. Oration 8, *Presbeutikos*, was written in Serbia and sent to a high-ranking official in Constantinople, possibly Nikephoros Choumnos. Oration 16, the funeral speech for Loukas, abbot of Chora, may have been delivered in front of the monks by someone else, since Metochites composed it while in exile outside Constantinople and sent it to the monks.

Metochites wrote Oration 15, a short preamble to an imperial chrysoboullon, upon the emperor's order. The text in the manuscript is incomplete, and its position in the collection is puzzling. Metochites undertook the compilation of his original orations during his time as megas logothetes, and he may have penned Oration 15 to conclude the collection; actually, this is far from certain.

Metochites wrote Orations 16–19 after falling from power. He sent Oration 17, the funeral speech for Joseph Rhakendytes, to a friend of his who had asked for it. It was probably never delivered before an audience. Orations 10, a protreptic speech, 13 and 14, challenging Nikephoros Choumnos, and 18, an essay on Demosthenes and Aelius Aristeides, have a more private character, but this does not preclude the possibility of their having been delivered at a *theatra*, a small private gatherings of scholars who were expected to listen to an author read his text and then offer opinions on it.

Justifiably included in this collection are the orations that are somewhat unconventional and, properly speaking, cannot be considered epideictic or panegyrical, such as Oration 10, *Ethikos*, and Oration 18; other scholars have also included among the epideictic orations Metochites' speeches of a more private character that were not intended to be delivered in front of large audiences. Close readings of some of these texts reveal much more than one might expect.

Paraphrases of Aristotle and the Stoikheiosis Astronomike

One group of Metochites' works is technical in nature, paraphrasing the Aristotelian treatises *De anima*, *Physica* and *Parva Naturalia*. He wrote them between 1320 and 1325 – that is, later in his career – for the sake of a limited audience interested in Aristotelian studies. On them, the late Byzantine polymath George Gemistos Pletho wrote, 'Let them say whatever they wish; no one is equal to Metochites, the Megas logothetes.' Most of them are either inadequately published or wholly unpublished.

Almost half of his *Stoikheiosis Astronomike*, an introduction to the science of astronomy, has been recently published, better informing everyone on a text that made Metochites so proud.[2] It is divided into two books and written on the basis of the Great Syntax. In writing it, Metochites also took into account the work of Theon.

Byzantine astronomers and scholars admired Metochites. Nikephoros Gregoras was grateful to his teacher for introducing him to the arcane doctrines of astronomy, while John Chortasmenos praised Metochites' attempt to provide his contemporaries with a concise version of the great astronomers' works. The text was written after 1316 – when Metochites took lessons with the astronomer Manuel Bryennios, who introduced him to astronomy – but before 1320.

Poems

Metochites probably wrote his poems between the death of Empress Eirene Palaiologina, in 1317, which he clearly refers to in Poem 7, and his own death. One or two of them may have been written before Eirene's passing. In any case, he composed the bulk of them after 1321. Metochites produced twenty long poems, written in the dactylic verse of Homer, which the Byzantines generally avoided, preferring instead the much more manageable iambic verse when writing long poems. Metochites dared to compose almost ten thousand dactylic verses in an idiosyncratic language, full of Homeric reminiscences, echoes from the various poems of Gregory of Nazianzus, and several wrong forms of obscure or archaic words transformed to fit the requirements of the verse. The last eight poems of the collection, which is preserved in Parisinus gr. 1776, a manuscript probably composed under Metochites' supervision, are addressed to the author himself, who wished to continue the tradition of the poems from Greek antiquity titled *Eis heauton*.

In the poems, the author examines the burning issue of the instability of human fate and attempts to explain the trials he has endured over the course of his life. He discusses the mysteries of divine providence and the judgement of God, who postpones our punishment or reward for our own profit. Metochites gives a pessimistic account of his life, full of great glories but also reversals and bitter disappointments. Each poem concludes with a prayer from the author to the Lord or the Virgin, protector of the monastery of Chora. The same applies to the two first poems of the collection, which may also be considered prayers of the author. The tone in these is more optimistic and triumphal. In Poem 1, Metochites presents a short accounting of his career, which culminated in the restoration of the monastery of Chora, in his view his greatest achievement. The tone of Poem 2 is sombre: he asks the Virgin to intercede on his behalf with her son, as a personal reward for his toiling for Chora's restoration. The poem offers a detailed description of the entire monastic complex.

Poems 3, 4, 11, 12 and 13 are poetic letters that Metochites addressed to various friends – Gregory, former archbishop of Bulgaria, Nikephoros Gregoras, the brothers Theodore and Nikephoros Xanthopouloi, and Leon Bardales, his kinsman. Some of the commonplaces found in Byzantine letters are also encountered here. In Poems 4 and 12, Metochites gives an account of his writings, with personal comments on them, providing his first evaluation of his own scholarly efforts. Poems 5 and 6 deal with St Athanasios and the three great prelates of the Byzantine church – Basil the Great, Gregory of Nazianzus and John Chrysostom. They resemble Metochites' orations for the saints preserved in Vindobonensis phil. gr. 95.

Poem 10 is a peculiar piece of literature – a praise of the science of harmony. Metochites begins with a general introduction, justifying study of the four mathematical sciences and explaining their superiority to physics, and then offers a brief description of the main characteristics of the laws of harmony, in all probability taken from Manuel Bryennios' textbook on the subject, and concludes with a majestic presentation of the way the laws of music govern the universe. There is no doubt that the poem relates to the controversy between Metochites and Nikephoros Choumnos concerning the value of physics and mathematics.

The reader is referred to *Theodorus Metochita: Carmina* (2016), an edition of the poems edited and translated by Ioannis Polemis.[3] The poems are as follows:

1. A glorification of the Lord, an autobiography of the author and a description of the restoration of the monastery of Chora
2. An address to Virgin Mary and on the monastery of Chora
3. To Gregory, archbishop of Bulgaria
4. To Nikephoros Gregoras
5. To St Athanasios of Alexandria
6. To the three prelates (Basil the Great, Gregory of Nazianzus and John Chrysostom)

7. Funeral poem for Empress Eirene Palaiologina
8. Funeral poem for Emperor Michael IX Palaiologos
9. Funeral poem for his son-in-law John Palaiologos
10. On the science of harmonics
11. To his friend Theodore Xanthopoulos
12. To his friend Nikephoros Xanthopoulos
13. To his kinsman and friend Leon Bardales

14–20. To himself [4]

Miscellanea (Semeioseis Gnomikai)

A group of Metochites' short essays on various subjects were first collected and published as *Miscellanea*, so titled by the first editors of the texts in the early nineteenth century, and later published as *Sententious Notes / Semeioseis Gnomikai*, by their modern editors. Some of the essays deal with historical subjects, others evaluate the merits and shortcomings of various authors, and still others address general social and political problems – for example, whether monarchy is preferable to democracy. Metochites also discusses the reasons for the decline of the empire and deplores the fate of the Roman state, a shadow of its former self. He even discusses metaphysical problems, such as the value, if any, of human existence. In all probability, these writings are a product of the later part of Metochites' life, or at least, the collection was published near the end of his public career. Some essays closely correspond to Metochites' orations, certain passages of which are incorporated into the essays almost verbatim. Metochites' literary model seems to have been Maximus of Tyre, an orator of the second century CE, under whose name a collection of short essays has been preserved. Maximus, like Metochites, dealt with a variety of subjects. Metochites was certainly familiar with this collection, although it was not particularly widespread in Byzantium. Of note, however, Metochites never mentions Maximus by name.

A prominent place in *Miscellanea* is accorded to Metochites' favourite authors. Some of the more interesting essays are devoted to Plato, Xenophon, Aristotle, Philo Judaeus, Josephus, Plutarch, Dio Chrysostom and Synesius of Cyrene; Metochites examines them both as thinkers and as successful authors, who may have served as models for his contemporaries. Surprisingly, Metochites does not devote a single essay to Gregory of Nazianzus, who appears to have been his literary model.

The new edition of the text has not yet been completed.[5] For the part of the text that has not yet been re-edited, see the 1821 edition, by Christian Gottried Müller and Gottlieb Kiessling.

NOTES

Introduction

1. On the Palaiologan period, see Angeliki E. Laiou, 'The Palaiologoi and the World Around Them (1261-1400)', in *The Cambridge History of the Byzantine Empire c.500-1492*, ed. J. Shepard (Cambridge: Cambridge University Press, 2008), 803-33; Angeliki E. Laiou, *Constantinople and the Latins. The Foreign Policy of Andronicus II 1282-1328*, Harvard Historical Studies 88 (Cambridge, MA: Harvard University Press, 1972); Costas N. Constantinides, *Higher education in Byzantium in the thirteenth and early fourteenth centuries (1204-ca 1310)*, Cyprus Research Centre, Texts and Studies of the History of Cyprus 11 (Nicosia: Cyprus Research Centre, 1982); Edmund B. Fryde, *The Early Palaeologan Renaissance 1261-c.1360*, The Medieval Mediterranean: Peoples, Economies and Cultures, 400-1453, 27 (Leiden: Brill, 2000).
2. The most important and pioneering presentation of Metochites' life and works remains that of Ihor Ševčenko, *Études sur la polémique entre Théodore Métochite et Nicéphore Choumnos*, Corpus Bruxellense Historiae Byzantinae, Subsidia 3 (Brussels: Byzanthion, 1962), 3-174. See also Ihor Ševčenko, 'Theodore Metochites, the Chora and the Intellectual Trends of His Time', in *The Kariye Djami*, vol. 4, *Studies in the Art of the Kariye Djami and Its Intellectual Background*, ed. P. Underwood (London: Routledge and Kegan Paul, 1975), 17-91, and Börje Bydén, *Theodore Metochites' Stoicheiosis Astronomike and the Study of Natural Philosophy and Mathematics in Early Palaiologan Byzantium*, Studia Graeca et Latina Gothoburgensia 66 (Gothenburg: Acta Universitatis Gothoburgensis, 2003), 33-8.
3. Ševčenko, *Études sur la polémique entre Théodore Métochite et Nicéphore Choumnos*, 126-44. The arguments of Kermanidis challenging the sequence are unconvincing. For them, see Markos Kermanidis *Episteme und Ästhetik der Raummodelierung in Literatur und Kunst des Theodoros Metochites: Ein frühpalaiologischer Byzantiner im Bezug zur Frühen Neuzeit*, Byzantinisches Archiv 37 (Berlin: De Gruyter, 2020), 27, n. 68.
4. See Ioannis Polemis, *Οἱ δύο βασιλικοὶ λόγοι: Εἰσαγωγή-Κριτικὴ ἔκδοση-Μετάφραση-Σημειώσεις* (Athens: Kanakis Publishers, 2007), 33-42.
5. Ioannis Polemis, ed., *Theodore Metochites: Poems. Introduction, Translation and Notes*, Corpus Christianorum in Translation 26 (Turnhout: Brepols, 2017), 9-10.
6. Smyrlis' paper is not yet in print. See Alexander Riehle, 'Literature, Politics and Manuscripts in Early Palaiologan Byzantium: Towards a Reassessment of the Choumnos-Metochites Controversy', *Travaux et Mémoires* 25, no. 1 (2021): 593, n. 12.
7. See Ioannis Polemis, *Θεόδωρος Μετοχίτης: Ἠθικὸς ἢ Περὶ παιδείας. Εἰσαγωγή-Κριτικὴ ἔκδοση-Μετάφραση-Σημειώσεις* (Athens: Kanakis Publishers, 1995), 49, n. 86.
8. See Margaret Mullett, *Theophylact of Ochrid: Reading the Letters of a Byzantine Archbishop*, Birmingham Byzantine and Ottoman Studies 2 (Aldershot: Variorum, 1997), 228.
9. Metochites: Poems, 302, Greek text 17, 259-61, and 335, Greek text 20, 176-83; Ioannis Polemis, ed., *Theodorus Metochita: Carmina*, Corpus Christianorum, Series Graeca 83 (Turnhout: Brepols, 2015), 294 and 334.

10 Ioannis Polemis and Eleni Kaltsogianni, *Theodorus Metochites: Orationes*, Bibliotheca Scriptorum Graecorum et Romanorum Teubneriana (Berlin: De Gruyter, 2019), 343 (Oration 9, 13.10–24).
11 Metochites: Orationes, 464 (Oration 11, 38.9–25). See also Metochites: Poems, 16–19.
12 Arthur M. Melzer, *Philosophy between the Lines: The Lost History of Esoteric Writing* (Chicago: University of Chicago Press, 2014), 11–52.
13 See Anthony Kaldellis, *The Argument of Psellos' Chronographia*, Studien und Texten zur Geistesgeschichte des Mittelalters 68 (Leiden: Brill, 1999), 1–22 and 34–41.
14 Krystina Kubina, *Die enkomiastische Dichtung des Manuel Philes: Form und Funktion des literarischen Lobes in der frühen Palaiologenzeit*, Byzantinisches Archiv 38 (Berlin: De Gruyter, 2020), 263.
15 Stratis Papaioannou, 'Authors (With an Excursus on Symeon Metaphrastes)', in *The Oxford Handbook of Byzantine Literature*, ed. S. Papaioannou (New York: Oxford University Press, 2021), 501.
16 Metochites: Poems, 251, Greek text 12, 203–6; Metochita: Carmina, 232.
17 See Jeffrey Michael Featherstone, *Theodore Metochites's Poems to Himself: Introduction, Text and Translation*, Byzantina Vindobonensia 23 (Vienna: Verlag der Österreichischen Akademie der Wissenschaften, 2000), 12–15; Jeffrey Michael Featherstone, 'Parisinus Graecus 1776: Metochites' Poems and the Chora', in *Kariye: From Theodore Metochites to Thomas Whittemore. One Monument, Two Monumental Personalities*, ed. B. Anit and I. A. Kisilik (Istanbul: Pera Museum, 2007), 76; Jeffrey Michael Featherstone, 'Metochites's Poems and the Chora', in *Kariye Camii, Yeniden / The Kariye Camii Reconsidered*, ed. H. A. Klein, R. G. Ousterhout and B. Pitarakis (Istanbul: Pera Museum, 2011), 216; and Christian Förstel, 'Theodore Metochites and His Books between the Chora and the Renaissance', in Klein, Ousterhout and Pitarakis, *Kariye Camii, Yeniden / The Kariye Camii Reconsidered*, 257–9.
18 See Metochites: Poems, 16–19, and Alexander Riehle, 'Epistolography as Autobiography: Remarks on the Letter Collections of Nikephoros Choumnos', *Parekbolai* 2 (2012): 19. See also the pertinent remarks on the letters of Maximos Planoudes in Ilias Taxidis, *Μάξιμος Πλανούδης: Συμβολή στη μελέτη του corpus των επιστολών του*, Βυζαντινά Κείμενα και Μελέτες 58 (Thessaloniki: Centre of Byzantine Studies, 2012), 294. On the 'recontextualization' of previous works of an author who recollected them after a certain time, see also Bradley K. Storin, *Self-Portrait in Three Colors. Gregory of Nazianzus's Epistolary Autobiography* (Oakland: University of California Press 2019), 24.
19 All translations of Metochites' texts quoted in this book are my own, unless otherwise indicated.
20 Sidonie Smith and Julia Watson, *Reading Autobiography. Guide for Interpreting Life Narratives*, 2nd edn (Minneapolis: University of Minnesota Press, 2010), 13.
21 Smith and Watson, *Reading Autobiography*, 32.
22 Paul Magdalino, 'Theodore Metochites, the Chora, and Constantinople', in Klein, Ousterhout and Pitarakis, *Kariye Camii, Yeniden / The Kariye Camii Reconsidered*, 171.
23 The attempt of Robert S. Nelson, 'Heavenly Allies at the Chora', *Gesta* 43, no. 1 (2004): 31–40, to recover the 'subtext' of some of the mosaics of Chora by comparing them to the relevant literary works of Metochites and other contemporaries is hardly convincing. The same applies to a similar attempt by Zaras, who tries to explain the depiction of the healing of two blind men at Chora on the basis of passages from Metochites on spiritual blindness. See Nektarios Zaras, 'Illness and Healing: The Healing Ministry Cycle in the Chora Monastery and the Literary Oeuvre of Theodore Metochites', *Dumbarton Oaks Papers* 75 (2021): 104.

24 Robert S. Ousterhout, 'Reading Difficult Buildings: The Lessons of Kariye Camii', in Klein, Ousterhout and Pitarakis, *Kariye Camii, Yeniden / The Kariye Camii Reconsidered*, 100–3.
25 See Floris Bernard, 'The Poems "To Oneself" of John Mauropous: Traditions and Self-representative Strategies', in *Byzantine Authors and Their Times*, ed. V. N. Vlyssidou (Athens: National Hellenic Research Foundation, 2021), 199–200. On the problems arising out of the autobiographical discourse in ancient and medieval literature, see also Louis Pernot, 'Periautologia: Problèmes et méthodes de l'éloge de soi-même dans la tradition éthique et rhétorique gréco-romaine', *Revue des Études Grecques* 111 (1998): 101–24, and Katherine Nelson, 'Self and Social Functions: Individual Autobiographic Memory and Collective Narrative', *Memory* 11 (2003): 125–36.
26 Niels Gaul, *Thomas Magistros und die spätbyzantinische Sophistik: Studien zum Humanismus urbaner Eliten in der frühen Palaiologenzeit*, Mainzer Veröffentlichungen zur Byzantinistik 10 (Wiesbaden: Harrassowitz, 2011), 34.
27 Stratis Papaioannou, 'The Epistolographic Self', in *A Companion to Byzantine Epistolography*, ed. A. Riehle (Leiden: Brill, 2020), 333.
28 Ingela Nilsson, 'Narrative: Theory and Practice', in *The Oxford Handbook of Byzantine Literature*, ed. S. Papaioannou (New York: Oxford University Press, 2021), 283–4.
29 Gaul, *Thomas Magistros und die spätbyzantinische Sophistik*, 38.
30 Gaul, *Thomas Magistros und die spätbyzantinische Sophistik*, 48–9. See also Riehle, 'Epistolography as Autobiography', 3.
31 Gaul, *Thomas Magistros und die spätbyzantinische Sophistik*, 50.
32 Anthony Storr, *The Essential Jung: Selected Writings* (London: Fontana Press, 1986), 100.
33 Storr, *Essential Jung*, 102.
34 Gaul, *Thomas Magistros und die spätbyzantinische Sophistik*, 122. See also the remarks of Sophia Kotzabassi, 'Epistolography and Rhetoric', in Riehle, *A Companion to Byzantine Epistolography*, 185, and Foteini Kolovou, Μιχαὴλ Χωνιάτης: Συμβολὴ στὴ μελέτη τοῦ βίου καὶ τοῦ ἔργου του. Τὸ corpus τῶν ἐπιστολῶν, Πονήματα 2 (Athens: Academy of Athens, 1999), 201–3.
35 Metochites devoted many chapters of his *Semeioseis Gnomikai* to these authors. See Karin Hult, 'Theodore Metochites as a Literary Critic', in *Interaction and Isolation in Late Byzantine Culture: Papers Read at a Colloquium Held at the Swedish Research Institute in Istanbul, 1–5 December, 1999*, ed. J. O. Rosenqvist, Transactions 13 (Stockholm: Swedish Research Institute in Constantinople; London: Distributed by I.B. Tauris, 2004), 44–56.
36 Sophia Xenophontos, 'Plutarch and Theodore Metochites', in *Brill's Companion to the Reception of Plutarch*, ed. S. Xenophontos and K. Oikonomopoulou (Leiden: Brill, 2019), 313–20, has convincingly demonstrated how Metochites ornamented his intellectual portrait with Plutarchan characteristics, transforming Plutarch into an appropriate persona for himself.
37 Gaul, *Thomas Magistros und die spätbyzantinische Sophistik*, 276.
38 Gaul, *Thomas Magistros und die spätbyzantinische Sophistik*, 380.
39 Gaul, *Thomas Magistros und die spätbyzantinische Sophistik*, 288. For a different, more balanced view, see Pantelis Golitsis, 'The Reappropriation of Philosophy in the Palaeologan Period', in *The Intellectual Life of the Palaeologan Period*, ed. S. Kotzabassi, Brill Companions to the Byzantine World 12 (Leiden: Brill 2023), 260.
40 Aglae Pizzone, 'Introduction', in *The Author in Middle Byzantine Literature: Modes, Functions, and Identities*, ed. A. Pizzone, Byzantinisches Archiv 28 (Berlin: De Gruyter, 2014), 4.

41 Margaret Mullett, 'In Search of the Monastic Author: Story-telling, Anonymity and Innovation in the 12th Century', in Pizzone, *The Author in Middle Byzantine Literature*, 171–2.
42 Bernard, 'The Poems "To Oneself" of John Mauropous', 213.
43 Bernard, 'The Poems "To Oneself" of John Mauropous', 213.
44 Metochites: Orationes, 390–3 (Oration 10, 58.1–60.19).
45 See, for example, the pertinent remarks by Martin M. Winkler, *The Persona in Three Satires of Juvenal*, Altertumswissenschaftliche Texte und Studien 10 (Hildesheim: Olms, 1983), 15–16.
46 Hans-Georg Beck, *Theodoros Metochites: Die Krise des byzantinischen Weltbildes im 14. Jahrhundert* (Munich: C. H. Beck, 1952), 110–12.
47 Beck, *Theodoros Metochites*, 49.
48 Herbert Hunger, 'Von Wissenschaft und Kunst de frühen Palaiologenzeit: Mit einem Exkurs über die Kosmike Delosis Theodoros' II Dukas Laskaris', *Jahrbuch der Osterreichischen Byzantinistischen Gesellschaft* 8 (1959): 138.
49 Herbert Hunger, 'Theodoros Metochites as Vorläufer des Humanismus', *Byzantinische Zeitschrift* 45 (1952): 18–19.
50 Ševčenko, 'Theodore Metochites, the Chora and the Intellectual Trends of His Time', 51–2.
51 Eva De Vries-Van der Velden, *Théodore Métochite: Une réévaluation* (Amsterdam: J. C. Gieben, 1987), 174–81.
52 Kermanidis, *Episteme und Ästhetik der Raummodelierung in Literatur und Kunst des Theodoros Metochites*, 142–3.
53 Kermanidis, *Episteme und Ästhetik der Raummodelierung in Literatur und Kunst des Theodoros Metochites*, 326–31.
54 Kermanidis, *Episteme und Ästhetik der Raummodelierung in Literatur und Kunst des Theodoros Metochites*, 327.
55 Kermanidis, *Episteme und Ästhetik der Raummodelierung in Literatur und Kunst des Theodoros Metochites*, 27–8, n. 68.
56 Kermanidis, *Episteme und Ästhetik der Raummodelierung in Literatur und Kunst des Theodoros Metochites*, 243, 274.
57 See Leo Strauss, *What Is Political Philosophy and Other Studies* (Chicago: University of Chicago Press, 1959), 63–4.
58 Sophia Xenophontos, 'Exploring Emotions in Late Byzantium: Theodore Metochites on Affectivity', *Byzantion* 91 (2021): 460–1.
59 Sophia Xenophontos, 'The Cultural Dynamics of the Term *Hellanodikes* in Palaiologan Byzantium', *Byzantinische Zeitschrift* 108, no. 2 (2015): 221–7.
60 Sententious Notes 9, Karin Hult, *Theodore Metochites on Ancient Authors and Philosophy: Semeioseis Gnomikai 1–26 & 71. A Critical Edition with Introduction, Translation, Notes and Indexes with a Contribution by B. Bydén*, Acta Universitatis Gothoburgensis (Gothenburg: University of Gothenburg, 2002), 89.
61 Sententious Notes 9, Hult, *Theodore Metochites on Ancient Authors and Philosophy*, 95.
62 Sententious Notes 3, Hult, *Theodore Metochites on Ancient Authors and Philosophy*, 37–9.
63 Sententious Notes 3, Hult, *Theodore Metochites on Ancient Authors and Philosophy*, 39.
64 Melzer, *Philosophy between the Lines*, 36.
65 Sententious Notes 61, Staffan Wahlgren, *Theodore Metochites' Sententious Notes: Semeioseis Gnomikai 61–70 & 72–81. A Critical Edition with Introduction, Translation, Notes, and Indexes* (Gothenburg: University of Gothenburg, 2018), 13.

66 Wahlgren, *Theodore Metochites' Sententious Notes*, 135–69 and 181–203.
67 Dimitar Angelov, *Imperial Ideology and Political Thought in Byzantium, 1204–1330* (Cambridge: Cambridge University Press, 2007), 141. See some other cases of Metochitean contradictions adduced in a recent article by S. MacPhee, 'Roaring Tempests of the Human Mind: Theodoros Metochites and the Sententious Notes', Academia.edu, 29 April 2022, 3–13.
68 Floris Bernard, 'The Ethics of Authorship: Some Tensions in the 11th Century', in Pizzone, *The Author in Middle Byzantine Literature*, 56–7.
69 Metochites: Orationes, 261 (Oration 6, 26–8).
70 Richard Schechner, *Performance Theory*, 2nd edn (London: Routledge, 2003), x.
71 See preliminary remarks by Puchner, *Φαινόμενα καὶ Νοούμενα*, 36, n. 9. Also see the older but extensive and still useful treatment of the subject by Beck, *Theodoros Metochites*, 96–114.
72 Metochites: Orationes, 413 (Oration 10, 83.8–17), Sophia Xenophontos, trans., *On Morals or Concerning Education: Theodore Metochites*, Dumbarton Oaks Medieval Library 61 (Cambridge, MA: Harvard University Press, 2020), 197.
73 Metochites: Poems, 59, Greek text 1, 302–3; Metochita: Carmina, 15.
74 Metochites: Poems, 63, Greek text 1, 383–90; Metochita: Carmina, 19.
75 See, for example, *Life of St. Constantine the Jew* 1, 16, Ioannis Polemis and Evelina Mineva, *Βυζαντινὰ ὑμνογραφικὰ καὶ ἁγιολογικὰ κείμενα: Νέα Ἔκδοση* (Athens: Kanakis Publishers, 2021), 537.
76 Metochites: Orationes, 30 (Oration 2, 12.24–8).
77 Metochites: Orationes, 48 (Oration 2, 23.40–1).
78 Metochites: Orationes, 118 (Oration 4, 7.22–5).
79 Schechner, *Performance Theory*, 14.
80 Metochites: Orationes, 122 (Oration 4, 10, 27). The same image appears in the Encomium of St George, written by Gregory of Cyprus, which Metochites used as a source. In any case, the image appears in other authors as well. See, for example, Manuel Gabalas, Letter B 44.14–15, Diether Roderich Reinsch, *Die Briefe des Matthaios von Ephesos im Codex Vindobonensis Theol. Gr. 174* (Berlin: Mielke, 1974), 161. For St George's encomium, see PG 142:305CD.
81 Metochites: Orationes, 562 (Oration 12, 8.10).
82 Metochites: Orationes, 569 (Oration 12, 13.3–4).
83 Metochites: Orationes, 642 (Oration 17, 10.29).
84 Metochites: Orationes, 667 (Oration 17, 34. 57).
85 Metochites: Orationes, 701 (Oration 19, 3.37–8).
86 Metochites: Orationes, 704 (Oration 19, 6.49).
87 Metochites: Orationes, 715 (Oration 19, 17.1–2).
88 Metochites: Orationes, 494 (Oration 11, 73.29–34).
89 Metochites: Orationes, 512 (Oration 11, 93.15–16).
90 Metochites: Orationes, 523 (Oration 11, 104.19–28).
91 Metochites: Orationes, 551 (Oration 11, 136.19–22).
92 Walter Puchner, *Greek Theatre between Antiquity and Independence: A History of Reinvention from the Third Century BC to 1830* (Cambridge: Cambridge University Press, 2017), 65–6.
93 Anthony Arthur Long, *From Epicurus to Epictetus: Studies in Hellenistic and Roman Philosophy* (Oxford: Clarendon Press, 2006), 14–15.
94 See Cedric A. J. Littlewood, *Self-representation and Illusion in Senecan Tragedy*, Oxford Classical Monographs (Oxford: Oxford University Press, 2004), 56–7.

95 On this particular aspect of the terminology of the theatre, which is encountered in Greek patristic texts, see Walter Puchner, *Φαινόμενα και Νοούμενα: Δέκα θεατρολογικά μελετήματα*, 2nd edn (Athens: Hellenika Grammata, 1999), 36–8. Metochites employs the terms *drama* and *skene* in a negative sense. See Metochites: Orationes, 250 (Oration 6, 54.23), and Metochites: Orationes, 411 (Oration 10, 80.27), respectively.

Chapter 1

1 See Kubina, *Die enkomiastische Dichtung des Manuel Philes*, 190–1.
2 On this term, see Martin Hinterberger, *Autobiographische Traditionen in Byzanz*, Wiener Byzantinistische Studien 22 (Vienna: Verlag der Österreichischen Akademie der Wissenschaften, 1999), 99–105.
3 Metochites: Poems, 47, Greek text 1 (title); Metochita: Carmina, 5.
4 See Hinterberger, *Autobiographische Traditionen in Byzanz*, 183–294; Michael Angold, 'The Autobiographical Impulse in Byzantium', *Dumbarton Oaks Papers* 52 (1998): 242–51; and Margaret Mullett, 'Constructing Identities in Twelfth-century Byzantium', in *Το Βυζάντιο ώριμο για αλλαγές: Επιλογές, ευαισθησίες και τρόποι έκφρασης από τον ενδέκατο στον δέκατο πέμπτο αιώνα*, ed. C. G. Angelidi, International Symposia 13 (Athens: National Research Foundation, Institute of Byzantine Research, 2004), 129–33.
5 This is not something unusual. See, for example, the autobiography of Gregory of Cyprus as analysed by Sophia Kotzabassi, 'Περὶ τοῦ καθ' ἑαυτὸν βίου ὡς ἀπ' ἄλλου προσώπου: Παρατηρήσεις στην αυτοβιογραφία του πατριάρχη Γρηγορίου Β' Κυπρίου', *Ελληνικά* 58, no. 2 (2008): 283–4.
6 Georg Misch, *Geschichte der Autobiographie*, vol. 1, *Das Altertum*, pt. 2 (Berlin: A. Franke Verlag, 1950), 386.
7 Metochites: Poems, 50–1, Greek text 1, 68–70; Metochita: Carmina, 7.
8 Metochites: Poems, 54, Greek text 1, 149; Metochita: Carmina, 10.
9 Metochites: Poems, 59, Greek text 1, 302; Metochita: Carmina, 15.
10 Metochites: Poems, 64, Greek text 1, 431; Metochita: Carmina, 20.
11 Metochites: Poems, 64, Greek text 1, 434; Metochita: Carmina, 20.
12 Metochites: Poems, 66, Greek text 1, 488; Metochita: Carmina, 22.
13 Metochites: Poems, 72, Greek text 1, 681; Metochita: Carmina, 29.
14 Metochites: Poems, 78, Greek text 1, 859, and 80, Greek text 1, 927; Metochita: Carmina, 35 and 37. See also the term *prophron* as employed in the text, Poem 1, 493; Metochita: Carmina, 22.
15 Metochites: Poems, 82, Greek text 1, 980; Metochita: Carmina, 39.
16 Metochites: Poems, 90, Greek text 1, 1268; Metochita: Carmina, 49.
17 On the pattern moulding the Byzantine autobiographic narratives, see Hinterberger, *Autobiographische Traditionen in Byzanz*, 85–6.
18 On the contribution of a good education to the creation of a distinct social group of intellectuals (*Bildungselite*) that strived for social advancement in this period, see Klaus-Peter Matschke and Franz Tinnefeld, *Die Gesellschaft im späten Byzanz: Gruppen, Strukturen und Lebensformen* (Cologne: Böhlau, 2001), 259–62.
19 Hinterberger, *Autobiographische Traditionen in Byzanz*, 89.
20 Metochites; Metochita: Carmina, lxxxiii–lxxxv.
21 See Hinterberger, *Autobiographische Traditionen in Byzanz*, 92–3.
22 Hinterberger, *Autobiographische Traditionen in Byzanz*, 135.
23 Metochites: Poems, 95, Greek text 2, 62; Metochita: Carmina, 54.

24 Metochites: Poems, 99, Greek text 2, 198; Metochita: Carmina, 59.
25 Metochites: Poems, 104, Greek text 2, 379–81; Metochita: Carmina, 54.
26 Misch, *Geschichte der Autobiographie*, 409.
27 Misch, *Geschichte der Autobiographie*, 410–11.
28 Sententious Notes 28.3.2, Karin Hult, *Theodore Metochites on the Human Condition and the Decline of Rome: Semeioseis Gnomikai 27–60. Critical Edition with Introduction, Translation, Notes, and Indexes* (Gothenburg: University of Gothenburg, 2016), 18, 1–3.
29 *Stoikheiosis Astronomike* 1, 1.23.386–97, Bydén, *Theodore Metochites' Stoicheiosis Astronomike and the Study of Natural Philosophy and Mathematics in Early Palaiologan Byzantium*, 429–30. See the pertinent remarks of Sofia Kotzabassi, 'Continuity and Evolution in Autobiographical Literature', in S. Kotzabassi (ed.), *The Intellectual Life of the Palaeologan Period*, Brill Companions to the Byzantine World 12 (Leiden: Brill 2023), 118–20.
30 Metochites: Orationes, 403 (Oration 10, 72.1–4).
31 Metochites: Orationes, 409 (Oration 10, 23–5), trans. Xenophontos, *On Morals or Concerning Education*, 185.
32 Metochites: Orationes, 400–4 (Oration 10, 68.1–72.28), trans. Xenophontos, *On Morals or Concerning Education*, 158–70.
33 Metochites: Orationes, 401 (Oration 10, 69.1–8), trans. Xenophontos, *On Morals or Concerning Education*, 161.
34 On this tension, see Bernard, 'The Ethics of Authorship', 41–52.
35 Metochites: Poems, 61–2, Greek text 1, 364–72; Metochita: Carmina, 18.
36 Metochites: Poems, 71, Greek text 1, 639–40; Metochita: Carmina, 27.
37 Metochites: Poems, 131, Greek text 4, 233–7; Metochita: Carmina, 93.
38 Metochites: Poems, 131–2, Greek text 4, 244–9; Metochita: Carmina, 93.
39 Metochites: Poems, 132, Greek text 4, 247–9; Metochita: Carmina, 93.
40 Metochites: Poems, 132–3, Greek text 4, 263–80; Metochita: Carmina, 94.
41 Markos Kermanidis, 'Allegorie und Lob der Physik: Das Proömium der Paraphrase des Theodoros Metochites zu naturwissenschaftlichen Schriften des Aristoteles', *Byzantinische Zeitschrift* 115, no. 1 (2022): 148.33–149.39.
42 Metochites: Poems, 251, Greek text 12, 172–9; Metochita: Carmina, 231.
43 Metochites: Poems, 251, Greek text 12, 193–9; Metochita: Carmina, 231–2.
44 Metochites: Poems, 251, Greek text 12, 199–208; Metochita: Carmina, 232.
45 Metochites: Poems, 251, Greek text 12, 209–17; Metochita: Carmina, 232.
46 Metochites: Poems, 252, Greek text 12, 245–51; Metochita: Carmina, 233–4.
47 Metochites: Poems, 253, Greek text 12, 257–8; Metochita: Carmina, 234.
48 Metochites: Poems, 254, Greek text 12, 312–15; Metochita: Carmina, 236; Metochites: Poems, 251, Greek text 12, 172–9; Metochita: Carmina, 231.
49 Metochites: Poems, 252, Greek text 12, 223–31; Metochita: Carmina, 233.
50 See, for example, Michael Roberts, *The Jeweled Style: Poetry and Poetics in Late Antiquity* (Ithaca, NY: Cornell University Press, 1989), 48–51.
51 See Kurt Treu, *Synesios von Kyrene: Ein Kommentar zu seinem 'Dion'* (Berlin: Akademie-Verlag, 1958), 97, who discusses a passage of Synesius' Dion, a treatise well known to Metochites. Several Byzantine authors employed imagery of the meadow of Kalliope. See, for example, Nikephoros Basilakes, Oration to Alexius Aristenus, in *Nicephori Basilacae: Orationes et Epistulae,* Bibliotheca Scriptorum Graecorum et Romanorum Teubneriana, ed. Antonio Garzya (Leipzig: Teubner, 1984), 17.23–4.
52 Metochites: Orationes, 60–2 (Oration 3, 1.1–3.22). On this comparison, see Ihor Ševčenko, 'Hagiography of the Iconoclast Period', in *Iconoclasm: Papers Given at the 9th*

Spring Symposium of Byzantine Studies, University of Birmingham, March 1975, ed. A. Bryer and J. Herrin (Birmingham: Centre for Byzantine Studies, University of Birmingham, 1977), 10–27, and 34, n. 49. Manuel Philes, a contemporary of Metochites, entertains certain doubts about whether a painter can adequately represent an angel, 2, 192.1–4, E. E. Miller, ed., *Manuelis Philae Carmina ex codicibus Escurialensibus, Florentinis, Parisinis et Vaticanis nunc primum edidit*, vol. 1 (Paris, 1855; repr., Amsterdam: A. M. Hakkert, 1967), 357–8.

53 Metochites: Orationes, 109–10 (Oration 4, 1.27–32). On the motif of the contest between singers and poets, see Ernst R. Curtius, *European Literature and the Latin Middle Ages*, trans. W. R. Trask, Bollingen Series 36 (Princeton: Princeton University Press, 1952), 190. In Byzantium the comparison of an author with an athlete or a musician was commonplace. See, for example, Poem 19, 1 of Theodore Prodromos, where both motifs appear side by side, Wolfram Hörandner, *Theodoros Prodromos: Historische Gedichte*, Wiener Byzantinistische Studien 11 (Vienna: Verlag der Österreichischen Akademie der Wissenschaften, 1974), 310.

54 Metochites: Poems, 306, Greek text 18, 1–10; Metochita: Carmina, 300. The comparison is ancient. See Euripides, *Iphigeneia Taurensis*, 1095. Byzantine authors mostly employed it in funeral orations. See, for example, Theodorus Hexapterygus, Oration to Stephanos Choregetopoulos, Alexandros Sideras, ed., *25 unedierte byzantinische Grabreden* (Thessaloniki: Paratērētēs, 1991), 226.26–227.16.

55 Metochites: Orationes, 429 (Oration 10, 101.1–24), trans. Xenophontos, *On Morals or Concerning Education*, 243–5.

56 Metochites: Poems, 63, Greek text 1, 402–4; Metochita: Carmina, 19.

57 Angelov, *Imperial Ideology and Political Thought in Byzantium*, 161.

58 Metochites: Poems, 131, Greek text 4, 210–21; Metochita: Carmina, 92.

59 Angelov, *Imperial Ideology and Political Thought in Byzantium*, 165.

60 Martin Hinterberger, 'Studien zu Theodoros Metochites: Gedicht I – Des Meeres und des Lebens Wellen – Die Angst von der Neid – Die autobiographische Texte-Sprache', *Jahrbuch der Osterreichischen Byzantinistik* 51 (2001): 307–14.

61 *Stoikheiosis Astronomike* 1.1.35–53, Bydén, *Theodore Metochites' Stoicheiosis Astronomike and the Study of Natural Philosophy and Mathematics in Early Palaiologan Byzantium*, 418.

62 Metochites: Orationes, 390 (Oration 10, 57.17–58.33), trans. Xenophontos, *On Morals or Concerning Education*, 127–9.

63 See Ioannis Polemis, Θεόδωρος Μετοχίτης: Ἠθικὸς ἢ Περὶ παιδείας. Εἰσαγωγή-Κριτικὴ ἔκδοση-Μετάφραση-Σημειώσεις, 2nd edn (Athens: Kanakis Publishers, 2002), 144*–145*, and Karin Metzler, 'Pagane Bildung im christlichen Byzanz: Basileios von Kaisareia, Michael Psellos und Theodoros Metochites', in *Theatron: Rhetorische Kultur in Spätantike und Mittelalter*, ed. M. Grünbart, Millenium-Studien 13 (Berlin: De Gruyter, 2007), 300, n. 86.

64 See Manolis Borbouhakis, 'The End of ἐπίδειξις: Authorial Identity and Authorial Intention in Michael Choniates' Πρὸς τοὺς αἰτιωμένους τὸ ἀφιλένδεικτον', in Pizzone, *The Author in Middle Byzantine Literature*, 204–14.

65 Brian Stock, *Augustine's Inner Dialogue: The Philosophical Soliloquy in Late Antiquity* (Cambridge: Cambridge University Press, 2010), 71–2.

66 Stock, *Augustine's Inner Dialogue*, 71.

67 Metochites: Orationes, 77 (Oration 3, 12.26–30). See also Misch, *Geschichte der Autobiographie*, 451.

68 See Metochita: Carmina, xx.

69 Bernard, 'The Poems "To Oneself" of John Mauropous', 211–14.
70 See, for example, Poems 91 and 92: Floris Bernard and Christopher Livanos, *The Poems of Christopher of Mytilene and John Mauropous*, Dumbarton Oaks Medieval Library 50 (Cambridge, MA: Harvard University Press, 2018), 492–503.
71 See Stock, *Augustine's Inner Dialogue*, 63–76.
72 Misch, *Geschichte der Autobiographie*, 631–4.
73 Metochites: Poems, 318, Greek text 19, 1–5; Metochita: Carmina, 314.
74 Metochites: Poems, 318–19, Greek text 19, 6–45; Metochita: Carmina, 314–15.
75 Metochites: Poems, 319–25, Greek text 19, 46–251; Metochita: Carmina, 315–25.
76 Metochites: Poems, 325, Greek text 19, 252; Metochita: Carmina, 322.
77 Metochites: Poems, 325, Greek text 19, 267–8; Metochita: Carmina, 323.
78 Metochites: Poems, 326, Greek text 19, 279; Metochita: Carmina, 323.
79 Metochites: Poems, 327, Greek text 19, 320–6; Metochita: Carmina, 325.
80 Metochites: Poems, 327, Greek text 19, 327–37; Metochita: Carmina, 325.
81 Metochites: Poems, 318, Greek text 19, 395–6; Metochita: Carmina, 327.
82 Metochites: Poems, 330, Greek text 20, 1–2; Metochita: Carmina, 328.
83 Metochites: Poems, 331, Greek text 20, 32–53; Metochita: Carmina, 329.
84 Metochites: Poems, 332, Greek text 20, 61–2; Metochita: Carmina, 330.
85 Metochites: Poems, 332, Greek text 20, 90–1; Metochita: Carmina, 331.
86 Metochites: Poems, 334, Greek text 20, 157–60; Metochita: Carmina, 333.
87 Metochites: Poems, 335–6, Greek text 20, 205–14; Metochita: Carmina, 335.
88 Metochites: Poems, 336, Greek text 20, 227–8; Metochita: Carmina, 335.
89 Metochites: Poems, 260–1, Greek text 13, 155–74; Metochita: Carmina, 242–m 3.
90 Metochites: Poems, 261–2, Greek text 13, 188–204; Metochita: Carmina, 244.
91 Metochites: Poems, 261, Greek text 13, 189; Metochita: Carmina, 244.
92 Michel Foucault, 'Different Spaces', in *Aesthetics, Method, and Epistemology: Essential Works of Foucault, 1954–1984*, ed. James D. Faubion, vol. 2, trans. Robert Hurley (New York: The New Press, 1998), 175–85.
93 Metochites: Orationes, 454 (Oration 11, 29.6–8).
94 Metochites: Orationes, 523 (Oration 11, 104.19–24). See also Myrto Veikou and Ingela Nilsson, 'Ports and Harbours as Heterotopic Entities in Byzantine Literary Texts', in *Harbours as Objects of Interdisciplinary Research: Archaeology + History + Geoscience*, ed. C. von Carnap-Bornheim, F. Daim, P. Ettel and U. Warnke, RGZM-Tagungen 34 (Mainz: Verlag des Römisch-Germanischen Zentralmuseums, 2018), 269–70, on the heterotopic attributes of ports and harbours in Byzantine literary texts as places where knowledge is accumulated, but also as liminal places between danger and security.
95 Metochites: Orationes, 449–50 (Oration 11, 23.16–27). Some elements of this image appear in the Oration for Michael VIII Palaiologos of Gregory of Cyprus (PG 142:349C).
96 Metochites: Orationes, 453 (Oration 11, 28.1–17).
97 Smith and Watson, *Reading Autobiography*, 44.
98 Metochites: Orationes, 282–3 (Oration 7, 21.1–22.11).
99 Metochites: Poems, 117, Greek text 3, 141–4; Metochita: Carmina, 79.
100 Metochites: Poems, 117, Greek text 3, 135–6; Metochita: Carmina, 78.
101 Metochites: Poems, 119–20, Greek text 3, 196–212; Metochita: Carmina, 81.
102 Metochites: Poems, 119–20, Greek text 3, 196–212; Metochita: Carmina, 81.
103 Metochites: Poems, 119, Greek text 3, 204–5; Metochita: Carmina, 81.
104 Metochites: Orationes, 509–10 (Oration 11, 90.1–91.20).

105 Metochites: Poems, 241 and 262, Greek text 11, 215, and Greek text 13, 195; Metochita: Carmina, 221 and 244, respectively.
106 Metochites: Poems, 238-9, Greek text 11, 148-55; Metochita: Carmina, 218.
107 Metochites: Poems, 261-2, Greek text 13, 188-204; Metochita: Carmina, 244.
108 I employ the term *figura* in the sense presented by Erich Auerbach, *Figura*, in *Gesammelte Aufsätze zur Romanischen Philologie* (Bern: Francke, 1967), 65.
109 Metochites: Poems, 110, Greek text 2, 576; Metochita: Carmina, 72.
110 Metochites: Poems, 322-4, Greek text 19, 156-239; Metochita: Carmina, 319-22.
111 Metochites: Poems, 329, Greek text 19, 392-5; Metochita: Carmina, 327.
112 Auerbach, *Figura*, 65-74.
113 Metochites: Poems, 303-4, Greek text 17, 302-26; Metochita: Carmina, 296-7. See also Herodotus 3, 40-3.
114 Metochites: Poems, 303-5, Greek text 17, 327-65; Metochita: Carmina, 297-8.
115 Metochites: Poems, 304, Greek text 17, 355; Metochita: Carmina, 298.
116 Metochites: Poems, 319, Greek text 19, 30-45; Metochita: Carmina, 315.
117 Ousterhout, 'Reading Difficult Buildings', 98.
118 Metochites: Poems, 234, Greek text 10, 1011; Metochita: Carmina, 212. Compare with Metochites: Poems, 231, Greek text 10, 935; Metochita: Carmina, 209.
119 Metochites: Poems, 52, Greek text 1, 89; Metochita: Carmina, 8, and Metochites: Poems, 53, Greek text 1, 116; Metochita: Carmina, 9.
120 Metochites: Poems, 82, Greek text 1, 998; Metochita: Carmina, 40. See also Metochites: Poems, 102, Greek text 2, 313; Metochita: Carmina, 63.
121 Delight at the spectacle of Chora: Metochites: Poems, 98, Greek text 2, 162; Metochita: Carmina, 57. Delight of man's contemplating the world: Metochites: Poems, 232-3, Greek text 10, 965-6; Metochita: Carmina, 210.
122 Metochites: Orationes, 429 (Oration 10, 101.22).
123 Metochites: Poems, 92, Greek text 2, 1305-9; Metochita: Carmina, 51.
124 Metochites: Poems, 95-6, Greek text 2, 62-74; Metochita: Carmina, 54.
125 Metochites: Poems, 253, Greek text 12, 257; Metochita: Carmina, 234.
126 Metochites: Poems, 251, Greek text 12, 204; Metochita: Carmina, 232.
127 On similar phenomena in Western medieval literature, see Burt Kimmelman, *The Poetics of Authorship in the Later Middle Ages: The Emergence of the Modern Literary Persona*, Studies in the Humanities 21 (New York: Peter Lang, 1996), 96.

Chapter 2

1 Stratis Papaioannou, *Michael Psellos: Rhetoric and Authorship in Byzantium* (Cambridge: Cambridge University Press, 2013), 152.
2 Metochites: Orationes, 267 (Oration 7, 1.2).
3 Metochites: Orationes, 301 (Oration 8, 7.34).
4 Metochites: Orationes, 330 (Oration 9, 2.10).
5 Metochites: Orationes, 611 (Oration 16, 1.13).
6 Metochites: Orationes, 147 (Oration 4, 27.2).
7 Metochites: Orationes, 147 (Oration 4, 27.18-19).
8 This is a free translation. Metochites: Orationes, 143-4 (Oration 4, 25.7-42)
9 Ioannis Polemis, Θεόδωρος Μετοχίτης: Βυζάντιος ἢ Περὶ τῆς βασιλίδος μεγαλοπόλεως. Κοσμολογία καὶ ρητορικὴ κατὰ τὸν ΙΔ΄ αἰῶνα - Εἰσαγωγή, κριτικὴ ἔκδοση, μετάφραση, σημειώσεις (Thessaloniki: Zitros Publishers, 2013), 31-40.

10 Metochites: Orationes, 118 (Oration 4, 7.24–6).
11 Metochites: Poems, 63–4, Greek text 1, 412–36; Metochita: Carmina, 19–20.
12 Metochites: Poems, 74, Greek text 1, 738–49; Metochita: Carmina, 31.
13 Metochites: Poems, 86–7, Greek text 1, 1120–37; Metochita: Carmina, 44–5.
14 Metochites: Orationes, 115 (Oration 4, 4.3–13).
15 Metochites: Poems, 327, Greek text 19, 320, 334; Metochita: Carmina, 325.
16 See, for example, Metochites: Orationes, 656 (Oration 17, 24.53–4). The same idea appears in Metochites: Orationes, 193 (Oration 6, 16.9–10). Michael Gabras praises Metochites for stressing this combination in his oration for Gregory. See Epistle 84, 34: Georgios Fatouros, *Die Briefe des Michael Gabras (ca. 1290–nach 1350)*, vol. 2, *Text*, Wiener Byzantinistische Studien 10.2 (Vienna: Österreichische Akademie der Wissenschaften, 1973), 136. The same combination appears in the Oration for Gregory of Nazianzus of Thomas Magistros, PG 145:232BC.
17 Metochites: Orationes, 638 (Oration 17, 6.1–6).
18 Metochites: Orationes, 639–40 (Oration 4, 8.3–7).
19 Metochites: Orationes, 663–4 (Oration 17, 32.2–4).
20 Metochites: Poems, 64, Greek text 1, 421; Metochita: Carmina, 20.
21 Metochites: Orationes, 424 (Oration 4, 12.48).
22 Metochites: Orationes, 664 (Oration 17, 32.13).
23 Metochites: Orationes, 667 (Oration 17, 34.53–6).
24 Metochites: Orationes, 640–1 (Oration 17, 9.1–18).
25 Metochites: Orationes, 641 (Oration 17, 10.4).
26 Metochites: Orationes, 647 (Oration 17, 15.4).
27 Metochites: Orationes, 648 (Oration 17, 16.2).
28 Metochites: Orationes, 647 (Oration 17, 15.10–17).
29 Metochites: Orationes, 653 (Oration 17, 22.53–4).
30 Metochites: Orationes, 653–4 (Oration 17.23, 1–20).
31 Metochites: Orationes, 653 (Oration 17, 22.51–2).
32 Metochites: Orationes, 654 (Oration 17, 24.8–10).
33 Metochites: Orationes, 657 (Oration 17, 26.7–8).
34 Metochites: Orationes, 667 (Oration 17, 34.57).
35 Metochites: Orationes, 668–9 (Oration 17, 36.1–33).
36 Metochites: Orationes, 700 (Oration 19, 2.50–6).
37 Metochites: Orationes, 701 (Oration 19, 3.37–8).
38 Metochites: Orationes, 703 (Oration 19, 6.12–13).
39 E.g. Metochites: Orationes, 118 (Oration 4, 7.20), 119 (Oration 4, 7, 45).
40 Metochites: Orationes, 705 (Oration 19, 8.7–9).
41 Metochites: Orationes, 706 (Oration 19, 8.33).
42 Metochites: Orationes, 712 (Oration 19, 14.8–17).
43 Metochites: Orationes, 715 (Oration 19, 17.6).

Chapter 3

1 Metochites: Poems, 104, Greek text 2, 365–84; Metochita: Carmina, 65.
2 Metochites: Poems, 117, Greek text 3, 142, 150; Metochita: Carmina, 79.
3 Michel Foucault, *The Care of the Self*, vol. 3 of *The History of Sexuality*, trans. R. Hurley, repr. edn (New York: Vintage, 1988), 41.
4 Foucault, *Care of the Self*, 42.

5   Foucault, *Care of the Self*, 43.
6   Foucault, *Care of the Self*, 64–7.
7   See Foucault, *Care of the Self*, 94.
8   Metochites: Orationes, 383 (Oration 10, 50.1–8), trans. Xenophontos, *On Morals or Concerning Education*, 107.

Chapter 4

1   Metochites: Orationes, 147–8 (Oration 4, 27.1–37).
2   Metochites: Orationes, 124–5 (Oration 4, 12.68–97).
3   PG 141:24D.
4   PG 141:24C.
5   Giovanni Mercati, *Notizie di Procoro e Demetrio Cidone, Manuele Caleca e Teodoro Meliteniota ed altri appunti per la storia della teologia e della letteratura bizantina del secolo XIV*, Studi e Testi 56 (Vatican City: Vatican Apostolic Library, 1931), 370, 40–2.
6   On the innovative aspects of Metochites' poetry, see Ioannis Vassis, 'Spirituality and Emotion: Poetic Trends in the Palaeologan Period', in S. Kotzabassi (ed.), *A Companion to the Intellectual Life of the Palaeologan Period*, Brill's Companions to the Byzantine World 12 (Leiden: Brill 2023), 182.
7   Metochites: Orationes, 578 (Oration 13, 3.1–21).
8   Metochites: Orationes, 580–2 (Oration 13, 6.1–49).
9   Metochites: Orationes, 579 (Oration 13, 4.8–13).
10 Metochites: Orationes, 584 (Oration 13, 10.1–2).
11 Metochites: Orationes, 585 (Oration 13, 11.6–19).
12 Metochites: Orationes, 586 (Oration 13, 12.1–18).
13 Metochites: Orationes, 587 (Oration 13, 14.5–8).
14 See Martin Hinterberger, *Phthonos: Mißgunst, Neid und Eifersucht in der byzantinischer Literatur*, Serta Graeca 29 (Wiesbaden: Dr Ludwig Reichert Verlag, 2013), 324.
15 Metochites: Orationes, 595 (Oration 14, 9.12–17).
16 Metochites: Orationes, 596 (Oration 14, 10.22).
17 Metochites: Orationes, 598 (Oration 14, 12.5–10).
18 Metochites: Orationes, 603 (Oration 14, 17.16–21).
19 Metochites: Orationes, 604 (Oration 14, 18.32–5).
20 Metochites: Orationes, 606 (Oration 14, 20.25–48).
21 Metochites: Orationes, 608 (Oration 14, 21.33–9).
22 Riehle, 'Literature, Politics and Manuscripts in Early Palaiologan Byzantium', 603–4.
23 Riehle, 'Literature, Politics and Manuscripts in Early Palaiologan Byzantium', 599.
24 Metochites: Orationes, 586 (Oration 13, 12.1–18).
25 Metochites: Orationes, 595 (Oration 14, 9.15).
26 Metochites: Orationes, 586–7 (Oration 13, 13.11–33).
27 Metochites: Orationes, 587 (Oration 13, 13.15–16).
28 Metochites: Orationes, 584 (Oration 13, 9.33–45).
29 Metochites: Orationes, 584–5 (Oration 13, 10.1–15).
30 Metochites: Orationes, 586 (Oration 13, 13.4–5).
31 Jean François Boissonade, ed., *Anecdota graeca*, vol. 3 (Paris, 1831; repr., Hildesheim: Georg Olms Verlagsbuchhandlung, 1962), 356–7.
32 Boissonade, *Anecdota graeca*, 3:359.

33 Boissonade, *Anecdota graeca*, 3:361.
34 Boissonade, *Anecdota graeca*, 3:362.
35 Boissonade, *Anecdota graeca*, 3:368.
36 Boissonade, *Anecdota graeca*, 3:368–70.
37 Boissonade, *Anecdota graeca*, 3:371.
38 Boissonade, *Anecdota graeca*, 3:373.
39 Boissonade, *Anecdota graeca*, 3:373.
40 Boissonade, *Anecdota graeca*, 3:380–1.
41 Boissonade, *Anecdota graeca*, 3:359.
42 Boissonade, *Anecdota graeca*, 3:360
43 Boissonade, *Anecdota graeca*, 3:373.
44 Boissonade, *Anecdota graeca*, 3:358.
45 Boissonade, *Anecdota graeca*, 3:367–9.
46 Boissonade, *Anecdota graeca*, 3:373.

Chapter 5

1 On the chronology of this work, see Ihor Ševčenko, 'The Logos on Gregory of Nazianzus by Theodore Metochites', in *Geschichte und Kultur der Palaiologenzeit: Referate des Internationales Symposions zu Ehren von H. Hunger*, ed. W. Seibt (Vienna: Verlag der Österreichischen Akademie der Wissenschaften, 1996), 222–3.
2 Metochites: Orationes, 178 (Oration 6, 3.6–17).
3 Metochites: Orationes, 178 (Oration 6, 3.19–20).
4 Metochites: Poems, 251–2, Greek text 12, 218–22; Metochita: Carmina, 232–3.
5 Metochites: Orationes, 265–6 (Oration, 6, 61.1–15).
6 Letter 84, 26–51, Fatouros, *Die Briefe des Michael Gabras*, 135–6.
7 Metochites: Poems, 10–11, and Metochita: Carmina, xlix–liii.
8 Metochites: Orationes, 195–6 (Oration 6, 18.1–17).
9 Metochites: Orationes, 196–7 (Oration 6, 18.30–42).
10 Metochites: Orationes, 197 (Oration 6, 18.44–5).
11 Metochites: Orationes, 197 (Oration 6, 18.50–1).
12 Metochites: Orationes, 197–8 (Oration 6, 18.74–5).
13 Metochites: Orationes, 198 (Oration 6, 18.75–82).
14 Metochites: Orationes, 198 (Oration 6, 19, 1–9).
15 Metochites: Orationes, 198–9 (Oration 6, 19.10–25).
16 Metochites: Orationes, 199 (Oration 6, 19.25–37).
17 Metochites: Orationes, 199 (Oration 6, 19.32–5).
18 George A. Kennedy, *Greek Rhetoric under Christian Emperors* (Princeton: Princeton University Press, 1983), 96–7.
19 Hermogenes, *On Ideas* B, Hugo Rabe, ed., *Hermogenes opera: Adiectae sunt II tabulae*, Bibliotheca Scriptorum Graecorum et Romanorum Teubneriana (Leipzig: Teubner, 1913), 404.6–7.
20 Hermogenes, *On Ideas* B, Rabe, *Hermogenes opera*, 409.24–411.11.
21 Hermogenes, *On Ideas* B, Rabe, *Hermogenes opera*, 408.14–16.
22 Metochites: Orationes, 199–200 (Oration 6, 20.7–18).
23 Metochites: Orationes, 200 (Oration 6, 20.18–37).
24 Metochites: Orationes, 645 (Oration 17, 13.39–44).

25 Metochites: Orationes, 265 (Oration 6, 60.134–8). The importance of man's natural qualities was stressed both by Hermogenes and by his predecessors. See Kennedy, *Greek Rhetoric under Christian Emperors*, 97.
26 PG 45:220A.
27 PG 45:248A.
28 PG 45:245C.
29 PG 45:245C.
30 PG 45:327A.
31 Papaioannou, *Michael Psellos*, 69–87.
32 Metochites: Orationes, 196 (Oration 6, 18.36).
33 Metochites: Orationes, 197 (Oration 6, 18.73).
34 Metochites: Orationes, 197 (Oration 6, 18.72).
35 Metochites: Orationes, 197 (Oration 6, 18.72).
36 Metochites: Orationes, 198–9 (Oration 6, 19.23–4).
37 Metochites: Orationes, 198 (Oration 6, 19.1–22).
38 Metochites: Orationes, 198 (Oration 6, 19.19).
39 Metochites: Orationes, 197 (Oration 6, 18.51).
40 See, for example, Metochites: Orationes, 645 (Oration 17, 13.48).
41 Metochites: Orationes, 603–4 (Oration 14, 18.8–32). For a different interpretation, see Przemyslaw Marciniak, 'Byzantine Theatron: A Place of Performance?', in *Theatron: Rhetorische Kultur in Spätantike und Mittelalter*, ed. M. Grünbart, Millenium-Studien 13 (Berlin: De Gruyter, 2007), 281–2.
42 On this terminology, see Manolis Bourbouhakis, 'Rhetoric and Performance', in *The Byzantine World*, ed. P. Stephenson (London: Routledge, 2010), 175–87.
43 *Stoikheiosis Astronomike* 1.1.49, Bydén, *Theodore Metochites' Stoicheiosis Astronomike and the Study of Natural Philosophy and Mathematics in Early Palaiologan Byzantium*, 418.
44 Metochites: Orationes, 675–6 (Oration 18, 3.1–16). On the oration's chronology, see Marcello Gigante, *Teodoro Metochites Saggio critic su Demostene e Aristide* (Milan: Istituto editoriale cisalpino, 1969), 10.
45 Metochites: Orationes, 677–8 (Oration 18, 5.14–26).
46 Metochites: Orationes, 678 (Oration 18, 5.25–44).
47 Metochites: Orationes, 679 (Oration 18, 6.10–28).
48 Metochites: Orationes, 679–80 (Oration 18, 7.1–18).
49 Metochites: Orationes, 682–3 (Oration 18, 11.12–42).
50 Metochites: Orationes, 683 (Oration 18, 11.43–4).
51 Metochites: Orationes, 683–4 (Oration 18, 11.56–12, 25).
52 Metochites: Orationes, 685 (Oration 18, 13.5–8).
53 Metochites: Orationes, 685 (Oration 18, 13.8–15).
54 Metochites: Orationes, 688–90 (Oration 18, 15.22–84)
55 Metochites: Orationes, 690 (Oration 18, 16.5–10).
56 Metochites: Orationes, 695 (Oration 18, 18.73–84).
57 Metochites: Orationes, 584 (Oration 13, 9.33–45).
58 Metochites: Orationes, 685 (Oration 18, 13.5).
59 Metochites: Orationes, 687 (Oration 18, 14.9–19):
60 Metochites: Orationes, 198–9 (Oration 6, 19.1–37).
61 Metochites: Orationes, 585 (Oration 13, 11, 8–19).
62 Metochites: Orationes, 198 (Oration 6, 19.14–17).
63 Metochites: Orationes, 688 (Oration 18, 15.22).

64 Metochites: Orationes, 691 (Oration 18, 16.17–26).
65 Jakov Ljubarskij, 'How Should a Byzantine Text Be Read?', in *Rhetoric in Byzantium: Papers from the Thirty-fifth Spring Symposium of Byzantine Studies, Exeter College, University of Oxford, March 2001*, ed. E. Jeffreys (Aldershot: Ashgate, 2003), 121.
66 Metochites: Orationes, 694 (Oration 18, 18.49–52).
67 Louis Pernot, 'Mimesis, rhétorique et politique dans l'essai de Théodore Métochite sur Démosthène et Aelius Aristide', *Quaderni dell'Accademia Pontaniana* 47 (2006): 119, despite pointing out that Metochites identifies himself with Aristeides, fails to understand the meaning of such an identification. Neither the Antonine Roman Empire of the second century CE nor the Byzantine Empire of the fourteenth century were so admirable for Metochites!
68 Metochites: Orationes, 677–8 (Oration 18, 5.14–44).
69 Metochites: Orationes, 681 (Oration 18, 11.1–6).
70 Metochites: Orationes, 688–90 (Oration 18, 15.22–84).
71 Metochites: Orationes, 691 (Oration 18, 16.16–18).
72 Hermogenes, *On Invention* A, 1, Rabe, *Hermogenes opera*, 93.9–94.3.
73 Metochites: Orationes, 678 (Oration 18, 6.5).
74 Although this participle does not refer to Aristeides, it is clear that he is the target of Metochites' criticism. See Metochites: Orationes, 681 (Oration 18, 10.10). By contrast, in Metochites: Orationes, 682 (Oration 18, 11.33), the participle clearly refers to him.
75 Metochites: Orationes, 695 (Oration 18, 18.68–73).
76 Metochites: Orationes, 694–5 (Oration 18, 18.58–68).
77 See Kaldellis, *Argument of Psellos'* Chronographia, 31–4.
78 Metochites: Orationes, 682 (Oration 18, 11.13–14).
79 Metochites: Orationes, 677–8 (Oration 18, 5.14–44).
80 Metochites: Orationes, 518–22 (Oration 11, 99.1–102.25).
81 Metochites: Orationes, 674 (Oration 18, 2.1–19).
82 Metochites: Orationes, 689 (Oration 18, 15.54–5).
83 Metochites: Orationes, 682 (Oration 18, 11.34–5).
84 Metochites: Orationes, 679 (Oration 18, 6.8–28).
85 Metochites: Orationes, 680 (Oration 18, 8.1–19).
86 Metochites: Orationes, 695 (Oration 18, 18.68–80).
87 Metochites: Orationes, 678 (Oration 18, 5.29–30).
88 Metochites: Orationes, 681 (Oration 18, 11.1–2).
89 Metochites: Orationes, 160 (Oration 5, 17.26–7).
90 Metochites: Orationes, 464 (Oration 11, 38.28–9).
91 Metochites: Orationes, 680–1 (Oration 18, 9.1–16).
92 Metochites: Orationes, 681 (Oration 18, 10.1–13).
93 Metochites: Orationes, 681 (Oration 18, 10.9).
94 Metochites: Orationes, 681 (Oration 18, 10.8).

Chapter 6

1 Papaioannou, *Michael Psellos*, 39.
2 Metochites: Poems, 60–2, Greek text 1, 308–82; Metochita: Carmina, 16–18.
3 Metochites: Orationes, 195–200 (Oration 6, 18.1–20.37).
4 Metochites: Orationes, 644–6 (Oration 17, 13.1–79).
5 Metochites: Poems, 124–30, Greek text 4, 24–196; Metochita: Carmina, 85–92.

6　Papaioannou, *Michael Psellos*, 85–7.
7　Papaioannou, *Michael Psellos*, 39.
8　Papaioannou, *Michael Psellos*, 48–50.
9　Papaioannou, *Michael Psellos*, 103–6.
10　Papaioannou, *Michael Psellos*, 118.
11　Pizzone, 'Introduction', *The Author in Middle Byzantine Literature*, 8–9.
12　Stratis Papaioannou, 'Voice, Signature, Mask: The Byzantine Author', in Pizzone, *The Author in Middle Byzantine Literature*, 26–7.

Chapter 7

1　Metochites: Poems, 164–6; Greek text 6, 500–42; Metochita: Carmina, 132–3.
2　Metochites: Poems, 114, Greek text 3, 59–71; Metochita: Carmina, 76.
3　Metochites: Poems, 118, Greek text 3, 155–61; Metochita: Carmina, 79.
4　Metochites: Poems, 324, Greek text 19, 213–27; Metochita: Carmina, 321.
5　Metochites: Poems, 87–8, Greek text 1, 1162–73; Metochita: Carmina, 46.
6　Metochites: Orationes, 631 (Oration 16, 20.1–19).
7　Metochites: Orationes, 688 (Oration 18, 15.25–6).
8　Metochites: Orationes, 45 (Oration 2, 21.41–6). Remarkably similar are the encounters of Theoleptos of Philadelpheia described by Nikephoros Choumnos in his Funeral Oration for the prelate. See Jean François Boissonade, *Anecdota graeca*, vol. 5 (Paris, 1833; repr., Hildesheim: Georg Olms Verlagsbuchhandlung, Hildesheim, 1962), 208.
9　Sententious Notes 60, Hult, *Theodore Metochites on the Human Condition and the Decline of Rome*, 217.
10　Metochites: Poems, 167, Greek text 6, 590–7; Metochita: Carmina, 135.
11　Metochites: Poems, 166, Greek text 6, 579; Metochita: Carmina, 134.
12　Metochites: Poems, 167, Greek text 6, 603–4; Metochita: Carmina, 135.
13　Metochites: Poems, 168, Greek text 6, 639 (cf. 6, 611); Metochita: Carmina, 136 (cf. 135).
14　Metochites: Poems, 169, Greek text 6, 644; Metochita: Carmina, 137.
15　Metochites: Poems, 169, Greek text 6, 645; Metochita: Carmina, 137.
16　Metochites: Poems, 169, Greek text 6, 645–50; Metochita: Carmina, 137.
17　Metochites: Orationes, 645 (Oration 17, 13.39–44).
18　Metochites: Poems, 125, Greek text 4, 25–35; Metochita: Carmina, 86.
19　Metochites: Poems, 150, Greek text 5, 455; Metochita: Carmina, 114.
20　Metochites: Poems, 169, Greek text 6, 643; Metochita: Carmina, 137.
21　Metochites: Poems, 149, Greek text 5, 429–30; Metochita: Carmina, 113.
22　See, for example, Metochites: Poems, 155, Greek text 6, 159–63; Metochita: Carmina, 120.
23　Metochites: Poems, 149, Greek text 5, 437–55; Metochita: Carmina, 113–14.
24　Metochites: Orationes, 195 (Oration 6, 17.31–45).
25　Metochites: Orationes, 351 (Oration 10, 7.4–9).
26　Metochites: Orationes, 157–8 (Oration 5, 13.4–14.22).
27　Metochites: Orationes, 172 (Oration 5, 32.3–8).
28　Metochites: Orationes, 172–3 (Oration 5, 32.3–8).
29　Metochites: Orationes, 596 (Oration 14, 10.15–19).
30　See Melzer, *Philosophy between the Lines*, 1–8.
31　Metochites: Poems, 251, Greek text 12, 199–206; Metochita: Carmina, 232.

32 Metochites: Orationes, 400–4 (Oration 10, 68.1–72.28), trans. Xenophontos, *On Morals or Concerning Education*, 158–70.
33 Anne-Marie Malingrey, '*Philosophia*': *Étude d'une groupe des mots dans la littérature grecque, des Présocratiques au IVe siècle après J.-C.* Études et Commentaires 40 (Paris: Klincksieck, 1961), 59–9 and 81–5.
34 Ernst H. Kantorowicz, 'Die Wiederkehr gelehrter Anachorese in Mittelalter', in *Selected Studies* (Locust Valley, NY: J. J. Augustin Publishers, 1965), 339–44.
35 Free translation. Metochites: Orationes, 387–8 (Oration 10, 54, 1–33), trans. Xenophontos, *On Morals or Concerning Education*, 119–21.
36 Metochites: Poems, 249, Greek text 12, 152, Metochita: Carmina, 230. On the metaphor of the feast, see Alberto Grilli, *Il problema della vita contemplativa nel mondo Greco-romano* (Milan: Fratelli Bocca, 1953), 328; Pierre Hadot, *Philosophy as a Way of Life*, ed. A. I. Davidson, trans. Michael Chase (Oxford: Blackwell Publishers, 1995), 181–2 and 264–5. See also A. J. Festugière, *Le Dieu cosmique*, vol. 2 of *La révélation d'Hermès trismégiste* (Paris: Librairie Lecoffre, 1949), 233–8.
37 See A. J. Festugière, *L'idéal religieux des Grecs et l'évangile* (Paris: J. Gabalda, 1932), 129, and n. 1; Pierre Boyancé, *Études sur le 'Songe de Scipion'*, Bibliothèque des universités du Midi 20 (Bordeaux: Feret et Fils, 1936), 116–19; and Robert Joly, *Le thème philosophique des genres de vie dans l'Antiquité Classique*, Académie royale de Belgique, Classe des Lettres et des Sciences Morales et Politiques. Mémoires, 2nd ser., 51.3 (Brussels: Palais des Académies, 1956), 35–9.
38 On this theme, see Festugière, *Le Dieu cosmique*, 441–59.
39 See especially Festugière, *Le Dieu cosmique,* 153–95, for an explanation of the intellectual background of this trend of Hellenistic spirituality.
40 A. J. Festugière, *Hermétisme et mystique païenne* (Paris: Aubier-Montaigne, 1967), 26–7. See also A. J. Festugière, 'Les thèmes du *Songe de Scipion*', in *Eranos Rudbergianus: Opuscula philologica Gunnaro Rudberg A.D. XVI Kal. Nov. anno MCMXLV dedicate* (Gothenburg: Elander Boktryckeri Aktiebolag, 1946), 375–85.
41 On the early fathers, see Joshua Gareth Lollar, '"To See into the Life of Things": The Contemplation of Nature in Maximus the Confessor's *Ambigua* to John', vol. 1 (PhD diss., University of Notre Dame, 2011), 117–205. See also Michel Spanneut, *Le stoïcisme des pères de l'église: De Clément de Rome à Clément d'Alexandrie* (Paris: Le Seuil, 1957), 274–85.
42 Free translation. Philo Judaeus, *De specialibus legibus* 3.1, Leopold Cohn and Paul Wendland, *Philonis Alexandrini opera quae supersunt*, vol. 5, editio minor (Berlin: Reimer, 1906), 129.6–130.5. See also Festugière, *Le Dieu cosmique*, 551–3.
43 Hadot, *Philosophy as a Way of Life*, 238–50.
44 Philo Judaeus, *De vita contemplativa* 27, Leopold Cohn and Paul Wendland, *Philonis Alexandrini opera quae supersunt*, vol. 6, editio minor (Berlin: Reimer, 1915), 37.11–17. Recently Zaras, 'Illness and Healing', 85–119, has attempted to interpret the iconographical circle of the monastery of Chora as an expression of Metochites' intellectual preoccupations. It is an interesting idea, but the way Zaras tries to prove his views is hardly convincing. He even tries to explain the presence of John the Baptist in a mosaic as the model of the spirituality, adducing the passage of Philo in question referring to the Therapeutai; however, to interpret the passage of Metochites we discussed above as a cryptic reference to John the Baptist, as Zaras (p. 90) tries to do, has no basis.
45 See Festugière, *Le Dieu cosmique*, 561–72.
46 Metochites: Orationes, 424 (Oration 10, 96.5–21), trans. Xenophontos, *On Morals or Concerning Education*, 230.

47 See Daniel S. Richter, *Cosmopolis: Imagining Community in Late Classical Athens and the Early Roman Empire* (Oxford: Oxford University Press, 2011), 61–86.
48 See, for example, Michel Spanneut, *Permanence du stoïcisme: De Zénon à Malraux* (Gembloux: J. Duculot, 1973), 152–3, on the appearence of this theory in the works of the church fathers.
49 Philo Judaeus, *Septem contra Thebas* 2.248, Leopold Cohn and Paul Wendland *Philonis Alexandrini opera quae supersunt*, vol. 3, editio minor (Berlin: Reimer, 1898), 281.22–7. On this theme in the works of Philo, see Festugière, *Le Dieu cosmique*, 537–40.
50 Interestingly, Michael Gabras stresses this particular aspect in a letter to Metochites, discussing the soul of the recipient of his letter. See Letter 179, 58–74, Fatouros, *Die Briefe des Michael Gabras*, 300.
51 On the Stoic connection between microcosm and macrocosm, see Spanneut, *Le stoïcisme des pères de l'église*, 414–16.
52 Metochites was not alone in this respect. Gregory of Cyprus complains in his autobiography about his inability to pursue his studies because of his public duties. See William Lameere, *La tradition manuscrite de la correspondance de Grégoire de Chypre patriarche de Constantinople (1283–1289)* (Brussels: Palais des académies, 1937), 189.9–16. The same applies to the Autobiography of Nikephoros Blemmydes, see ch. 38, 6–8, Joseph Munitiz, *Nicephori Blemmydae Autobiographia, sive, Curriculum vitae; necnon, Epistula universalior*, Corpus Christianorum, Series Graeca 13 (Turnhout: Brepols; Leuven: Leuven University Press, 1984), 21–2.
53 Metochites: Orationes, 362 (Oration 10, 21.1–13), trans. Xenophontos, *On Morals or Concerning Education*, 49.
54 See, for example, Maximus Confessor, *Capita de caritate* 4.1 (PG 90:1048B).
55 Philo Judaeus, *De vita contemplativa* 20, Cohn and Wendland [Reiter?], *Philonis Alexandrini opera quae supersunt*, 6:36.7–11. See also Grilli, *Il problema della vita contemplativa nel mondo Greco-romano*, 190.
56 See Festugière, *Le Dieu cosmique*, 527–8.
57 Metochites: Poems, 126–7, Greek text 4, 89–122; Metochita: Carmina, 88–9.
58 On the background of this thought, see Joly, *Le thème philosophique des genres de vie dans l'Antiquité Classique*, 43–52, and Myrto Dragona-Monachou, *The Stoic Arguments for the Existence and the Providence of the Gods* (Athens: National and Capodistrian University of Athens, Faculty of Arts, 1976), 147–51 and 227–30.
59 See some relevant texts in Festugière, *Le Dieu cosmique*, 213–32.
60 See David T. Runia, *Philo of Alexandria and the Timaeus of Plato* (Leiden: Brill, 1986), 458–61, where the motif of 'admiration of the cosmos, praise for the creator' is discussed.
61 Christian Gottried Müller and Gottlieb Kiessling, eds, *Miscellanea philosophica et historica: Textum e codice Cizensi descripsit, lectionisque varietatem ex aliquot aliis acodicibus enotattam adiecit C. G. Müller. Editio auctoris morte praeventa, cui praefatus est Th. Kiessling* (Leipzig: 1821), 581.
62 Müller and Kiessling, *Miscellanea philosophica et historica*, 581–2.
63 Maximus of Tyre, Oration 10, 6–8, ed. Michael Trapp, *Maximus Tyrius: Dissertationes*, Bibliotheca Scriptorum Graecorum et Romanorum Teubneriana (Leipzig: Teubner, 1994), 77. On this theme, see Hadot, *Philosophy as a Way of Life*, 241, and J. D. P. Bolton, *Aristeas of Proconnesus* (Oxford: Clarendon Press, 1962), 121–3. A similar example appears in the Oration for Gregory of Nazianzus of Thomas Magistros (PG 145:264D).
64 See Spanneut, *Le stoïcisme des pères de l'église*, 216–22.

65 Metochites: Orationes, 388 (Oration 10, 54.31–3), trans. Xenophontos, *On Morals or Concerning Education*, 121.
66 Metochites: Poems, 228–30, Greek text 10, 843–86; Metochita: Carmina, 206–7.
67 See Spanneut, *Le stoïcisme des pères de l'église*, 362–79.
68 On this term, see Spanneut, *Le stoïcisme des pères de l'église*, 296–301, and Spanneut, *Permanence du stoicism*, 151–2. See also Lars Thunberg, *Microcosm and Mediator: The Theological Anthropology of Maximus the Confessor*, foreword by A. M. Allchin, 2nd edn (Chicago: Open Court Publishing Co., 1995), 64–6, and Lollar, '"To See into the Life of Things"', 392, on the meaning of the term in Maximus the Confessor.
69 Metochites: Orationes, 387 (Oration 10, 54.16–17).
70 Metochites: Poems, 219, Greek text 10, 510–12; Metochita: Carmina, 194.
71 Gerhard Richter, *Theodoros Dukas Laskaris, der naturliche Zusammenhang: Ein Zeugnis von Stand der byzantinischen Philosophie in der Mitte des 13. Jahrhunderts* (Amsterdam: Adolf M. Hakkert, 1989), 161.
72 Xenophontos, 'Exploring Emotions in Late Byzantium', 449–51, examines the same problem, treating the intellectual presuppositions and sources of Metochites' opinions on spiritual delight.
73 Metochites: Orationes, 382 (Oration 10, 48.16–34), trans. Xenophontos, *On Morals or Concerning Education*, 103–5.
74 Metochites: Orationes, 384 (Oration 10, 50.15–32), trans. Xenophontos, *On Morals or Concerning Education*, 109.
75 This view was shared by his contemporary Thomas Magistros, *On Kingship* 25.1147–70, Paola Volpe Cacciatore, *[Toma Magistro's] La regalità: Testo critico, introduzione e indici* (Naples: M. D'Auria Editore, 1997), 74–5.
76 Synesius of Cyrene, *Dion* 8.2, ed. Jacques Lamoureux and Noël Aujoulat, *Synésios de Cyrène,* vol. 4, *Opuscules I* (Paris: Les Belles Lettres, 2004), 159.
77 Gerhard Podskalsky, *Theologie und Philosophie in Byzanz: Die Streit um die theologische Methodik in der spätbyzantinischen Geistesgeschichte (14/15. Jh.), seine systematischen Grundlagen und seine historische Entwicklung* (Munich: C. H. Beck, 1977), 34–48.
78 See Kimmelman, *Poetics of Authorship in the Later Middle Ages*, 72.
79 See Maximos Planoudes, Letter 68, Pietro Luigi Leone, *Maximi monachi Planudis epistulae* (Amsterdam: A. M. Hakkert, 1991), 104.19–23, where he speaks about the delight of the soul of anyone dealing with the four mathematical lessons.
80 Stavros Kourousis, *Τὸ ἐπιστολάριον Ἀνδρονίκου Λακαπηνοῦ-Γεωργίου Ζαρίδου καὶ ὁ ἰατρὸς-ἀκτουάριος Ἰωάννης Ζαχαρίας: Μελέτη φιλολογική* (Athens: Scientific Society of Athens, 1988), 452–6.
81 Kourousis, *Τὸ ἐπιστολάριον Ἀνδρονίκου Λακαπηνοῦ*, 206–42.
82 Kourousis, *Τὸ ἐπιστολάριον Ἀνδρονίκου Λακαπηνοῦ*, 463–83.
83 See Papaioannou, *Michael Psellos*, 140–52.
84 Kaldellis, *Argument of Psellos'* Chronographia, 154–66.
85 Kaldellis, *Argument of Psellos'* Chronographia, 161.
86 Metochites: Orationes, 619 (Oration 16, 8.8–11)
87 Metochites: Poems, 98, Greek text 2, 161–85; Metochita: Carmina, 57–8.
88 See the pertinent remarks of Beck, *Theodoros Metochites*, 28–49, on some similar passages in the edition of Miller and Kiessling, *Miscellanea philosophica et historica*. By contrast, the opinion of De Vries-Van der Velden, *Théodore Métochite*, 174, and n. 115, are too tenuous, taking at face value some negative assessments of the contemplative life in the same work.
89 Metochites: Orationes, 389–90 (Oration 10, 57, 1–31).

90 Metochites: Orationes, 390–1 (Oration 10, 58, 1–26).
91 Metochites: Orationes, 392 (Oration 10, 59, 15–18).
92 Maximilian Treu, 'Der Philosoph Joseph', *Byzantinische Zeitschrift* 8 (1899): 34.3–35.27.
93 For background on this comparison in Greek thought, see Grilli, *Il problema della vita contemplativa nel mondo Greco-romano*, 33–164, and Joly, *Le thème philosophique des genres de vie dans l'Antiquité Classique*, 40–127.
94 Although certain intellectuals distanced themselves from this uncompromising stance, see Manuel Gabalas, Letter B 4.15–18, Reinsch, *Die Briefe des Matthaios von Ephesos im Codex Vindobonensis Theol. Gr. 174*, 86. Manuel argues that the philosopher must also involve himself in political affairs, citing Plato as his authority.
95 Anton Elter, 'Hermodotus et Mousocles dialogi primum editi', in *Natalicia regis augustissimi Guilelmi II ab universitate Fridericia Guilelmi Rhenana a. 1898 concelebranda* (Bonn: Ex Caroli Georgi typographeo academico, 1898), 50.431–6.
96 Ludwig Schopen, ed., *Ioannis Cantacuzeni eximperatoris historiarum libri IV*, vol. 1, *Graeca et Latine*, Corpus Scriptorum Historiae Byzantinae (Bonn: Weber, 1828), 8.19–9.10.
97 Treu, 'Der Philosoph Joseph', 34.7–36.14.
98 Boissonade, *Anecdota graeca*, 3:188–9.
99 Metochites: Orationes, 350 (Oration 10, 6.1–16).
100 Metochites: Orationes, 392–3 (Oration 10, 60.1–19).
101 Metochites: Orationes, 395–7 (Oration 10, 64.1–59).
102 Metochites: Orationes, 398 (Oration 10, 66.1–23).
103 Metochites: Orationes, 399–400 (Oration 10, 67.20–39).
104 Despite the reservations of Alexander Riehle, 'Funktionen der byzantinischen Epistolographie. Studien zu den Briefen und Briefsammlungen des Nikephoros Chumnos (ca. 1260–1327' (https://edoc.ub.uni-muenchen.de/16879/) (PhD diss., Ludwig-Maximilians-Universität München, 2011): 81*, and Gaul, *Thomas Magistros und die spätbyzantinische Sophistik*, 303–5.
105 Boissonade, *Anecdota graeca*, 5:287. See the new edition of Riehle, 'Die Briefsammlungen des Nikephoros Chumnos', 49.29–50.3.
106 Metochites: Orationes, 633 (Oration 17, title).
107 Thomas Pratsch, *Der hagiographische Topos: Griechische Heiligenviten in mittelbyzantinischer Zeit*, Millenium-Studien 6 (Berlin: De Gruyter, 2005) 117–22.
108 Metochites: Orationes, 640 (Oration 17, 8.23–30).
109 Pratsch, *Der hagiographische Topos*, 147–54.
110 Metochites: Orationes, 641 (Oration 17, 10.1–13).
111 Metochites: Orationes, 654–5 (Oration 17, 24.8–24).
112 Life of St Athanasios, A 41.1–21, Jacques Noret, *Vitae duae antiquae sancti Athanasii Athonitae*, Corpus Christianorum, Series Graeca 9 (Turnhout: Brepols; Leuven: Leuven University Press, 1982), 20–1.
113 Metochites: Orationes, 647 (Oration 17, 5.1–7).
114 Metochites: Orationes, 648–51 (Oration 17, 17.1–21.32).
115 Metochites: Orationes, 652–3 (Oration 17, 22.1–65).
116 Ioannis Polemis, 'Life of St George of Chozeva', in Ἀνθολόγιο βυζαντινῆς πεζογραφίας (Athens: Papazisis Publishers, 2018), 292–3. See also Tim Vivian, ed., *Journeying into God. Seven Early Monastic Lives*, Translated with Introductions, (Minneapolis: Fortress Press 1996), 93.
117 Metochites: Orationes, 655 (Oration 17, 24.14–16).

118 Metochites: Orationes, 656 (Oration 17, 25.1–3).
119 Palladius, *Lausaikon* 21.1–14, ed. G. J. M. Bartelink, *[Palladius'] La storia lausiaca: Testo critico e commento,* 4th edn (Milan: Fondazione Lorenzo Valla, 1990), 104–14. A similar story appears in the Autobiography of Blemmydes, 40.1–16, Munitiz, *Nicephori Blemmydae Autobiographia,* 22, but there the monk under Blemmydes' protection attempts to assassinate him!
120 Metochites: Orationes, 657–8 (Oration 17, 26.1–28).
121 Metochites: Orationes, 664–5 (Oration 17, 32.33–42).
122 Pratsch, *Der hagiographische Topos*, 140–3.
123 Metochites: Orationes, 642 (Oration 17, 10.28–30).

Chapter 8

1   Metochites: Orationes, 454 (Oration 11, 19.6–10).
2   Metochites: Orationes, 457–8 (Oration 11, 32.1–14).
3   Metochites: Orationes, 468 (Oration 11, 42.14–15).
4   Metochites: Orationes, 471 (Oration 11, 47.10–14).
5   Metochites: Orationes, 480–1 (Oration 11, 58.13–22).
6   Metochites: Orationes, 495 (Oration 11, 74.13–20).
7   Metochites: Orationes, 501–2 (Oration 11, 80.33–48).
8   Metochites: Orationes, 503 (Oration 11, 83.1–2).
9   Metochites: Orationes, 510 (Oration 11, 91.18–23).
10 Metochites: Orationes, 510 (Oration 11, 91.1–4).
11 See Spanneut, *Le stoïcisme des pères de l'église*, 388–91.
12 Spanneut, *Le stoïcisme des pères de l'église*, 388–9, with the relevant bibliography cited in notes. See also Gaul, *Thomas Magistros und die spätbyzantinische Sophistik*, 146.
13 *Quis rerum divinarum heres sit* 55, Wendland, *Philonis Alexandrini opera quae supersunt*, 3:11.7–9.
14 *Enneades* 5, 9.13.2–3, Paul Henry and Han-Rudolf Schwyzer, *Plotini opera*, vol. 2, *Enneades IV–V*, Museum Lessianum Series, Philosophica 34 (Paris: Desclée de Brouwer et Cie; Bruxelles: L'Édition Universelle, 1959), 426.
15 Metochites: Orationes, 519 (Oration 11, 99.10).
16 Metochites: Orationes, 513 (Oration 11, 94.1–4)
17 Metochites: Orationes, 518 (Oration 11, 98.10–14).
18 Metochites: Orationes, 387 (Oration 10, 54.11–17).
19 Thomas Magistros, Epistle 1 (PG 145:405B).
20 See, for example, Festugière, *Le Dieu cosmique*, 271–8; Jens Pfeiffer, *Contemplatio Caeli: Untersuchungen zum Motiv der Himmelsbetrachtung in lateinischen Texten der Antike und des Mittelalters*, Spolia Berolinensia 12 (Hildesheim: Weidmann, 1994), 50–2; and Malcolm Schofield, *The Stoic Idea of a City*, with a new foreword by Martha C. Nussbaum and a new epilogue by the author (Chicago: University of Chicago Press, 1999), 57–92.
21 See, for example, Festugière, *L'idéal religieux des Grecs et l'évangile*, 272–5.
22 Metochites: Orationes, 510 (Oration 11, 91.2).
23 Ernst H. Kantorowicz, *The King's Two Bodies: A Study in Medieval Political Theology*, with a new preface by W. C. Jordan (Princeton: Princeton University Press, 1981), 207–32.

24 See, for example, Joseph Moreau, *L'âme du monde de Platon aux stoïciens* (Paris: Les Belles Lettres, 1939), 2–55; Festugière, *Le Dieu cosmique*, 123–29; and Jean Pépin, *Théologie cosmique et théologie chrétienne (Ambroise, Exam. I 1, 1–4)* (Paris: Presses Universitaires de France, 1964), 198–9.
25 Kantorowicz, *The King's Two Bodies*, 472–5.
26 PG 140:1409A–1416B.
27 Metochites: Orationes, 505 (Oration 11, 85.9–16).
28 Metochites: Orationes, 113 (Oration 4, 2.76–81).
29 Metochites: Orationes, 431 (Oration 11, 4.1–3).
30 Metochites: Orationes, 471 (Oration 11, 47, 13–14).
31 Metochites: Orationes, 411 (Oration 10, 81.1–8).
32 Metochites: Orationes, 14 (Oration 1, 17.1–24).
33 Metochites: Orationes, 282 (Oration 7, 21.15).
34 Metochites: Orationes, 282 (Oration 7, 21.15–16).
35 Müller and Kiessling, *Miscellanea philosophica et historica*, 613 and 634–5.
36 Kantorowicz, *The King's Two Bodies*, 459, n. 24.
37 Sententious Notes 37–39, Hult, *Theodore Metochites on the Human Condition and the Decline of Rome*, 64–82.
38 Gaul, *Thomas Magistros und die spätbyzantinische Sophistik*, 191–2.
39 Metochites: Orationes, 519–20 (Oration 11, 100.1–35).
40 Metochites: Orationes, 520 (Oration 11, 100.20).
41 Metochites: Orationes, 520 (Oration 11, 101.1–7).
42 Metochites: Orationes, 520 (Oration 11, 101.10–11).
43 Metochites: Orationes, 521 (Oration 11, 101.23).
44 Metochites: Orationes, 519 (Oration 11, 99.13–20).
45 *Republic* 514a–518b.

Chapter 9

1 Metochites: Poems, 215, Greek text 10, 416–17; Metochita: Carmina, 190.
2 Müller and Kiessling, *Miscellanea philosophica et historica*, 264. On the image of the feast, see Pierre Hadot, *Le voile d'Isis: Essai sur l'histoire de l'idée de nature* (Paris: Gallimard, 2004), 194–5.
3 See Dimitar Angelov, *The Byzantine Hellene: The Life of Emperor Theodore Laskaris and Byzantium in the Thirteenth Century* (Cambridge: Cambridge University Press, 2019), 184–8. On some aspects of the idea of nature in the Byzantine romances, see Carolina Cupane, '"Natura formatrix": Umwege eines rhetorischen Topos', in *Byzantios: Festschrift für Herbert Hunger zum. 70 Geburtstag dargebracht von Schülern und Mitarbeitern*, ed. W. Hörandner, J. Koder, O. Kresten and E. Trapp (Vienna: E. Becvar, 1984), 37–52.
4 See Charlotte Köckert, *Christliche Kosmologie und kaiserzeitliche Philosophie*, Studien und Texte zu Antike und Christentum 56 (Tübingen: Mohr Siebeck, 2009), 438–46 and 522–3.
5 M.-D. Chenu, *Nature, Man, and Society in the Twelfth Century: Essays on New Theological Perspectives in the Latin West*, with a preface by E. Gilson, selected, edited and translated by J. Taylor and L. K. Little (Toronto: University of Toronto Press, in association with the Medieval Academy of America, 1997), 4–13. He seems to identify

nature with God as the ancient Stoics did. See Dragona-Monachou, *Stoic Arguments for the Existence and the Providence of the Gods*, 138-47.
6   Chenu, *Nature, Man, and Society in the Twelfth Century*, 20-2.
7   Chenu, *Nature, Man, and Society in the Twelfth Century*, 33. See also Ruth Finckh, *Minor Mundus Homo: Studien zur Mikrokosmos in der mittelalterischen Literatur*, Palaestra 306 (Göttingen: Vandenhoeck & Ruprecht, 1999), 24-61.
8   See Bydén, *Theodore Metochites' Stoicheiosis Astronomike and the Study of Natural Philosophy and Mathematics in Early Palaiologan Byzantium*, 216-62; Jurgen Mittelstrass, *Die Rettung der Phänome: Ursprung und Geschichte eines antikes Forschungsprinzip* (Berlin: De Gruyter, 1962), 164-73; Dominique O'Meara, *Pythagoras Revived: Mathematics and Philosophy in Late Antiquity* (Oxford: Clarendon Press, 1989), 44-5, and 181-94; and Hadot, *Le voile d'Isis*, 71 and 171.
9   The two meanings of the term 'nature' have been thoroughly discussed elsewhere. For more, see Bydén, *Theodore Metochites' Stoicheiosis Astronomike and the Study of Natural Philosophy and Mathematics in Early Palaiologan Byzantium*, 263-361.
10 On nature as a negative thing in medieval Western thought, see Étienne Gilson, 'Le Moyen Âge et le naturalisme antique', in *Moyen Âge et Renaissance au Collège de France: Leçons inaugurals*, ed. P. Toubert, M. Zink and O. Bombard (Paris: Fayard, 2009), 268-9. The same applies to the term 'world' (κόσμος), which is used by Metochites with various meanings, both positive and negative, in his works.
11 See Gilson, 'Le Moyen Âge et le naturalisme antique', 269-71.
12 Metochites: Orationes, 423 (Oration 10, 95.1-5).
13 Metochites: Orationes, 423 (Oration 10, 95.17-20).
14 Metochites: Orationes, 424 (Oration 10, 96.15-16).
15 Metochites: Orationes, 350-2 (Oration 10, 7.1-34).
16 Metochites: Orationes, 386 (Oration 10, 52.18).
17 Metochites: Orationes, 425 (Oration 10, 97.4-6).
18 Metochites: Orationes, 410 (Oration 10, 80.11).
19 Metochites: Orationes, 361 (Oration 10, 19.9-10).
20 Metochites: Orationes, 363 (Oration 10, 22.5-8), trans. Xenophontos, *On Morals or Concerning Education*, 51.
21 Müller and Kiessling, *Miscellanea philosophica et historica*, 732. See also Ševčenko, 'Theodore Metochites, the Chora and the Intellectual Trends of His Time', 47.
22 See also Teresa Shawcross, 'Theories of Decline from Metochites to Ibn Khaldun', in *The Cambridge Intellectual History of Byzantium*, ed. A. Kaldellis and N. Siniossoglou (Cambridge: Cambridge University Press, 2017), 621-8.
23 Metochites: Orationes, 283 (Oration 7, 22.20-2).
24 On the development of this concept in classical antiquity, see Sue Blundell, *The Origins of Civilization in Greek and Roman Thought* (London: Croom Helm, 1986), 203-24.
25 On *Hodoiporikon* and its connection with autobiography, see Margaret Mullett, 'In Peril on the Sea: Travel Genres and the Unexpected', in *Travel in the Byzantine World: Papers from the Thirty-fourth Spring Symposium of Byzantine Studies, Birmingham, April 2000*, ed. R. Macrides (Aldershot: Ashgate, 2002), 261, and Angold, 'The Autobiographical Impulse in Byzantium', 253.
26 Metochites: Orationes, 322 (Oration 8, 30.18-23).
27 Metochites: Orationes, 322 (Oration 8, 30.28-31).
28 On Metochites' attitude towards foreigners, which is far from the traditional Byzantine one, see Panagiotis A. Agapitos, Karin Hult and Ole L. Smith, eds, *Theodoros Metochites on Philosophic Irony and Greek History* (Nicosia: Department of Greek

Studies, Philosophy and History, University of Cyprus; Gothenburg: Department of Classical Studies, Gothenburg University, 1996), 14–15.
29 Chenu, *Nature, Man, and Society in the Twelfth Century*, 24.
30 Kaldellis, *Argument of Psellos'* Chronographia, 93–7.
31 Sententious Notes 58.1, Hult, *Theodore Metochites on the Human Condition and the Decline of Rome*, 184.20–1.
32 Sententious Notes 58.1, Hult, *Theodore Metochites on the Human Condition and the Decline of Rome*, 184.21–4.
33 Sententious Notes 58.1, Hult, *Theodore Metochites on the Human Condition and the Decline of Rome*, 186.10–11.
34 Sententious Notes 58.11, Hult, *Theodore Metochites on the Human Condition and the Decline of Rome*, 202.29–204.1.
35 Metochites: Orationes, 520–1 (Oration 11, 101.1–28).
36 Hubert Dreyfus and Sean Dorrance Kelly, *All Things Shining: Reading the Western Classics to Find Meaning in a Secular Age* (New York: Free Press, 2011), 18.
37 Sophocles, *Oedipus Coloneus* 1225–8.
38 Richard J. Jebb, *Sophocles: The Plays and Fragments with Critical Notes, Commentary and Translation in English Prose*, vol. 2, *The Oedipus Coloneus* (Cambridge: Cambridge University Press, 1928), 194.
39 Fragment 449, 4–6, ed. Richard Kannicht, *Tragicorum Graecorum Fragmenta*, vol. 5, *Euripides* (Göttingen: Vandehoeck & Ruprecht, 2004), 487.
40 Annette Harder, *Euripides' Kresphontes and Archelaos: Introduction, Text and Commentary* (Leiden: Brill, 1985), 93–4, where several passages of Greek authors sharing this pessimistic view of human life are adduced.
41 *Ethica Nicomachea* 1177a12–33.

Conclusion

1 Leo Strauss, *The Rebirth of Classical Political Rationalism: An Introduction to the Thought of Leo Strauss. Essays and Lectures by Leo Strauss Selected and Introduced by T. L. Pangle* (Chicago: University of Chicago Press, 1989), 64.
2 Boissonade, *Anecdota graeca*, 3:356–7.
3 Sententious Notes 1.1, Hult, *Theodore Metochites on Ancient Authors and Philosophy*, 20.23–22.2. This seems to be the view of his student Nikephoros Gregoras, too. See his *Antilogia* 115–16, Pietro Luigi Leone, 'Nicephori Gregorae *Antilogia* et *Solutiones quaestionum*', *Byzantion* 40 (1970): 483.
4 Mircea Eliade, *A History of Religious Ideas*, vol. 1, *From the Stone Age to the Eleusinian*, trans. W. R. Trask (Chicago: University of Chicago Press, 1978), 82.
5 Ševčenko, 'Theodore Metochites, the Chora and the Intellectual Trends of His Time', 40.

Appendix

1 Metochites: Orationes.
2 See Emmanuel A. Paschos and Christos Simelidis, *Introduction to Astronomy by Theodore Metochites (Stoicheiosis Astronomike 1.5–30)* (Hackensack, NJ: World Scientific Publishing, 2017), 2–3.

3 Metochita: Carmina. All the poems are newly translated.
4 Metochites: Poems.
5 Hult, *Theodore Metochites on Ancient Authors and Philosophy*; Hult, *Theodore Metochites on the Human Condition and the Decline of Rome*; and Wahlgren, *Theodore Metochites' Sententious Notes*.

BIBLIOGRAPHY

Primary resources: Texts and editions

Theodore Metochites

Agapitos, Panagiotis A., Karin Hult and Ole L. Smith, eds. *Theodoros Metochites on Philosophic Irony and Greek History*. Nicosia: Department of Greek Studies, Philosophy and History, University of Cyprus; and Gothenburg: Department of Classical Studies, Gothenburg University, 1996.

Featherstone, Jeffrey Michael. *Theodore Metochites's Poems to Himself: Introduction, Text and Translation*. Byzantina Vindobonensia 23. Vienna: Verlag der Österreichischen Akademie der Wissenschaften, 2000.

Gigante, Marcello. *Teodoro Metochites Saggio critic su Demostene e Aristide*. Milan: Istituto editoriale cisalpino, 1969.

Hult, Karin. *Theodore Metochites on Ancient Authors and Philosophy: Semeioseis Gnomikai 1–26 & 71. A Critical Edition with Introduction, Translation, Notes and Indexes with a Contribution by B. Bydén*. Acta Universitatis Gothoburgensis. Gothenburg: University of Gothenburg, 2002.

Hult, Karin. *Theodore Metochites on the Human Condition and the Decline of Rome: Semeioseis Gnomikai 27–60. Critical Edition with Introduction, Translation, Notes and Indexes*. Gothenburg: University of Gothenburg, 2016.

Müller, Christian Gottried, and Gottlieb Kiessling, eds. *Miscellanea philosophica et historica: Textum e codice Cizensi descripsit, lectionisque varietatem ex aliquot aliis acodicibus enotattam adiecit C. G. Müller. Editio auctoris morte praevanta, cui praefatus est Th. Kiessling*. Leipzig: 1821.

Paschos, Emmanuel A., and Christos Simelidis. *Introduction to Astronomy by Theodore Metochites (Stoicheiosis Astronomike 1.5–30)*. Hackensack, NJ: World Scientific Publishing, 2017.

Polemis, Ioannis. *Θεόδωρος Μετοχίτης: Ἠθικὸς ἢ Περὶ παιδείας. Εἰσαγωγή-Κριτικὴ ἔκδοση-Μετάφραση-Σημειώσεις*. Athens: Kanakis Publishers, 1995.

Polemis, Ioannis. *Θεόδωρος Μετοχίτης: Ἠθικὸς ἢ Περὶ παιδείας. Εἰσαγωγή-Κριτικὴ ἔκδοση-Μετάφραση-Σημειώσεις*. 2nd edn. Athens: Kanakis Publishers, 2002.

Polemis, Ioannis. *Οἱ δύο βασιλικοὶ λόγοι: Εἰσαγωγή-Κριτικὴ ἔκδοση-Μετάφραση-Σημειώσεις*. Athens: Kanakis Publishers, 2007.

Polemis, Ioannis. *Θεόδωρος Μετοχίτης: Βυζάντιος ἢ Περὶ τῆς βασιλίδος μεγαλοπόλεως. Κοσμολογία καὶ ρητορικὴ κατὰ τὸν ΙΔ΄ αἰῶνα – Εἰσαγωγή, κριτικὴ ἔκδοση, μετάφραση, σημειώσεις*. Thessaloniki: Zitros Publishers, 2013.

Polemis, Ioannis, ed. *Theodorus Metochita: Carmina*. Corpus Christianorum, Series Graeca 83. Turnhout: Brepols, 2015.

Polemis, Ioannis, ed. *Theodore Metochites: Poems. Introduction, Translation and Notes*. Corpus Christianorum in Translation 26 Malingrey 1961. Turnhout: Brepols, 2017.

Polemis, Ioannis, and Eleni Kaltsogianni, eds. *Theodorus Metochites: Orationes.* Bibliotheca Scriptorum Graecorum et Romanorum Teubneriana. Berlin: De Gruyter, 2019.

Wahlgren, Staffan. *Theodore Metochites' Sententious Notes: Semeioseis Gnomikai 61–70 & 72–81. A Critical Edition with Introduction, Translation, Notes and Indexes.* Gothenburg: University of Gothenburg, 2018.

Xenophontos, Sophia, trans. *On Morals or Concerning Education: Theodore Metochites.* Dumbarton Oaks Medieval Library 61. Cambridge, MA: Harvard University Press, 2020.

Additional authors

Bartelink, G. J. M., ed. *[Palladius'] La storia lausiaca: Testo critico e commento.* 4th edn. Milan: Fondazione Lorenzo Valla, 1990.

Bernard, Floris, and Christopher Livanos. *The Poems of Christopher of Mytilene and John Mauropous.* Dumbarton Oaks Medieval Library 50. Cambridge, MA: Harvard University Press, 2018.

Boissonade, Jean François, ed. *Anecdota graeca.* Vol. 3. Paris, 1831. Reprint, Hildesheim: Georg Olms Verlagsbuchhandlung, 1962.

Boissonade, Jean François, ed. *Anecdota graeca.* Vol. 5. Paris, 1833. Reprint, Hildesheim: Georg Olms Verlagsbuchhandlung, Hildesheim, 1962.

Cacciatore, Paola Volpe. *[Toma Magistro's] La regalità: Testo critico, introduzione e indici.* Naples: M. D'Auria Editore, 1997.

Wendland Paul, ed. *Philonis Alexandrini opera quae supersunt.* Vol. 3. Editio minor. Berlin: Reimer, 1898.

Cohn Leopold, ed. *Philonis Alexandrini opera quae supersunt.* Vol. 5. Editio minor. Berlin: Reimer, 1906.

Cohn Leopold, and Reiter Siegfried, eds. *Philonis Alexandrini opera quae supersunt.* Vol. 6. Editio minor. Berlin: Reimer, 1915.

Elter, Anton. 'Hermodotus et Mousocles dialogi primum editi'. In *Natalicia regis augustissimi Guilelmi II ab universitate Fridericia Guilelmi Rhenana a. 1898 concelebranda,* cols. 5–54. Bonn: Ex Caroli Georgi typographeo academico, 1898.

Fatouros, Georgios. *Die Briefe des Michael Gabras (ca. 1290–nach 1350).* Vol. 2, *Text.* Wiener Byzantinistische Studien 10.2. Vienna: Österreichische Akademie der Wissenschaften, 1973.

Garzya, Antonio, ed. *Nicephori Basilacae: Orationes et Epistulae.* Bibliotheca Scriptorum Graecorum et Romanorum Teubneriana. Leipzig: Teubner, 1984.

Henry, Paul, and Hans-Rudolf Schwyzer. *Plotini opera.* Vol. 2, *Enneades IV–V.* Museum Lessianum Series, Philosophica 34. Paris: Desclée de Brouwer et Cie; Bruxelles: L'Édition Universelle, 1959.

Hörandner, Wolfram. *Theodoros Prodromos: Historische Gedichte.* Wiener Byzantinistische Studien 11. Vienna: Verlag der Österreichischen Akademie der Wissenschaften, 1974.

Lameere, William. *La tradition manuscrite de la correspondance de Grégoire de Chypre patriarche de Constantinople (1283–1289).* Brussels: Palais des académies, 1937.

Lamoureux, Jacques, and Noël Aujoulat, eds. *Synésios de Cyrène.* Vol. 4, *Opuscules I.* Paris: Les Belles Lettres, 2004.

Leone, Pietro Luigi. *Maximi monachi Planudis epistulae.* Amsterdam: A. M. Hakkert, 1991.

Leone, Pietro Luigi. 'Nicephori Gregorae *Antilogia* et *Solutiones quaestionum*'. *Byzantion* 40 (1970): 471–516.

Maximus Confessor. *Capita de caritate*. In *Patrologia cursus completa . . . Series graeca*, edited by J.-P. Migne, 90:960–1080. Paris: Petit-Montrouge, 1857–83.

Miller, E. E., ed. *Manuelis Philae Carmina ex codicibus Escurialensibus, Florentinis, Parisinis et Vaticanis nunc primum edidit*. Vol. 1. Paris, 1855. Reprint, Amsterdam: A. M. Hakkert, 1967.

Munitiz, Joseph. *Nicephori Blemmydae Autobiographia, sive, Curriculum vitae; necnon, Epistula universalior*. Corpus Christianorum, Series Graeca 13. Turnhout: Brepols; Leuven: Leuven University Press, 1984.

Noret, Jacques. *Vitae duae antiquae sancti Athanasii Athonitae*. Corpus Christianorum, Series Graeca 9. Turnhout: Brepols; Leuven: Leuven University Press, 1982.

PG (*Patrologia cursus completa . . . Series graeca*, edited by J.-P. Migne. 166 vols. Paris: Petit-Montrouge, 1857–83).

Polemis, Ioannis. '*Life* of St. George of Chozeva'. In Ἀνθολόγιο βυζαντινῆς πεζογραφίας, 237–364. Athens: Papazisis Publishers, 2018.

Rabe, Hugo, ed. *Hermogenes opera: Adiectae sunt II tabulae*. Bibliotheca Scriptorum Graecorum et Romanorum Teubneriana. Leipzig: Teubner, 1913.

Reinsch, Diether Roderich. *Die Briefe des Matthaios von Ephesos im Codex Vindobonensis Theol. Gr. 174*. Berlin: Mielke, 1974.

Schopen, Ludwig, ed. *Ioannis Cantacuzeni eximperatoris historiarum libri IV*. Vol. 1, *Graeca et Latine*. Corpus Scriptorum Historiae Byzantinae. Bonn: Weber, 1828.

Sideras, Alexandros, ed. *25 unedierte byzantinische Grabreden*. Thessaloniki: Paratērētēs, 1991.

Trapp, Michael, ed. *Maximus Tyrius: Dissertationes*. Bibliotheca Scriptorum Graecorum et Romanorum Teubneriana. Leipzig: Teubner, 1994.

Vivian, Tim, 'The *Life* of Saint George of Chozeva 1-42, 57–60'. In *Journeying into God. Seven Early Monastic Lives*, 71–105. Translated, with Introductions. Minneapolis: Fortress Press, 1996.

Secondary sources

Angelov, Dimitar. *Imperial Ideology and Political Thought in Byzantium, 1204–1330*. Cambridge: Cambridge University Press, 2007.

Angelov, Dimitar. *The Byzantine Hellene: The Life of Emperor Theodore Laskaris and Byzantium in the Thirteenth Century*. Cambridge: Cambridge University Press, 2019.

Angold, Michael. 'The Autobiographical Impulse in Byzantium'. *Dumbarton Oaks Papers* 52 (1998): 52–73.

Auerbach, Erich. *Figura*. In *Gesammelte Aufsätze zur Romanischen Philologie*, 55–92. Bern: Francke, 1967.

Beck, Hans-Georg. *Theodoros Metochites: Die Krise des byzantinischen Weltbildes im 14. Jahrhundert*. Munich: C. H. Beck, 1952.

Bernard, Floris. 'The Ethics of Authorship: Some Tensions in the 11th Century'. In *The Author in Middle Byzantine Literature: Modes, Functions, and Identities*, edited by A. Pizzone, 41–60. Byzantinisches Archiv 28. Berlin: De Gruyter, 2014.

Bernard, Floris. 'The Poems "To Oneself" of John Mauropous: Traditions and Self-representative Strategies'. In *Byzantine Authors and Their Times*, edited by V. N. Vlyssidou, 199–222. Athens: National Hellenic Research Foundation, 2021.

Blundell, Sue. *The Origins of Civilization in Greek and Roman Thought*. London: Croom Helm, 1986.
Bolton, J. D. P. *Aristeas of Proconnesus*. Oxford: Clarendon Press, 1962.
Bourbouhakis, Manolis. 'Rhetoric and Performance'. In *The Byzantine World*, edited by P. Stephenson, 175–87. London: Routledge, 2010.
Bourbouhakis, Manolis. 'The End of ἐπίδειξις: Authorial Identity and Authorial Intention in Michael Choniates' Πρὸς τοὺς αἰτιωμένους τὸ ἀφιλένδεικτον'. In *The Author in Middle Byzantine Literature: Modes, Functions, and Identities*, edited by A. Pizzone, 201–24. Byzantinisches Archiv 28. Berlin: De Gruyter, 2014.
Boyancé, Pierre. *Études sur le 'Songe de Scipion'*. Bibliothèque des universités du Midi 20. Bordeaux: Feret et Fils, 1936.
Bydén, Börje. *Theodore Metochites' Stoicheiosis Astronomike and the Study of Natural Philosophy and Mathematics in Early Palaiologan Byzantium*. Studia Graeca et Latina Gothoburgensia 66. Gothenburg: Acta Universitatis Gothoburgensis, 2003.
Chenu, M.-D. *Nature, Man, and Society in the Twelfth Century: Essays on New Theological Perspectives in the Latin West*. With a preface by E. Gilson, selected, edited, and translated by J. Taylor and L. K. Little. Toronto: University of Toronto Press, in association with the Medieval Academy of America, 1997.
Constantinides, Costas, N. *Higher education in Byzantium in the thirteenth and early fourteenth centuries (1204–ca. 1310)*. Texts and Studies of the History of Cyprus, 11. Nicosia: Cyprus Research Centre, 1982.
Cupane, Carolina. '"Natura formatrix": Umwege eines rhetorischen Topos'. In *Byzantios: Festschrift für Herbert Hunger zum. 70 Geburtstag dargebracht von Schülern und Mitarbeitern*, edited by W. Hörandner, J. Koder, O. Kresten and E. Trapp, 37–52. Vienna: E. Becvar, 1984.
Curtius, Ernst R. *European Literature and the Latin Middle Ages*. Translated by W. R. Trask. Bollingen Series 36. Princeton: Princeton University Press, 1952.
De Vries-Van der Velden, Eva. *Théodore Métochite: Une réévaluation*. Amsterdam: J. C. Gieben, 1987.
Dragona-Monachou, Myrto. *The Stoic Arguments for the Existence and the Providence of the Gods*. Athens: National and Capodistrian University of Athens, Faculty of Arts, 1976.
Dreyfus, Hubert, and Sean Dorrance Kelly. *All Things Shining: Reading the Western Classics to Find Meaning in a Secular Age*. New York: Free Press, 2011.
Eliade, Mircea. *A History of Religious Ideas*. Vol. 1, *From the Stone Age to the Eleusinian*. Translated by W. R. Trask. Chicago: University of Chicago Press, 1978.
Featherstone, Jeffrey M. 'Parisinus Graecus 1776: Metochites' Poems and the Chora'. In *Kariye: From Theodore Metochites to Thomas Whittemore. One Monument, Two Monumental Personalities*, edited by B. Anit and I. A. Kisilik, 75–95. Istanbul: Pera Museum, 2007.
Featherstone, Jeffrey M. 'Metochites's Poems and the Chora'. In *Kariye Camii, Yeniden / The Kariye Camii Reconsidered*, edited by H. A. Klein, R. G. Ousterhout and B. Pitarakis, 215–39. Istanbul: Pera Museum, 2011.
Festugière, A. J. *L'idéal religieux des Grecs et l'évangile*. Paris: J. Gabalda, 1932.
Festugière, A. J. 'Les thèmes du *Songe de Scipion*'. In *Eranos Rudbergianus: Opuscula philologica Gunnaro Rudberg A.D. XVI Kal. Nov. anno MCMXLV dedicate*, 370–88. Gothenburg: Elander Boktryckeri Aktiebolag, 1946.
Festugière, A. J. *Le Dieu cosmique*. Vol. 2 of *La révélation d'Hermès trismégiste*. Paris: Librairie Lecoffre, 1949.

Festugière, A. J. *Hermétisme et mystique païenne*. Paris: Aubier-Montaigne, 1967.
Finckh, Ruth. *Minor Mundus Homo: Studien zur Mikrokosmos in der mittelalterischen Literatur*. Palaestra 306. Göttingen: Vandenhoeck & Ruprecht, 1999.
Förstel, Christian. 'Theodore Metochites and His Books between the Chora and the Renaissance'. In *Kariye Camii, Yeniden / The Kariye Camii Reconsidered*, edited by H. A. Klein, R. G. Ousterhout and B. Pitarakis, 257–84. Istanbul: Pera Museum, 2011.
Foucault, Michel. *The Care of the Self*. Vol. 3 of *The History of Sexuality*, translated by R. Hurley. Reprint edn. New York: Vintage, 1988.
Foucault, Michel. 'Different Spaces'. In Foucault, Michel, *Aesthetics, Method, and Epistemology: Essential Works of Foucault, 1954–1984*. Edited by James D. Faubion, Volume 2, trans. Robert Hurley, 175–85. New York: The New Press, 1998.
Fryde, Edmund B. *The Early Palaeologan Renaissance 1261–c.1360*. The Medieval Mediterranean: Peoples, Economies and Cultures, 400–1453, 27. Leiden: Brill, 2000.
Gaul, Niels. *Thomas Magistros und die spätbyzantinische Sophistik: Studien zum Humanismus urbaner Eliten in der frühen Palaiologenzeit*. Mainzer Veröffentlichungen zur Byzantinistik 10. Wiesbaden: Harrassowitz, 2011.
Gilson, Étienne. 'Le Moyen Âge et le naturalisme antique'. In *Moyen Âge et Renaissance au Collège de France: Leçons inaugurals*, edited by P. Toubert, M. Zink and O. Bombard, 257–78. Paris: Fayard, 2009.
Golitsis, Pantelis. 'The Reappropriation of Philosophy in the Palaeologan Period'. In *The Intellectual Life of the Palaeologan Period*, edited by S. Kotzabassi. Brill Companions to the Byzantine World 12, 252–80. Leiden: Brill, 2023.
Grilli, Alberto. *Il problema della vita contemplativa nel mondo Greco-romano*. Milan: Fratelli Bocca, 1953.
Hadot, Pierre. *Philosophy as a Way of Life*, edited by A. I. Davidson, translated by Michael Chase. Oxford: Blackwell Publishers, 1995.
Hadot, Pierre. *Le voile d'Isis: Essai sur l'histoire de l'idée de nature*. Paris: Gallimard, 2004.
Harder, Annette. *Euripides' Kresphontes and Archelaos: Introduction, Text and Commentary*. Leiden: Brill, 1985.
Hinterberger, Martin. *Autobiographische Traditionen in Byzanz*. Wiener Byzantinistische Studien 22. Vienna: Verlag der Österreichischen Akademie der Wissenschaften, 1999.
Hinterberger, Martin. 'Studien zu Theodoros Metochites: Gedicht I – Des Meeres und des Lebens Wellen – Die Angst von der Neid – Die autobiographische Texte-Sprache'. *Jahrbuch der Österreichischen Byzantinistik* 51 (2001): 285–319.
Hinterberger, Martin. *Phthonos: Mißgunst, Neid und Eifersucht in der byzantinischer Literatur*. Serta Graeca 29. Wiesbaden: Dr Ludwig Reichert Verlag, 2013.
Hult, Karin. 'Theodore Metochites as a Literary Critic'. In *Interaction and Isolation in Late Byzantine Culture: Papers Read at a Colloquium Held at the Swedish Research Institute in Istanbul, 1–5 December, 1999*, edited by J. O. Rosenqvist, 44–56. Transactions 13. Stockholm: Swedish Research Institute in Constantinople; London: Distributed by I.B. Tauris, 2004.
Hunger, Herbert. 'Theodoros Metochites as Vorläufer des Humanismus'. *Byzantinische Zeitschrift* 45 (1952): 4–19.
Hunger, Herbert. 'Von Wissenschaft und Kunst de frühen Palaiologenzeit: Mit einem Exkurs über die Kosmike Delosis Theodoros' II Dukas Laskaris'. *Jahrbuch der Osterreichischen Byzantinistischen Gesellschaft* 8 (1959): 123–55.
Jebb, Richard J. *Sophocles: The Plays and Fragments with Critical Notes, Commentary and Translation in English Prose*. Vol. 2, *The Oedipus Coloneus*. Cambridge: Cambridge University Press, 1928.

Joly, Robert. *Le thème philosophique des genres de vie dans l'Antiquité Classique.* Académie royale de Belgique. Classe des Lettres et des Sciences Morales et Politiques. Mémoires. 2nd ser., 51.3. Brussels: Palais des Académies, 1956.

Kaldellis, Anthony. *The Argument of Psellos' Chronographia.* Studien und Texten zur Geistesgeschichte des Mittelalters 68. Leiden: Brill, 1999.

Kannicht, Richard, ed. *Tragicorum Graecorum Fragmenta.* Vol. 5, *Euripides.* Göttingen: Vandehoeck & Ruprecht, 2004.

Kantorowicz, Ernst H. 'Die Wiederkehr gelehrter Anachorese in Mittelalter'. In *Selected Studies*, 339–51. Locust Valley, NY: J. J. Augustin Publishers, 1965.

Kantorowicz, Ernst H. *The King's Two Bodies: A Study in Medieval Political Theology.* With a new preface by W. C. Jordan. Princeton: Princeton University Press, 1997.

Kennedy, George A. *Greek Rhetoric under Christian Emperors.* Princeton: Princeton University Press, 1983.

Kermanidis, Markos. *Episteme und Ästhetik der Raummodelierung in Literatur und Kunst des Theodoros Metochites: Ein frühpalaiologischer Byzantiner im Bezug zur Frühen Neuzeit.* Byzantinisches Archiv 37. Berlin: De Gruyter, 2020.

Kermanidis, Markos. 'Allegorie und Lob der Physik: Das Proömium der Paraphrase des Theodoros Metochites zu naturwissenschaftlichen Schriften des Aristoteles'. *Byzantinische Zeitschrift* 115, no. 1 (2022): 143–83.

Kimmelman, Burt. *The Poetics of Authorship in the Later Middle Ages: The Emergence of the Modern Literary Persona.* Studies in the Humanities 21. New York: Peter Lang, 1996.

Köckert, Charlotte. *Christliche Kosmologie und kaiserzeitliche Philosophie.* Studien und Texte zu Antike und Christentum 56. Tübingen: Mohr Siebeck, 2009.

Kolovou, Foteini. *Μιχαὴλ Χωνιάτης: Συμβολὴ στὴ μελέτη τοῦ βίου καὶ τοῦ ἔργου του. Τὸ corpus τῶν ἐπιστολῶν.* Πονήματα 2. Athens: Academy of Athens, 1999.

Kotzabassi, Sophia. 'Περὶ τοῦ καθ' ἑαυτὸν βίου ὡς ἀπ' ἄλλου προσώπου: Παρατηρήσεις στην αυτοβιογραφία του πατριάρχη Γρηγορίου Β΄ Κυπρίου'. *Ἑλληνικά* 58, no. 2 (2008): 279–92.

Kotzabassi, Sophia. 'Epistolography and Rhetoric'. In *A Companion to Byzantine Epistolography*, edited by A. Riehle, 177–99. Leiden: Brill, 2020.

Kotzabassi, Sophia. 'Continuity and Evolution in Autobiographical Literature'. In *The Intellectual Life of the Palaeologan Period*, edited by S. Kotzabassi. Brill Companions to the Byzantine World 12, 112–32. Leiden: Brill, 2023.

Kourousis, Stavros. *Τὸ ἐπιστολάριον Ἀνδρονίκου Λακαπηνοῦ-Γεωργίου Ζαρίδου καὶ ὁ ἰατρὸς-ἀκτουάριος Ἰωάννης Ζαχαρίας: Μελέτη φιλολογική.* Athens: Scientific Society of Athens, 1988.

Kubina, Krystina. *Die enkomiastische Dichtung des Manuel Philes: Form und Funktion des literarischen Lobes in der frühen Palaiologenzeit.* Byzantinisches Archiv 38. Berlin: De Gruyter, 2020.

Laiou, Angeliki E. *Constantinople and the Latins. The Foreign Policy of Andronicus II 1282–1328.* Harvard Historical Studies 88. Cambridge, MA: Harvard University Press, 1972.

Laiou, Angeliki E. 'The Palaiologoi and the World Around Them (1261–1400)'. In *The Cambridge History of the Byzantine Empire c.500–1492*, edited by J. Shepard, 803–33. Cambridge: Cambridge University Press, 2008.

Littlewood, Cedric A. J. *Self-representation and Illusion in Senecan Tragedy.* Oxford Classical Monographs. Oxford: Oxford University Press, 2004.

Ljubarskij, Jakov. 'How Should a Byzantine Text Be Read?'. In *Rhetoric in Byzantium: Papers from the Thirty-fifth Spring Symposium of Byzantine Studies, Exeter College,*

University of Oxford, March 2001, edited by E. Jeffreys, 117–25. Aldershot: Ashgate, 2003.

Lollar, Joshua Gareth. '"To See into the Life of Things": The Contemplation of Nature in Maximus the Confessor's *Ambigua* to John'. Vol. 1. (PhD diss., University of Notre Dame, 2011).

Long, Anthony Arthur. *From Epicurus to Epictetus: Studies in Hellenistic and Roman Philosophy*. Oxford: Clarendon Press, 2006.

MacPhee, S. 'Roaring Tempests of the Human Mind: Theodoros Metochites and the Sententious Notes'. Academia.edu, 29 April 2022.

Magdalino, Paul. 'Theodore Metochites, the Chora, and Constantinople'. In *Kariye Camii, Yeniden / The Kariye Camii Reconsidered*, edited by H. A. Klein, R. G. Ousterhout and B. Pitarakis, 169–87. Istanbul: Pera Museum, 2011.

Magdalino, Paul. 'The Beauty of Antiquity in Late Byzantine Praises of Constantinople'. In *Villes de toute beauté: L'ekphrasis des cités dans les littératures byzantine et byzantino-slaves. Actes de colloque international, Prague, 25–26 novembre 2011*, edited by P. Odorico and C. Messis, 101–21. Paris: Centre d'études byzantines, néo-helléniques et sud-est européennes, École des hautes études en sciences sociales, 2012.

Malingrey, Anne-Marie. *'Philosophia': Étude d'une groupe des mots dans la littérature grecque, des Présocratiques au IVe siècle après J.-C.* Études et Commentaires 40. Paris: Klincksieck, 1961.

Marciniak, Przemyslaw. 'Byzantine Theatron: A Place of Performance?'. In *Theatron: Rhetorische Kultur in Spätantike und Mittelalter*, edited by M. Grünbart, 277–85. Millenium-Studien 13. Berlin: De Gruyter, 2007.

Matschke, Klaus-Peter, and Franz Tinnefeld. *Die Gesellschaft im späten Byzanz: Gruppen, Strukturen und Lebensformen*. Cologne: Böhlau, 2001.

Melzer, Arthur M. *Philosophy between the Lines: The Lost History of Esoteric Writing*. Chicago: University of Chicago Press, 2014.

Mercati, Giovanni. *Notizie di Procoro e Demetrio Cidone, Manuele Caleca e Teodoro Meliteniota ed altri appunti per la storia della teologia e della letteratura bizantina del secolo XIV*. Studi e Testi 56. Vatican City: Vatican Apostolic Library, 1931.

Metzler, Karin. 'Pagane Bildung im christlichen Byzanz: Basileios von Kaisareia, Michael Psellos und Theodoros Metochites'. In *Theatron: Rhetorische Kultur in Spätantike und Mittelalter*, edited by M. Grünbart, 287–303. Millenium-Studien 13. Berlin: De Gruyter, 2007.

Misch, Georg. *Geschichte der Autobiographie*, Vol. 1, *Das Altertum*, pt. 2. Berlin: A. Franke Verlag, 1950.

Mittelstrass, Jurgen. *Die Rettung der Phänome: Ursprung und Geschichte eines antikes Forschungsprinzip*. Berlin: De Gruyter, 1962.

Moreau, Joseph. *L'âme du monde de Platon aux stoïciens*. Paris: Les Belles Lettres, 1939.

Mullett, Margaret. *Theophylact of Ochrid: Reading the Letters of a Byzantine Archbishop*. Birmingham Byzantine and Ottoman Studies 2. Aldershot: Variorum, 1997.

Mullett, Margaret. 'In Peril on the Sea: Travel Genres and the Unexpected'. In *Travel in the Byzantine World: Papers from the Thirty-fourth Spring Symposium of Byzantine Studies, Birmingham, April 2000*, edited by R. Macrides, 259–84. Aldershot: Ashgate, 2002.

Mullett, Margaret. 'Constructing Identities in Twelfth-century Byzantium'. In *Το Βυζάντιο ώριμο για αλλαγές: Επιλογές, ευαισθησίες και τρόποι έκφρασης από τον ενδέκατο στον δέκατο έμπτο αιώνα*, edited by C. G. Angelidi, 129–44. International Symposia 13. Athens: National Research Foundation, Institute of Byzantine Research, 2004.

Mullett, Margaret. 'In Search of the Monastic Author: Story-telling, Anonymity and Innovation in the 12th Century'. In *The Author in Middle Byzantine Literature: Modes, Functions, and Identities*, edited by A. Pizzone, 171–98. Byzantinisches Archiv 28. Berlin: De Gruyter, 2014.

Nelson, Katherine. 'Self and Social Functions: Individual Autobiographic Memory and Collective Narrative'. *Memory* 11 (2003): 125–36.

Nelson, Robert S. 'Heavenly Allies at the Chora'. *Gesta* 43, no. 1 (2004): 31–40.

Nilsson, Ingela. 'Narrative: Theory and Practice'. In *The Oxford Handbook of Byzantine Literature*, edited by S. Papaioannou, 273–93. New York: Oxford University Press, 2021.

O'Meara, Dominique. *Pythagoras Revived: Mathematics and Philosophy in Late Antiquity*. Oxford: Clarendon Press, 1989.

Ousterhout, Robert S. 'Reading Difficult Buildings: The Lessons of Kariye Camii'. In *Kariye Camii, Yeniden / The Kariye Camii Reconsidered*, edited by H. A. Klein, R. G. Ousterhout and B. Pitarakis, 95–128. Istanbul: Pera Museum, 2011.

Papaioannou, Stratis. *Michael Psellos: Rhetoric and Authorship in Byzantium*. Cambridge: Cambridge University Press, 2013.

Papaioannou, Stratis. 'Voice, Signature, Mask: The Byzantine Author'. In *The Author in Middle Byzantine Literature: Modes, Functions, and Identities*, edited by A. Pizzone, 21–40. Byzantinisches Archiv 28. Berlin: De Gruyter, 2014.

Papaioannou, Stratis. 'The Epistolographic Self'. In *A Companion to Byzantine Epistolography*, edited by A. Riehle, 333–52. Leiden: Brill, 2020.

Papaioannou, Stratis. 'Authors (With an Excursus on Symeon Metaphrastes)'. In *The Oxford Handbook of Byzantine Literature*, edited by S. Papaioannou, 483–524. New York: Oxford University Press, 2021.

Pépin, Jean. *Théologie cosmique et théologie chrétienne (Ambroise, Exam. I 1, 1–4)*. Paris: Presses Universitaires de France, 1964.

Pernot, Louis. 'Periautologia: Problèmes et méthodes de l'éloge de soi-même dans la tradition éthique et rhétorique gréco-romaine'. *Revue des Études Grecques* 111 (1998): 101–24.

Pernot, Louis. 'Mimesis, rhetorique et politique dans l'essai de Theodore Metochite Sur Demosthene et Aristide'. *Quaderni dell'Accademia Pontaniana* 47 (2006): 107–20.

Pfeiffer, Jens. *Contemplatio Caeli: Untersuchungen zum Motiv der Himmelsbetrachtung in lateinischen Texten der Antike und des Mittelalters*. Spolia Berolinensia 12. Hildesheim: Weidmann, 1994.

Pizzone, Aglae. 'Introduction'. In *The Author in Middle Byzantine Literature: Modes, Functions, and Identities*, edited by A. Pizzone, 3–18. Byzantinisches Archiv 28. Berlin: De Gruyter, 2014.

Podskalsky, Gerhard. *Theologie und Philosophie in Byzanz: Die Streit um die theologische Methodik in der spätbyzantinischen Geistesgeschichte (14/15. Jh.), seine systematischen Grundlagen und seine historische Entwicklung*. Munich: C. H. Beck, 1977.

Polemis, Ioannis, and Evelina Mineva, *Βυζαντινὰ ὑμνογραφικὰ καὶ ἁγιολογικὰ κείμενα: Νέα Ἔκδοση*. Athens: Kanakis Publishers, 2021.

Pratsch, Thomas. *Der hagiographische Topos: Griechische Heiligenviten in mittelbyzantinischer Zeit*, Millenium-Studien 6. Berlin: De Gruyter, 2005.

Puchner, Walter. *Φαινόμενα και Νοούμενα: Δέκα θεατρολογικὰ μελετήματα*. 2nd edn. Athens: Hellenika Grammata, 1999.

Puchner, Walter. *Greek Theatre between Antiquity and Independence: A History of Reinvention from the Third Century BC to 1830*. Cambridge: Cambridge University Press, 2017.

Rhoby, Andreas. 'Theodoros Metochites' *Byzantios* and Other City *Encomia* of the 13th and 14th Centuries'. In *Villes de toute beauté: L'ekphrasis des cités dans les littératures byzantine et byzantine-slaves. Actes de colloque international, Prague, 25–26 novembre 2011*, edited by P. Odorico and C. Messis, 81–99. Paris: Centre d'études byzantines, néo-helléniques et sud-est européennes, École des hautes études en sciences sociales, 2012.

Richter, Daniel S. *Cosmopolis: Imagining Community in Late Classical Athens and the Early Roman Empire*. Oxford: Oxford University Press, 2011.

Richter, Gerhard. *Theodoros Dukas Laskaris, der naturliche Zusammenhang: Ein Zeugnis von Stand der byzantinischen Philosophie in der Mitte des 13. Jahrhunderts*. Amsterdam: Adolf M. Hakkert, 1989.

Riehle, Alexander. 'Funktionen der byzantinischen Epistolographie: Studien zu den Briefen und Briefsammlungen des Nikephoros Choumnos (ca. 1260–1327) https://edoc.ub.uni-muenchen.de/16879/ (PhD diss., Ludwig-Maximilians-Universität München, 2011).

Riehle, Alexander. 'Epistolography as Autobiography: Remarks on the Letter Collections of Nikephoros Choumnos'. *Parekbolai* 2 (2012): 1–22.

Riehle, Alexander. 'Literature, Politics and Manuscripts in Early Palaiologan Byzantium: Towards a Reassessment of the Choumnos-Metochites Controversy'. *Travaux et Mémoires* 25, no. 1 (2021): 591–624.

Roberts, Michael. *The Jeweled Style: Poetry and Poetics in Late Antiquity*. Ithaca, NY: Cornell University Press, 1989.

Runia, David T. *Philo of Alexandria and the Timaeus of Plato*. Leiden: Brill, 1986.

Schechner, Richard. *Performance Theory*. 2nd edn. London: Routledge, 2003.

Schofield, Malcolm. *The Stoic Idea of a City*. With a new foreword by Martha Nussbaum and a new epilogue by the author. Chicago: University of Chicago Press, 1999.

Ševčenko, Ihor. *Études sur la polémique entre Théodore Métochite et Nicéphore Choumnos*. Corpus Bruxellense Historiae Byzantinae. Subsidia 3. Brussels: Byzanthion, 1962.

Ševčenko, Ihor. 'Theodore Metochites, the Chora and the Intellectual Trends of His Time'. In *The Kariye Djami*. Vol. 4, *Studies in the Art of the Kariye Djami and Its Intellectual Background*, edited by P. Underwood, 19–91. London: Routledge and Kegan Paul, 1975.

Ševčenko, Ihor. 'Hagiography of the Iconoclast Period'. In *Iconoclasm: Papers Given at the 9th Spring Symposium of Byzantine Studies, University of Birmingham, March 1975*, edited by A. Bryer and J. Herrin, 1–42. Birmingham: Centre for Byzantine Studies, University of Birmingham, 1977.

Ševčenko, Ihor. 'The Logos on Gregory of Nazianzus by Theodore Metochites'. In *Geschichte und Kultur der Palaiologenzeit: Referate des Internationales Symposions zu Ehren von H. Hunger*, edited by W. Seibt, 221–33. Vienna: Verlag der Österreichischen Akademie der Wissenschaften, 1996.

Shawcross, Teresa. 'Theories of Decline from Metochites to Ibn Khaldun'. In *The Cambridge Intellectual History of Byzantium*, edited by A. Kaldellis and N. Siniossoglou, 615–32. Cambridge: Cambridge University Press, 2017.

Smith, Sidonie, and Julia Watson. *Reading Autobiography. Guide for Interpreting Life Narratives*. 2nd edn. Minneapolis: University of Minnesota Press, 2010.

Spanneut, Michel. *Le stoïcisme des pères de l'église: De Clement de Rome à Clément d'Alexandrie*. Paris: Le Seuil, 1957.

Spanneut, Michel. *Permanence du stoïcisme: De Zénon à Malraux*. Gembloux: J. Duculot, 1973.

Stock, Brian. *Augustine's Inner Dialogue: The Philosophical Soliloquy in Late Antiquity.* Cambridge: Cambridge University Press, 2010.

Storin, Bradley K., *Self-Portrait in Three Colors. Gregory of Nazianzus's Epistolary Autobiography.* Oakland: University of California Press 2019.

Storr, Anthony. *The Essential Jung: Selected Writings.* London: Fontana Press, 1986.

Strauss, Leo. *What Is Political Philosophy and Other Studies.* Chicago: University of Chicago Press, 1959.

Strauss, Leo. *The Rebirth of Classical Political Rationalism: An Introduction to the Thought of Leo Strauss. Essays and Lectures by Leo Strauss Selected and Introduced by T. L. Pangle.* Chicago: University of Chicago Press, 1989.

Taxidis, Ilias. *Μάξιμος Πλανούδης: Συμβολή στη μελέτη του corpus των επιστολών του*, Βυζαντινά Κείμενα και Μελέτες 58. Thessaloniki: Centre of Byzantine Studies, 2012.

Thunberg, Lars. *Microcosm and Mediator: The Theological Anthropology of Maximus the Confessor.* Foreword by A. M. Allchin. 2nd edn. Chicago: Open Court Publishing Co., 1995.

Treu, Kurt. *Synesios von Kyrene: Ein Kommentar zu seinem 'Dion'.* Berlin: Akademie-Verlag, 1958.

Treu, Maximilian. 'Der Philosoph Joseph'. *Byzantinische Zeitschrift* 8 (1899): 1–64.

Vassis, Ioannis. 'Spirituality and Emotion: Poetic Trends in the Palaeologan Period'. In *A Companion to the Intellectual Life of the Paleologan Period*, edited by S. Kotzabassi. Brill's Companions to the Byzantine World 12, 172–210. Leiden: Brill, 2023.

Veikou, Myrto, and Ingela Nilsson. 'Ports and Harbours as Heterotopic Entities in Byzantine Literary Texts'. In *Harbours as Objects of Interdisciplinary Research: Archaeology + History + Geoscience*, edited by C. von Carnap-Bornheim, F. Daim, P. Ettel and U. Warnke, 265–80. RGZM-Tagungen 34. Mainz: Verlag des Römisch-Germanischen Zentralmuseums, 2018.

Voudouri, Alexandra. 'Representations of Power in the Byzantios Oration of Theodore Metochites: Illusions and Realities'. *Parekbolai* 3 (2013): 107–30.

Winkler, Martin M. *The Persona in Three Satires of Juvenal.* Altertumswissenschaftliche Texte und Studien 10. Hildesheim: Olms, 1983.

Xenophontos, Sophia. 'The Cultural Dynamics of the Term *Hellanodikes* in Palaiologan Byzantium'. *Byzantinische Zeitschrift* 108, no. 2 (2015): 219–27.

Xenophontos, Sophia. 'Plutarch and Theodore Metochites'. In *Brill's Companion to the Reception of Plutarch*, edited by S. Xenophontos and K. Oikonomopoulou, 310–23. Leiden: Brill, 2019.

Xenophontos, Sophia. 'Exploring Emotions in Late Byzantium: Theodore Metochites on Affectivity'. *Byzantion* 91 (2021): 423–63.

Zaras, Nektarios. 'Illness and Healing: The Healing Ministry Cycle in the Chora Monastery and the Literary Oeuvre of Theodore Metochites'. *Dumbarton Oaks Papers* 75 (2021): 85–119.

INDEX

All works mentioned in the index are by Theodore Metochites unless otherwise attributed.

active life 123–4
Adversus Plotinum de anima (Choumnos, Nikephoros) 139
Aelius Aristeides 125
  miracles 98
  Panathenaikos 31, 131
  rhetorical style 71, 81–2, 83–7, 88, 90, 91, 153–4
  Sacred Orations 98
  Septem contra Thebas Aeschylus 111
Alexandria 134, 135
Andronikos II Palaiologos (Byzantine emperor) 1, 2, 41–2, 141–2
  abdication 6
  Greece 2
  legacy 3–4
  Metochites, relationship with 4–5, 18–19, 26, 48–9
  Ottoman threat 2
  qualities 100
  religion 2, 4
Andronikos III Palaiologos (Byzantine emperor) 3, 6, 41, 42
Anthony of Egypt, Saint 120
Antioch 134, 135
Antiochikos (Libanius) 131
Apology (Kydones, Demetrius) 65
Aristeas of Proconessus, myth of 114–15
Aristotle 16–17
  De anima 161
  Meteorologica 136
  Paraphrases of Aristotle 8, 30, 31, 161
  Parva Naturalia 161
  Physica 161
Asia Minor 38–9
Athanasios of Alexandria, Saint 99, 100
Athanasios of Ganos, Saint 121
Athanasios the Athonite 128

authors 9–10, 11, 12
  immortality of 123
Axiochus (Pseudo-Plato) 152

Babylon 134
Basil (the Great) of Caesarea, Saint 18, 73, 74, 95, 100
  rhetorical style 99
Beck, Hans-Georg
  Habilitationsschrift 13
being 152
Bekkos, John 4, 65
  On the Union of the Churches 65
Black Sea 38, 39
Bosphorus Straits 38, 39
Bryennios, Manuel 5
Byzantine Empire 1, 38–9
  authors 9–10, 123
  careers 48, 51–2
  civil war 3, 6
  debates 125
  decline 1, 3, 143, 157
  economy 4
  education 120, 122, 126
  ideology 157
  intellectuals 125, 127–8
  literary personae 9–11
  mimesis 11
  Ottoman threat 2, 3
  pronoia system 3
  religion 2, 33, 64–5, 120–2, 136
  rhetoric 9–10, 11, 89–91, 99
  sainthood in 48
  self-image 89–90
  Serbian threat 2–3
  social class 3, 11
  society 96
  sociolect 11
  theatre 9
  writings 9–10

Catalan Company 2
Chenu, M.-D. 150
Chora monastery 5, 8–9, 27, 40, 49–50, 97
   figurae 42, 43
   Kermanidis, Markos 14
   Palaiologan renaissance 121
   Zaras, Nektarios 181 n. 44
Choumnos, Nikephoros 8, 65–71, 77, 82,
   125–6, 127, 154, 162
   Adversus Plotinum de anima 139
   Metochites, relationship with 5–6,
      65–71, 77, 80–1, 82, 100, 126, 127,
      162
Christianity 53–4, 63, 95–6, 120–2, 139
   church as body of Christ 139–40
   Constantinople 134
   pleasure 117
   θεωρία (*theoria*) 107
city, the 111, 135–6, 139
Constantine the Great (Roman emperor)
   132, 133, 134, 141
Constantinople 2, 20, 38, 132–8, 139–41
   see also Chora monastery
   Hagia Sophia 39, 134, 139
   religion 124
contemplation 107–13
contemplative life 51, 123–4, 125
contradictions 7, 10–17
Cresphontes (Euripides) 152

De anima (Aristotle) 161
De somniis (Philo Judaeus) 111
De specialibus legibus (Philo Judaeus)
   109–10
De vita contemplative (Philo Judaeus) 110,
   112
de Vries-Van der Velden, Eva 13
death 151–2
debates 125
deconstructionism 11–12
Demetrius of Thessalonike, Saint 19, 46–8,
   49, 50, 63–4, 140
Demetrius I Poliorketes (king of
   Macedon) 42
Demosthenes 66, 67, 69, 125
   rhetorical style 81–3, 84–6, 87–8, 90,
      91, 153–4
digrammatology 14
Dio (Synesius of Cyrene) 121

Dio Chrysostom 152, 163
   Oration 23 152
Dion (Synesius of Cyrene) 119
Dreyfus, Hubert and Kelly, Sean Dorrance
   152

Eirene (Byzantine Empress) 5
elusiveness 10–11, 54, 55, 153
Encyclopaedia (Joseph Rhakendytes)
   123–4, 125
Epimenides, myth of 114–15
Epinomis (Pseudo-Plato) 108, 119, 151
ethopoiiai 9
Euripides 119
   Cresphontes 152

figurae 40, 41–3
Foucault, Michel 37, 57–8

Gabras, Michael 74–5
Gaul, Niels 143
George of Choziva, Saint 128
Greece 2
Greek learning 119–22
Gregoras, Nikephoros 46, 71
Gregory of Bulgaria 39, 46, 87, 97
Gregory of Cyprus 68, 69–70
Gregory of Nazianzus, Saint 18, 45, 46,
   73–9, 95, 100
   imitating 68, 69–71
   Miscellanea 163
   Oration 43 Funeral Oration for Basil
      the Great 73
   philosophy 76
   rhetorical style 68, 70–1, 75–9, 83, 90,
      99
   Thomas Magistros 77–8

Habilitationsschrift (Beck, Hans-Georg) 13
hagiographies 128, 129
Hamlet (Shakespeare, William) 152
Hermippos (Zacharias Aktouarios,
   Ioannes) 121
Hermogenes
   On Ideas 76, 83
   On Invention 85
Herodotus 152
heterotopies 37–41
historicism 14–15

History (Kantakouzenos, John) 124
History (Pachymeres, George) 121
human nature 148
humanistic monasticism 98
Hunger, Herbert 13

indexicality 14
individualism 57–8

John Chrysostom, Saint 95, 100
  rhetorical style 99
John of Didymoteichon, Saint 19–20, 46, 54–5, 97–8
Joseph Rhakendytes (Joseph the Philosopher) 19, 45–6, 51–4, 128–9
  Encyclopaedia 123–4, 125
  Metochites, relationship with 45, 52–3, 128, 129
Josephus 163
Jung, Carl 10

Kantakouzenos, John 3, 124
  History 124
Kermanidis, Markos 13–15
Kydones, Demetrius
  Apology 65

Lausaikon (Palladius) 129
Laws (Plato) 108
Libanius
  Antiochikos 131
life 151–2
Life of St Athanasios the Athonite (Athanasios) 128
Life of St Demetrius (Symeon Metaphrastes) 48
Life of St George of Choziva (Antony of Choziva) 128
Life of St Mary of Egypt, The (Sophronios of Jerusalem) 54
limit/limitless 38–9
literary/oratory style. *See* rhetorical style
literary personae 9–11
Loukas (abbot of Chora monastery) 45, 46, 97

Manifestation of the world (Κοσμικὴ Δήλωσις) (Theodore II Laskaris) 117

Marina, Saint 19
masks 9, 10, 54, 55, 122 see also *prosopon*
  Basil of Caesarea 18
  Gregory of Nazianzus 18
Maximianus (emperor of Rome) 47, 63
Maximus of Tyre 114, 163
Meteorologica (Aristotle) 136
Metochites, George 4–5, 65
Metochites, Theodore 1
  LIFE: birth 4; character 11, 25, 29–34, 36, 54, 59, 63; death 6, 52; education 4, 5, 28, 29; family 4–5, 27, 57, 65; house 40; self-image 12, 27, 34–7, 91, 96, 100–1, 102, 122–3, 126, 145, 15, 155, 157
  CAREER: 1, 4, 5, 26, 137; admiration for 161; as author 29–34, 91; criticism 69; downfall 6, 40, 41, 51; elusiveness 10–11, 42, 59, 90–1, 153, 155–7; glory/fame 30, 33, 52; masks 11, 15, 18, 34, 54, 106–7, 122, 129, 145, 153–7 as megas logothetes 5, 6; as monk 28; as philosopher 89; self-confidence 29–34, 36; as senator 49
  INTERESTS/VIEWS: 15, 16, 121, 155; active/contemplative life, opposition between 7, 12, 13, 28–9, 37, 45–6, 59, 75, 87, 97, 98, 101–2, 103, 105, 106–8, 112, 124–5, 126–7, 129, 137–8, 142, 144–5, 154–5; astronomy 5, 86, 109; being 147, 151–2, 156; Byzantine state 38; carnal pleasure 118, 119, 120; Chora monastery 5, 8–9, 14, 27, 40, 42, 43, 49–50, 97, 121, 181 n, 44; civilization 149–50; Constantinople 38, 39–40, 131–5, 136–8, 139–41, 142, 143, 154; contemplation 107–15; education 33–4, 89, 99–100, 101, 102, 103–5, 107–8, 113, 118; elusiveness 54, 55; emperors 141–3; *figurae* 40, 41–3; fortune 7, 35–7, 40, 41, 105; glory/fame 30, 33–4, 52; Greek learning 121–2; harmonious world 42–3, 115; harmonics 115–17; heterotopies 37–41; human nature 99–100, 148; innovation 63, 65; intellectuals 125–8; library

49–50, 97; masks, 18, 54, 55; mind, journey of 114–15; miracles 98; monasticism 98, 112, 122, 154; nature 99–100, 101, 109, 131, 135–6, 137–8, 147–51; oration 66, 80, 82–4, 153–4; philosophers 66; philosophy 89, 96, 104, 113, 156; pleasure/delight 58, 104, 116, 117–23; politics 42, 85–6, 123–7, 137–8, 140; reality 84, 115, 143–4; reason 106, 116, 148–9; religion 13, 26–7, 28, 32–3, 53–4, 64, 95–7, 98, 101, 102–3, 109, 111, 113, 116–17, 139–41, 151; rhetoric 89; rhetorical style 67–8, 69, 71, 76, 77, 78–9, 82–8, 89–91, 99; sanctity 54; solitariness 57–8; speech 16–18, 32; state, the 139–41, 142, 143; suffering 105, 106, 151; theatre 18–20; tradition 64–6; virtue 103 107–8, 111, 129; wisdom 95–6, 97, 101, 103–5, 106, 107–8, 123, 127; world, abandonment of 112; world, contemplating the 108, 111, 116–17, 140

RELATIONSHIPS: 45; Andronikos II 4–5, 18–19, 26, 45, 48–9; Choumnos, Nikephoros 5–6, 65–71, 77, 80–1, 82, 100, 126, 127, 162; Gregoras, Nikephoros 46; Joseph Rhakendytes 45, 52–3, 128, 129; Loukas 45; Milutin of Serbia 5; Thomas Magistros 123

WORKS: *See* works of Theodore Metochites

Michael VIII Palaiologos (Byzantine emperor) 1, 2, 4

Michael IX Palaiologos (Byzantine emperor) 5, 141

Michael the New Martyr of Egypt, Saint 19, 128

Milutin (Stefan Uroš, king of Serbia) 2–3, 5

mimesis 11

Miscellanea 31, 98, 114, 143, 154, 163 see also *Semeioseis Gnomikai / Sententious Notes*

being 151

chronology 6

nature 147

monasteries/monks 119–20 *see also* Chora monastery

founding of 97–8

humanistic monasticism 98

Mousokles 124

Müller, Christian Gottried and Kiessling, Gottlieb 163

nature 147–8, 150

imagery 135–6

study of 109

Nicaeus (Metochites, Theodore) 4

On Ideas (Hermogenes) 76, 83

On Invention (Hermogenes) 85

On kingship (Thomas Magistros) 123

On natural communion (Περὶ φυσικῆς κοινωνίας) (Theodore II Laskaris) 117

On the Union of the Churches (Bekkos, John) 65

Oration 23 (Dio Chrysostom) 152

Oration 43 Funeral Oration for Basil the Great (Gregory of Nazianzus) 73

orations 29, 43, 159–61

audience 7, 8, 29, 160–1

chronology 6, 159

Kermanidis, Markos 14

ordering 14

sea imagery 39

Oration 1 *Nicaeus,* ecomium of the city of Nicaea 4, 48–9, 141–2, 160

Oration 2 For St Marina 8, 14, 19, 30, 98, 160

Oration 3 For the archangel Michael and the angels 8, 14, 30, 32, 46, 160

Oration 4 For St Demetrius 8, 14, 19, 30, 32, 46–8, 50, 51, 63–4, 96, 140, 153, 160

Oration 5 First *basilikos*, praise of Emperor Andronikos II Palaiologos 7, 8, 14, 87, 100, 160

Oration 6 For St Gregory of Nazianzus 14, 18, 31, 45, 71, 73–6, 77, 79, 83, 90, 100, 153, 154, 160

Oration 7 Second basilikos, praise of Emperor Andronikos II Palaiologos 7, 8, 14, 38, 142, 149, 160
Oration 8 *Presbeutikos*, account of Metochites' diplomatic mission to Serbia 14, 85, 90, 150, 160
Oration 9 Funeral speech for Empress Theodora Palaiologina 7, 8, 14, 160
Oration 10 *Ethikos*, protreptic speech on education 7, 12, 13, 14, 20, 28–9, 31, 32, 33–4, 36, 43, 58, 69, 74, 90, 96, 100, 101–15, 116–17, 118, 120, 121, 122–3, 124, 126, 127, 129, 137–8, 140, 144, 147, 148, 149, 154, 155, 160–1
Oration 11 *Byzantios*, for Constantinople 12, 14, 20, 31, 38, 39, 47–8, 69, 74, 86, 87, 115, 124–5, 131–45, 148, 151, 154, 155, 160
Oration 12 For Michael the New Martyr of Egypt 8, 14 19, 46, 160
Oration 13 First speech against Nikephoros Choumnos 8, 14, 66, 67, 77, 82, 90, 153, 160–1
Oration 14 Second speech against Nikephoros Choumnos 8, 14, 66–7, 77, 80–1, 90, 100, 153, 160–1
Oration 15 Prologue to an imperial chrysoboullon 14, 160
Oration 16 Funeral speech for Loukas, abbot of the monastery of Chora 14, 96, 97, 122, 160
Oration 17 Funeral speech for Joseph Rhakendytes (Joseph the Philosopher) 14, 19, 45–6, 51–2, 53, 77–8, 96, 99, 125, 128–9, 153, 160
Oration 18 Comparison of Demosthenes and Aelius Aristeides 8, 14, 71, 81–8, 90, 97, 98, 115, 125, 127, 143–4, 153, 154, 160–1
Oration 19 For St John of Didymoteichon 8, 14, 19–20, 46, 54–5, 96, 160
oratory style. *See* rhetorical style
Ostrogorsky, Georg 3
Ottomans, the 2

Pachymeres, George
　History 121

Palaiologan renaissance 121
Palamas, Gregory 122
Panathenaikos (Aelius Aristeides) 31, 131
Papaioannou, Stratis 79
Paraphrases of Aristotle 8, 30, 31, 161
Parva Naturalia (Aristotle) 161
Pausanias 41, 42
περιουσία (property) 143, 144
persona 10
personae 9–11
Phaedrus (Plato) 113, 119
Philip II (king of Macedon) 41
Philo Judaeus 110, 112–13, 114, 163
　De somniis 111
　De specialibus legibus 109–10
　De vita contemplativa 110, 112
　Quis rerum divinarum heres sit 136
philosophy 110, 113–14, 126
　elusiveness 153
　politics 123, 124
Physica (Aristotle) 161
πίναξ 43
Planoudes, Maximus 121
Plato 66, 80, 103, 108–9, 123, 126, 136, 144
　see also Pseudo-Plato
　Laws 108
　Phaedrus 113
　philosophy 104
　pleasure 117–18
　reality 155
　Republic 47, 144
　Sophist 35
　Symposium 123
　Timaeus 108, 113, 114, 136
pleasure 117, 118
Plotinus 136, 139
Plutarch 163
poems 31–2, 69, 161–3
　audience 7–8, 15, 29
　chronology 6
　emotion in 15
　imagery 39
　sea imagery 39
　soliloquy in 35–7
　soul, addressing the 35–7
　themes 162
　Poem 1. A glorification of the Lord, an autobiography of the author and a description of the restoration of the

monastery of Chora 4, 5, 6, 8, 18, 20, 25–8, 29–30, 42, 43, 48, 49–50, 52, 153, 162
Poem 2. An address to Virgin Mary and on the monastery of Chora 6, 8, 27–8, 40, 42, 57, 96, 122, 162
Poem 3. To Gregory, archbishop of Bulgaria 6, 8, 39, 46, 57, 87, 96, 97, 153, 162
Poem 4. To Nikephoros Gregoras 6, 8, 30, 46, 99, 113, 162
Poem 5. To St Athanasios of Alexandria 6, 8, 95, 99–100, 162
Poem 6. To the three prelates (Basil the Great, Gregory of Nazianzus and John Chrysostom) 6, 8, 95–6, 99–100, 162
Poem 7. Funeral poem for Empress Eirene Palaiologina 6, 8
Poem 8. Funeral poem for Emperor Michael IX Palaiologos
Poem 9. Funeral poem for his son-in-law John Palaiologos 8
Poem 10. On the science of harmonics 42–3, 96, 115–17, 140, 147, 162
Poem 11. To his friend Theodore Xanthopoulos 8, 39, 162
Poem 12. To his friend Nikephoros Xanthopoulos 8, 30, 31–2, 43, 74, 121, 162
Poem 13. To his kinsman and friend Leon Bardales 8, 37, 39–40, 162
Poems 14–20. To himself 7–8, 35, 162
Poem 17. To himself 41–2
Poem 18. To himself 35
Poem 19. To himself 35–6, 40, 42, 50, 97
Poem 20. To himself 35, 36
poetry
 imagery 32
 soul, addressing the 35
Polemis, Ioannis
 Theodorus Metochites: Carmina 161
Polemis, Ioannis and Kaltsogianni, Eleni
 Theodorus Metochites: Orationes 159
πολιτεία (*politeiai*) 47–8, 49–50
politics 124
Polycrates of Samos 41

πράγματα (circumstances, realities of life) 84, 85, 143–4
progymnasmata 9, 17, 64
prosopon (mask, role) 18, 20
Psellos, Michael 10, 20, 79, 85, 89, 150
Pseudo-Plato
 Axiochus 152
 Epinomis 108, 119, 151
psychology 10

Quis rerum divinarum heres sit (Philo Judaeus) 136

reality 84–5, 115, 155
religion 2, 33, 64–5, 109–10, 113, 120–2, 136 see also Christianity
 being 152
 Constantinople 134
 monks 119–20
 Therapeutai, the 110
Republic (Plato) 47, 144
rhetoric 9–10, 11, 16–18, 32, 77, 89–91, 99
 political 90
rhetorical style 67–9, 70–1, 75–6
 Aelius Aristeides 71, 81–2, 83–7, 88, 90, 91, 153–4
 Basil (the Great) of Caesarea 99
 Demosthenes 81–3, 84–6, 87–8, 90, 91, 153–4
 epideictic 85, 86, 88, 90
 Gregory of Nazianzus 68, 70–1, 75–9, 83, 90, 99
 Hermogenes 76
 John Chrysostom 99
 political 90
 political/social reality affecting 81, 82, 84–8, 90, 91, 138, 143–4
Riehle, Alexander 67
Rome 134, 135

Sacred Orations (Aelius Aristeides) 98
science 66, 106, 117
Scythians, the 149
Semeioseis Gnomikai / Sententious Notes 28, 43, 163 see also *Miscellanea*
 Beck, Hans-Georg 13
 civilization 150
 contradictions 17
 nature 149

Septem contra Thebas Aeschylus (Aelius
    Aristeides) 111
Serbia 2–3, 150
Ševčenko, Ihor 6, 13, 67, 156–7, 159
Shakespeare, William
    Hamlet 152
Smyrlis, Kostis 6
social class 3
    sociolect 11
Socrates 103
soliloquies 34–7
sophism 87
Sophist (Plato) 35
Sophocles 152
Sophronios of Jerusalem
    Life of St Mary of Egypt, The 54
speech 16–18, 32 *see also* rhetoric
    freedom of 16, 17
Stilpo of Megara 42
Stoics the 20, 109, 111, 115
Stoikheiosis Astronomike 28, 33, 161
Symeon Metaphrastes, Saint
    Life of St Demetrius 48
Symposium (Plato) 123
Synesius of Cyrene 119–20, 163
    Dio 121
    Dion 119

theatre 9, 18–20
Theodore II Laskaris (emperor of Nicaea)
    Manifestation of the world (Κοσμικὴ
        Δήλωσις) 117
    On natural communion (Περὶ φυσικῆς
        κοινωνίας) 117
Theodorus Metochites: Carmina (Polemis,
    Ioannis) 161
Theodorus Metochites: Orationes (Polemis,
    Ioannis and Kaltsogianni, Eleni)
    159
θεωρία (*theoria*) 107–10, 121
Therapeutai, the 110
Thomas Magistros 34, 77–8, 143
    Metochites, relationship with 123
    On kingship 123

Thucydides 66, 67–8, 71, 82, 83
Timaeus (Plato) 108, 113, 114, 136
ἐπαφὴ (touch) 117
tradition 64–5

wisdom 95–6
works of Theodore Metochites 6–8, 90,
        159–63 see also *Miscellanea;*
        orations; poems; *Semeioseis
        Gnomikai / Sententious Notes*
    accidental encounter motif 54–5
    audience 7–8, 29, 115, 160 –1
    authorship 29–34
    chronology 6
    consistency/inconsistency 7, 12
    contradictions 17
    criticism 5–6, 66–71, 126, 127–8
    elusiveness 10–11
    emotion in 15
    fictions 9
    hagiographies 129
    masks 15, 106–7
    materialism 33
    mimesis 11
    motifs 54–5
    Paraphrases of Aristotle 8, 30, 31, 161
    personae 10–11
    portraits 45–55
    production/publication 7
    progymnasmata 17, 64
    soliloquies 34–7
    Stoikheiosis Astronomike 28, 33, 161
    theatre as metaphor 18–19, 53
    themes 7, 162
    writing patterns 12
    writing style 29–32, 67, 69, 70–1
world
    as city 111
    contemplating the 108–11, 113–14, 140

Xenophontos, Sophia 15

Zacharias Aktouarios, Ioannes 121
    Hermippos 121

www.ingramcontent.com/pod-product-compliance
Lightning Source LLC
Chambersburg PA
CBHW052113300426
44116CB00010B/1657